Setting Slavery's Limits

New Studies in Southern History

Series Editor: John David Smith, The University of North Carolina at Charlotte

Race and Masculinity in Southern Memory: History of Richmond, Virginia's Monument Avenue, 1948–1996
By Matthew Mace Barbee
Racial Cleansing in Arkansas, 1883–1924: Politics, Land, Labor, and Criminality
By Guy Lancaster
George Galphin and the Transformation of the George-South Carolina Backcountry
By Michael P. Morris
Race, Gender, and Film Censorship in Virginia, 1922–1965
By Melissa Ooten
Leisure, Plantations, and the Making of a New South: The Sporting Plantations of the South Carolina Lowcountry and Red Hills Region, 1900–1940
Edited by Julia Brock and Daniel Vivian
The Federal Theatre Project in the American South: The Carolina Playmakers and the Quest for American Drama
By Cecelia Moore
The Development of Southern Public Libraries and the African American Quest for Library Access, 1898–1963
By Dallas Hanbury
Backcountry Slave Trader: William James Smith's Enterprise, 1844–54
Edited by Philip Noel Racine and Frances Melton Racine
Setting Slavery's Limits: Physical Confrontations in Antebellum Virginia, 1801–1860
By Christopher H. Bouton

Setting Slavery's Limits

Physical Confrontations in Antebellum Virginia, 1801–1860

Christopher H. Bouton

LEXINGTON BOOKS
Lanham • Boulder • New York • London

To Mom and Dad

Published by Lexington Books
An imprint of The Rowman & Littlefield Publishing Group, Inc.
4501 Forbes Boulevard, Suite 200, Lanham, Maryland 20706
www.rowman.com

6 Tinworth Street, London SE11 5AL, United Kingdom

Copyright © 2020 The Rowman & Littlefield Publishing Group, Inc.

All rights reserved. No part of this book may be reproduced in any form or by any electronic or mechanical means, including information storage and retrieval systems, without written permission from the publisher, except by a reviewer who may quote passages in a review.

British Library Cataloguing-in-Publication Information Available

Library of Congress Cataloging-in-Publication Data

Names: Bouton, Christopher H., author.
Title: Setting Slavery's Limits : Physical Confrontations in Antebellum Virginia, 1801–1860 / Christopher H. Bouton.
Other titles: New studies in Southern history.
Description: Lanham, Maryland : Lexington Books, [2019] | Series: New studies in southern history | Includes bibliographical references and index. | Summary: "This study examines how slaves in antebellum Virginia, through physical confrontations with whites, fought to reassert some measure of control over their day-to-day lives. The author analyzes how while this violence came at a high cost, it also ensured the preservation of their humanity and set limits on their enslavement" — Provided by publisher.
Identifiers: LCCN 2019043114 (print) | LCCN 2019043115 (ebook) | ISBN 9781498579452 (cloth) | ISBN 9781498579469 (epub) ISBN 9781498579476 (pbk)
Subjects: LCSH: Slavery—Virginia—History—19th century. | Slaves—Virginia—History—19th century. | Interpersonal confrontation—Virginia—History—19th century. | Violence—Virginia—History—19th century.
Classification: LCC E445.V8 B66 2019 (print) | LCC E445.V8 (ebook) | DDC 306.3/62097550904—dc23
LC record available at https://lccn.loc.gov/2019043114
LC ebook record available at https://lccn.loc.gov/2019043115

Contents

Acknowledgments	vii
Introduction: Contextualizing Confrontations	ix
1 Paternalism and Physical Confrontations	1
2 Masculinity and Physical Confrontations	29
3 Resistance to Sexual Exploitation	59
4 Enslaved Women's Violence and the Household	89
5 Protecting White Supremacy	119
Epilogue: What Violence Meant to the Enslaved	151
Bibliography	159
Index	173
About the Author	179

Acknowledgments

My first thanks go to the archivists and staff at the various research institutions I visited. David Grabarek at the Library of Virginia deserves special thanks for helping me navigate through the Governors' Papers and other sources and thus making my trips to Richmond much more productive. The staff at the Library of Virginia went far and above the bounds of professional courtesy by promptly filling my never-ending waves of document requests. They retrieved box after box as I barreled my way through the Executive Papers of Virginia's governors. At the South Carolina Department of Archives and History in Columbia, Charles Lesser directed me to the Courts of Magistrates and Freeholders records. Mimi Miller at the Historic Natchez Foundation provided me with a database of slave cases, saving me precious time.

Over the course of my academic career, I incurred many debts, intellectual and otherwise that warrant recognition. My thanks go to those who participated in conference panels and offered words of encouragement. Tim Hack, Matt Hetrick, Stephanie Hill, Melissa Maestri, Jen Moses, Tom Sheeler, and Sally Stockdale all read early drafts of the chapters and offered helpful feedback. The University of Delaware provided financial support in the form of a University Dissertation Fellowship and summer research funding from the Dean's office and the Center for the Study of Diversity. My committee members Erica Armstrong-Dunbar, Christine Heyrman, and the late Anthony Kaye also warrant special thanks for their thoughtful and insightful critiques. Finally, I owe my greatest intellectual debt to Peter Kolchin. He fostered this project from an idea that emerged out of one of his seminars to a completed dissertation. If there is anything of historical value in the following pages, it is because of his thoughtful and critical eye. Any errors or mistakes that remain are solely my responsibility.

Special thanks also go out to Brian Hill, formerly of Lexington Books. He reached out to me and guided me through the proposal process. Eric Kuntzman and his assistant Ellen McDaniel have admirably continued to shepherd the book along to publication.

Writing a book is a solitary endeavor, but also an impossible one without the help of family and friends. Kim Nath and Allison Kreitzer have been friends since the beginning of our doctoral program. We've shared countless classes, meals, and bits of departmental gossip with one another. Thomas and Cera Fisher have lent a sympathetic ear and asked insightful questions that helped me clarify my arguments.

I would like to thank Hillary and Mayday for sharing the last several years of this project with me. My morning walk with Mayday is one of the highlights of my day. Further, her enthusiasm for laying in the hot sun is an inspiration to us all. Hillary has been my office companion for the past three years. Who knew a rabbit, rescued from our thoughtless neighbors, could be such a curious, fun, and occasionally destructive pet?

My great-grandmother, Louise Hussey was the research librarian at the Nantucket Historical Association and gave me the earliest push towards history. My grandparents Robert and Martha Bouton encouraged me to learn more about the Nantucket history, helping to set my on circuitous path to this book.

Casey Green has offered her constant love and encouragement. As a fellow historian, we have swapped stories, ideas, and frustrations. She has read significant portions of this book and offered feedback while teaching and finishing her own dissertation. Recently we learned a rule that has governed our relationship since, only one of us has to be sane at a given time. Every day spent with her is a joy.

Finally, I dedicate this book to my parents, Barney and Dale Bouton. They encouraged me to have confidence in myself and to pursue my own path. They have also lent their love and support as I struggled to explain the byzantine requirements governing graduate school, dissertation writing, and finally book publishing. They have always offered humor and much-needed perspective. They are the best parents I could ever have hoped for.

And Dad, I'm not sure the money from this book will pay for that window I broke as a kid. Maybe the next one will.

Introduction

Contextualizing Confrontations

Thomas Edwards was fat, so fat that Johnson and Jim, two of his slaves, could not carry his body across the swamp where they had killed him. On the afternoon of February 24, 1825, Edwards had left his home and walked into the nearby woods. He soon came upon Johnson and Jim, cutting and shaping logs and began to inspect their work. After sitting down on a stump, one of the men, likely Jim, came up behind Edwards and struck him in the head with a small ax. The other man, likely Johnson, then delivered the killing blow with a broad ax. Now faced with the problem of covering up their brutal crime, the two enslaved men settled on a gruesome solution. Armed with their axes and other woodcutting tools, they began dismembering Thomas Edwards. After severing his body at the waist, Johnson and Jim were still unable to move the upper half of their master's body. With darkness falling, the bondsmen "divided, longitudinally, that part of the trunk with the head attached to it."[1] After burying both parts of Edwards's torso in a nearby ditch, they dumped his legs in a gulley three quarters of a mile away. With the disposal of the body complete, Johnson returned to the Edwards home and Jim visited his wife at a nearby farm.

The next morning, Mrs. Edwards was growing concerned. Her husband had not returned home since leaving to check on Johnson and Jim. She encouraged her son, Isaac, to go and look for his father. Following Thomas Edwards's last known steps, Isaac Edwards walked into the woods and found Johnson and Jim working in their usual spot. Isaac asked the two bondsmen if they had seen their master. The enslaved men replied that they had not seen Thomas Edwards since the day before, when he inspected their work and then left to visit a neighbor. Skeptical of the slaves' explanation, Isaac Edwards began searching the area and quickly found proof of his father's demise. He discovered dried blood all over the area, including on a pile of previously shaped logs. While Johnson and

Jim continued their work, Edwards took a closer look at their clothing and saw that "Jim's pantaloons were bloody and Johnson's shirt had some blood upon that also."[2] Having realized what had happened to his father, Isaac Edwards quickly retreated back to his parents' house.

Isaac Edwards then recruited his brother, Warner, and several other white men to confront Johnson and Jim. Finding the bondsmen still at work, Isaac accused them of killing his father. At first, Johnson and Jim denied killing Thomas Edwards but soon found themselves being interrogated by the group of white men. While the court record is silent on the issue, the interrogators almost certainly beat Johnson and Jim to elicit a confession. After a time, the bondsmen confessed—that the other had killed their master. Jim claimed that Edwards "was killed and cut in two, and that Johnson killed him, upon which Johnson immediately spoke, and said that he did not kill his master, that Jim killed him."

Having learned the fate of Thomas Edwards, the white men split into two groups. One undertook a search for Edwards's body, while the other continued to question the two bondsmen. For their part, Johnson and Jim continued to blame one another for the murder. As James T. Shadwick, one of the interrogators, recalled, "Jim said that his master sent him after a saw, to one of the neighbors, and that while he was gone, Johnson killed his master." Johnson, for his part, said that "his master sent him off to finishing hawing a stock began before that time, and that while he was gone Jim killed his master."[3] Unsatisfied by the enslaved men's answers, the interrogators continued their interrogation of Johnson and Jim.

Only now they wanted to know what had happened to Thomas Edwards's body. The enslaved men continued to be evasive in their answers. Jim answered that "if his master was killed, he was killed just there, pointing to the end of the stock." The men then searched where Jim had indicated. A further search of the area, some 150 yards away from where the two bondsmen had been working revealed "the head and upper part of the body in a ditch." James Shadwick noticed that there were no tracks leading to the ditch, indicating the slaves had dismembered their master. Shadwick believed that no one "could have carried the body of Mr. Edwards, he being very large and the way over which the body was carried was a difficult one." Having found Thomas Edwards's upper half, the white men turned to the pressing question of finding his legs. As Isaac Edwards turned back to interrogate Johnson and Jim, he confronted a new problem. The enslaved men had stopped talking. Despite repeated questioning, the bondsmen "refused to tell where the legs were deposited."[4] After placing the slaves in custody, Isaac Edwards and his party found his father's legs in a gulley about three quarters of a mile away.

On March 3, 1825, only a week after the killing of Thomas Edwards, Johnson and Jim stood trial in the King William County Courthouse for the murder of their master. The one-hundred-year-old brick courthouse, one of the oldest in Virginia, played host to a special court, known as an oyer and terminer court, that handled criminal trials for the enslaved.[5] The rules governing slave trials differed significantly from those for white defendants. First, these trials occurred within days or a few weeks of the crime. White Virginians wanted to punish misbehaving slaves quickly to serve as a deterrent to others and demonstrate the power of the state. Additionally, oyer and terminer courts did not have juries. Rather five local justices of the peace served as judge and jury. King William County justices of the peace Christopher Johnson, Daniel Elliott, Philip Aylett Jr., John J. Roane, and Christopher Tompkins presided over Johnson and Jim's trial. William Armistead, the county's commonwealth attorney, served as the prosecutor and slaves were entitled to legal counsel. While some masters paid for lawyers for their slaves, the Edwards family refused to defend Johnson and Jim. As a result, the court appointed John Gaines and Thomas Grymes as Johnson and Jim's counsel.[6]

Criminal trials for slaves, conducted in oyer and terminer courts, were stacked against the enslaved. Virginia's slave code did not permit slaves to testify on their own behalf. Southern slave codes did not consider them capable of telling the truth. Southern legal scholar Thomas R.R. Cobb explained, "That the negro, as a general rule, is mendacious, is a fact too well established to require the production of proof, either from history, travels, or craniology."[7] As a result, Johnson and Jim never took the stand in their own defense. The law, however, did allow witnesses, white and slave alike, to relay conversations they had with the accused prior to the trial. Thus, the words of Johnson and Jim found their way into the trial transcript through the testimony of Isaac and Warner Edwards, James Shadwick, and Dina and Obadiah, two of Thomas Edwards's slaves. Slave laws allowed other slaves to testify in the criminal trials of other slaves, but they could not testify in criminal cases involving white defendants. While the testimony of African American slaves could not be used to condemn white men, it could be used to hang enslaved ones.

Johnson and Jim's trial began and concluded on March 3, 1825. After hearing the evidence, the five justices of the peace found the bondsmen guilty of murdering Thomas Edwards. Following the requirements of Virginia's slave code, they sentenced Johnson and Jim to hang. The justices then ordered a copy of the trial transcript be sent to Governor James Pleasants and his Executive Council for review. A change to the commonwealth's slave code in 1801 allowed Virginia's governors to review the death sentences of all slaves accused of capital crimes and reprieve their sentences to transportation out of the state.[8] Justices of the peace could also recommend the governor reprieve condemned bondsmen and women. Owners or other concerned citizens could write or petition the governor for pardons, reprieves, or request the governor to not interfere in the sentence. The five justices of the peace in Johnson and Jim's case did not recommend a reprieve and no one petitioned for mercy. On March 15, 1825, Governor Pleasants and his Executive Council reviewed Johnson and Jim's case and ten days later refused to reprieve the death sentence.[9] The two enslaved men were hanged on April 8, 1825. The commonwealth paid out $650 in compensation to Isaac and Warner Edwards. The only record of Johnson and Jim's execution is a receipt for the compensation located in the records of the Virginia Auditor of Public Accounts.[10]

The case garnered some coverage in local newspapers, where articles expressed outrage at the crime and offered lurid details about how Johnson and Jim dismembered their master. While the slaves' trial did not explore their motive for killing Thomas Edwards, one article offered insight into the cause of the confrontation. The article claimed that Edwards had gone into the woods to examine his bondsmen's work because "he had previously complained of their being lazy, and threatened some punishment upon them, if they continued to neglect their duty."[11] When confronted with the prospect of punishment, the article implied, Johnson and Jim struck their master with their axes and killed him.

In the late nineteenth and early twentieth centuries, historians of American slavery rarely researched physical confrontations like the one between Johnson and Jim and Thomas Edwards. These historians—excepting a small number of African-American and Marxist scholars—viewed southern plantations as akin to schools that elevated African Americans from barbarism to civilization. If scholars discussed slave violence at all, they saw it as proof of the racial inferiority of African Americans. This view reflected and reinforced the racism of the time by presenting the enslaved as largely content with their bondage.[12] This depiction manifested itself in popular depictions of slavery like the characters seen in Margaret Mitchell's *Gone with the Wind*, minstrel shows, and popular children's literature like *The Story of Little Black Sambo*.

In the 1950s, scholars began challenging the notion of slave docility and the Sambo stereotype. The earliest of these historians argued that white slaveholders, rather than being the gentle masters of plantation lore, brutalized their slaves. This scholarship largely relied on the same evidence that earlier historians employed and thus suffered from similar problems. By relying on sources written by whites—journals, plantation records, newspapers, diaries—their work focused more on white perceptions of slave behavior rather than how the enslaved actually behaved.[13] Stanley Elkins, employing research into the horrors of German concentration camps, argued that American slavery was so dehumanizing toward African Americans that it reduced them to childlike Sambos, dependent solely on their masters for survival.[14]

During the 1960s and 1970s, amid the tumult of the Civil Rights movement, the controversy generated by the Elkins thesis launched a thousand dissertations. Instead of stressing slave docility, historians emphasized slave agency, pointing out the areas where the enslaved exercised control over their own lives. Historians argued that African American slaves did not live in a closed system, as Elkins had argued, but rather formed their own communities and identities outside of the master-slave relationship. They created families, practiced their faith, and built support networks where they shared information, food, and aided one another in times of joy and sorrow. One of the leaders of this wave of slavery revisionism, John W. Blassingame, concluded that "rather than identifying with and submitting totally to his master, the slave held onto many remnants of his African culture, gained a sense of worth in the quarters, spent most of his time free from surveillance by whites, controlled important aspects of his life, and did some personally meaningful things on his own volition."[15]

This wave of revisionism, however, soon pushed the argument for slave agency past the breaking point. Some scholars argued enslaved African Americans had created their own culture and community that thrived without white interference. One scholar even introduced "the paradox of the free slave."[16] Slavery, it seemed, had done little damage to the slaves themselves. While these historians had engaged in valuable and necessary work in destroying the myth of slave contentment and docility, some had also taken their arguments too far by swapping out one unrealistic view of slavery for another. This idyllic slave community flattened the immense diversity of the experiences of the enslaved. As Peter Kolchin observed, "On the face of it, the revisionist portrait of the slave community seems distorted if not implausible. In reading about it one rarely comes across child abuse, wife beating, and unhappy, or even squalid and mundane, families; one encounters little black cruelty or meanness, few bullies, thieves, and rapists, or just dull, plodding, uninteresting people."[17] Kolchin has argued that historians should balance the insights of the revisionists with the recognition that slavery circumscribed the lives of the enslaved in significant ways.

While some of the revisionists pushed their view of slave agency too far, they reintroduced sources like slave interviews and autobiographies that previous generations of historians had dismissed as abolitionist propaganda. These sources opened up the first serious examination of physical confrontations. But the scattered nature of the sources, few autobiographies or interviews contained more than one example, made in-depth examinations difficult.

Autobiographies and interviews with ex-slaves offer valuable insights into the slave experience provided historians approach them with an appropriate level of diligence. Slave autobiographies, mostly published in the late antebellum period, reflected the political goals of their authors, who sought the support of Northern abolitionists, attack slavery, and persuade the Northern public of the evils of bondage. At one point in his famed autobiography, Frederick Douglass described the brutal activities of one of his overseers, a Mr. Severe.[18] This heavy handed thematic connection between name and personality strains credibility, but Douglass's description of the overseer's cruelty aligns with other descriptions by ex-slaves.[19] Autobiographies also generally came from a small slice of the slave population—young, male runaways from Border States.[20] Thus they presented a limited view of the experiences of the enslaved.

Ex-slave interviews, conducted in the 1930s as part of the Federal Writer's Project, offered a wider range of enslaved voices, but present their own challenges.[21] The interviews, conducted over seventy years after emancipation, faced issues of failing or distorted memories. As psychologists Christopher Chabris and Daniel Simons have written regarding human memory, "What is stored in memory is not an exact replica of reality, but a re-creation of it."[22] Seventy years of experiences, including Reconstruction, Jim Crow, and the Great Depression, colored ex-slaves' memories about their bondage. Additionally, many of the interviewers were white and some were even descendants of slave owners and ex-slaves may have softened the horrors of their enslavement for fear of offending their interviewers.[23] The challenges presented by these sources, however, are not unique in the study of history. Rather as the eminent Southern historian C. Vann Woodward wrote regarding the WPA sources, "The necessary precautions, however, are no more elaborate or burdensome than those required by many other types of sources. . . . They are certainly not great enough to justify continued neglect of this valuable evidence on black history in America."[24]

In recent decades, scholars have mined southern legal records for their insights into the lives of the enslaved, opening up new avenues for historical research.[25] Legal records, like those from Virginia that provide the bulk of evidence for this book, have their own strengths and weaknesses. Southern court systems offered few avenues for the enslaved to defend themselves.[26] As mentioned above, oyer and terminer courts denied slaves the right to testify in their own defense. But trial transcripts, like those found in the Executive Papers of Virginia's governors, were filled with firsthand accounts of confrontations of recent events. The trial of Johnson and Jim occurred a week after the murder of Thomas Edwards compared to the years that passed between the events described in slave interviews and autobiographies and the participants' recollection of those events. Additionally, court clerks and justices of the peace sought to accurately record testimony to satisfy the demands of Virginia's governors for complete transcripts. Some masters and lawyers made detailed legal arguments regarding the disposition of slave trials and relied on transcripts to point out incidents where justices of the peace and commonwealth attorneys failed to live up to their obligations. Virginian's governors took these pleas seriously and occasionally pardoned or reprieved the death sentences of convicted slaves.

Physical confrontations existed on a continuum of bondspeople's resistance to enslavement. Historians have identified four major categories of slave resistance: rebellion, running away, confrontations, and day-to-day resistance.[27] These forms of resistance varied in their risks, rewards, and outcomes. Slave rebellion carried the greatest risk and greatest reward.[28] Yet compared to slavery elsewhere in the Western hemisphere or to serfdom in Russia, American slaves rebelled far less often.[29] This was not because enslaved African Americans were more docile or more content with their bondage. Rather the realities of slavery in the United States, especially in a comparative context, made such rebellions rare. The United States, unlike elsewhere in the world, featured a resident master class, small holdings of slaves, and an armed white population.[30] Additionally, the swift and brutal retribution enacted by Virginia authorities in the aftermath of Gabriel's Plot in 1800 and the Nat Turner Revolt in 1831 served as a reminder to Virginia's slaves of the dangers of rebellion. These realities led enslaved Virginians to recognize the futility of rebellion.

Forms of day-to-day resistance, such as feigning illness or stupidity, sabotage, and theft of owners' property, while common strategies, offered only temporary relief of the horrors of bondage. While offering some relief to overworked or abused slaves, day-to-day resistance could not permanently alter the dynamics of enslavement. Slaves who feigned illness once in a while could get away with it. But repeatedly playing sick attracted the attention of owners and overseers, who had no qualms about whipping the slaves under their command. Additionally, day-to-day resistance strategies often shifted the burdens of labor onto other bondspeople who had to pick up the slack of their missing comrades.[31] These actions could create tensions between slaves and divide already weak slave communities. Day-to-day resistance also confirmed preexisting racial stereotypes regarding African Americans. As Peter Kolchin has argued, day-to-day resistance served "to reinforce among whites the notion that blacks were by nature lazy, foolish and thieving."[32] Day-to-day resistance could bring temporary but not permanent relief of the unrelenting horrors of bondage.

Physical confrontations and running away represented an intermediate form of resistance. Their advantage came from their frequency as well as their ability to alter the dynamics of slavery without necessarily triggering the brutal repression used to put down slave rebellions. The evidence for slave flight is voluminous. Frederick Douglass famously escaped slavery by borrowing a sailor's uniform and free papers. Harriet Jacobs hid in her grandmother's attic for seven years before escaping to the North. Henry "Box" Brown mailed himself in a crate from Richmond to Philadelphia.[33] Besides flight to the

North, bondspeople also engaged in temporary truancy. In response to punishments or to express displeasure with their owners, slaves ran away for days and weeks at a time. They hid out in nearby woods or swamps or hid themselves with relatives. Martha Showvely, an ex-slave from Virginia, recalled how her uncle ran away after his master beat him. She explained, "De massa beat him, an' he ran away. He went up in the woods an' dug him a hole in de ground an' covered it with leaves."[34] Fears of truant slaves and those escaping to the North prompted white southerners to constantly agitate for fugitive slave laws throughout the history of the United States.[35] It is in this middle ground where the enslaved could exert the most control over their lives.

In examining physical confrontations in Virginia from 1801 to 1860, a few trends become apparent. The vast majority of Virginia's enslaved population did not violently resist. On the whole, bondspeople accepted their circumstances. They surrendered parts of their lives to accommodate to the world in which they lived. They worked without pay, obeyed their owners, and showed deference to whites and the ideology of white supremacy. This acceptance of their reality, however, does not mean that enslaved Virginians were the Sambos of the Elkins's thesis, so brutalized by the oppressiveness of enslavement that they were reduced to servile-like dependency. Rather enslaved Virginians knew there was little they could do to overthrow the system of racialized slavery—it would take a war to accomplish that goal—but they could protect, as best they could, themselves from white intrusions into their lives. They also recognized that the power of their masters and mistresses was contextual. Masters and mistresses had a lot more power and control over their slaves in the fields and households than they did in the quarters. In these spaces, the enslaved married, raised children, and built communal traditions apart from white interference. In the areas where they interacted with whites, bondsmen and women established expectations regarding punishment, the treatment of themselves and their family members, and who would control the day-to-day rhythms of their lives. In other words, they survived by setting limits on their enslavement. And when whites pushed past those limits, the enslaved fought to restore them.

The weakness of slave communities, however, prevented the establishment of clearly delineated standards of white behavior. Instead, bondspeople shared a general sense of acceptable and unacceptable white behaviors. This left individual slaves to set personal boundaries for themselves. Some rejected any efforts of whites to punish them, while others accepted punishment only from their owners. Some men avenged the rape of their wives. Others did not. Some enslaved women patiently endured beatings from their mistresses while others beat their mistresses right back. It is not surprising that the boundaries of acceptable behavior and the outbreak of violence largely depended on the slaves themselves. As mentioned above, the African

American slave community was relatively fragile compared to others found in other slave societies. Owners held slaves on small holdings and lived alongside them. This reality made it difficult for the development of a unified slave community that could collectively resist oppression. Additionally, whites would not tolerate any collection resistance by the slaves as it too closely resembled slave rebellion.

These extraordinary acts of violence brought the ordinary concerns of enslaved Virginians into focus.[36] When they engaged in confrontations, the vast majority of enslaved men and women did not seek to overthrow their masters and claim their freedom—though they certainly wished for it. Rather they sought to reassert some measure of control over their day-to-day lives. They agreed to work for their owners while trying to avoid physical abuse. They protected their rights to work without overseers or to visit family members on weekends. They married and built families largely without interference from whites, but rapes or other attacks on family members threatened the worlds that the enslaved constructed apart from their owners' oppression. While Virginia's slave code did not recognize slave marriages, rights to visit family members, or that enslaved women could be raped, over the decades whites had acknowledged their importance as part of give and take that mediated the master-slave relationship. When whites intruded in these areas, bondsmen and women reacted violently to reestablish their rights. And through this violence, the enslaved revealed precisely what they held most dear.

The legacy of physical confrontations is complicated. On the individual level, they afforded the enslaved greater control over their day-to-day lives and pushed back against the worst excesses of bondage. This valuable breathing room allowed for the enslaved to protect their families and ensure the preservation of their humanity. On the collective level, however, slave violence worked in two ways. First, physical confrontations reified rather than overthrew the Southern social order. While slave violence set limits on the worst brutalities of bondage, it did little to bring about the end of slavery. Slaves who resisted and survived their confrontations, may have won better treatment like Frederick Douglass in his famous confrontation with Edward Covey, but they were still slaves. That physical confrontations were not some form of revolutionary violence should not be surprising. Their goal was not revolution, but restoration—restoration of a tenuous status quo that provided the enslaved enough room to survive and also served as a reminder to others of what would happen if masters pushed their power too far.

The following chapters will explore these issues in greater depth. The first chapter will explore how paternalism—owners' interest and interference in the lives of their slaves—shaped slave violence. Paternalism created a series of reciprocal obligations between slaves and their owners. The enslaved labored, obeyed their owners' orders, and accommodated themselves to the brutal reality of their lives. In exchange, masters were supposed to provide food, not whip too much, and allow their bondspeople the opportunity to create semi-autonomous lives. Owners, however, frequently failed to live up to their end of the bargain. They whipped mercilessly, underfed their slaves, and interfered in all aspects of their slaves' lives. In response, the enslaved fought back. They rejected indiscriminate punishments. The presence of overseers and hired-out owners complicated these relationships even further. Overseers and hired-out owners and had little regard for slaves' expectations governing work and punishment. These differing expectations could result in conflict. Masters who ignored their paternalistic obligations pushed the enslaved toward violence. In a world of unremitting cruelty, slaves risked everything and killed their masters rather than endure any more mistreatment.

The second chapter will investigate enslaved men and their masculinity. In antebellum Virginia, the presence of enslaved men, who obeyed their owners' orders, allowed their bodies to be physically mutilated, and were legally the property of whites, undergirded white southern masculinity. Whites defined their masculinity in opposition to the degraded status of their slaves. If slaves submitted, white men dominated. Despite the claims of whites, enslaved men developed their own definitions of what it meant to be a man. Due to the relative weakness of the slave community to create and enforce communal standards of behavior, this definition of masculinity varied from bondsman to bondsman, but shared some general characteristics. Some enslaved men only permitted their owners to punish them and violently resisted when anyone else tried to. Some avenged the whippings and punishments of their family members. Enslaved men also believed that violence and a willingness to engage in it represented a key component of masculinity. They took pride in their own resistance and in the violence of other bondsmen.

The third chapter shifts its focus to enslaved women and their response to sexual assault. Southern whites, as they had done with enslaved men, constructed their own understandings of bondswomen's femininity. These views, which had developed over hundreds of years, stressed that enslaved women were sexually promiscuous. This view of African American women's sexuality justified all manner of white men's abuses and interference. It shifted the blame for the rapes and sexual assaults that pervaded antebellum slavery away from the perpetrators, white men, and onto the victims, African American women. The realities under which enslaved women lived and worked reinforced these views. In a slave society with a naturally reproducing population and without access to new supplies of African slaves, white masters took a special interest in slave women's reproductivity. Enslaved children were the key to increased wealth either through their labor or sale. Bondswomen frequently found their bodies exposed to whites while receiving punishment, working, or being sold. Slave-traders tied the value of enslaved women to the condition of their bodies. Young, pretty girls fetched high prices on the market for their use as sexual companions for wealthy whites. These realities reinforced white stereotypes regarding slave women's promiscuity.

Enslaved women attempted to resist sexual exploitation at the hands of whites. They fought back, ran away, and sought allies to protect themselves from rape. In some cases, bondswomen managed to ward off sexual exploitation through violence or the intercession of other whites. They often sought help from their mistresses, but white women shared no sense of gender solidarity with African Americans. White supremacy idolized elite white women and cast them in a reverential light. Benefitting from their white skin, these white women had little reason to systematically push back against sexual exploitation. Whatever rage they had often manifested itself in violence against African American women and children rather than their cheating husbands. It was easier to punch down at slaves than up at their husbands. As a result, enslaved women rarely successfully warded off sexual assault.

The fourth chapter considers enslaved women's violence within the context of the household. Slaveholding white women bore the responsibility for organizing and running their households. They had to ensure that meals were prepared, beds made, and create a tranquil and pleasant atmosphere. Yet elite white women performed very little of the actual work within their households. Enslaved women provided the bulk of the labor that kept southern households functioning. They cooked meals, swept floors, supervised children, mended clothes, and performed any other number of household tasks. During their lifetime most female slaves spent some time working in the household under their mistresses' supervision. Mistresses understood their role as educating their lazy and stupid slaves. If African American women were ever to rise from their degraded status, it would be because of the discipline instilled by their mistresses. As it turns out, southern households were not the havens of domestic bliss found in Lost Cause propaganda like *Gone With the Wind*.

Rather mistresses beat and whipped their enslaved women for the smallest infractions. They chided their bondswomen for their poor work habits and incompetence. White mistresses viewed these behaviors as further proof of African American women's natural inferiority. Moreover, they came to understand enslaved women's failure to live up to expectations as a threat to white women's place in the household. This resistance represented not only a problem of labor management but could undermine the entire household. As a result, white women savagely sought to keep their bondswomen in line. They misconstrued enslaved women's resistance to their working conditions as a character flaw rather than what it truly was—an effort to push back against the limits of their enslavement. In doing so, bondswomen revealed the fragile foundations upon which white women's power rested. Without enslaved women's labor, white women could not claim the mantle of femininity for themselves.

The fifth chapter examines the ways in which physical confrontations divided white Virginians and revealed their deepest anxieties over their communities and the future of slavery itself. The chapter focuses on three specific cases where individual male slaves were convicted by oyer and terminer courts and sentenced to hang. In each case, Virginia's governors, using their executive powers, reprieved the slaves, against the wishes of local elites. These cases all highlighted white concerns regarding the future of white supremacy. The first case from Princess Anne County in 1818 and 1819 involved Mingo, a male slave, who interacted with slaves and whites alike all the while terrorizing white farmers and participating in a murder-for-hire plot. His ability to move freely across the color line played into pervasive fears of runaways and the threat of a racial alliance between slaves and poor whites to overthrow the slave regime. The second case, from Louisa County, in 1828, dealt with the disappearance of an orphaned white girl and the allegation that Sydnor, a mixed-race slave, had sexually exploited her for profit, with the knowledge of local elites. The last case involved the commutation of Jordan Hatcher, a slave convicted of killing his overseer in a Richmond tobacco factory. The commutation became a flashpoint between Virginia's first democratically elected governor, from the western part of the state where slaveholding was not prominent, and the eastern elites in the legislature, who feared any loss of government support for slavery.

In each of these instances, white Virginians proved willing to do whatever they deemed necessary to preserve white supremacy. In Mingo's case, they lynched a slave who had been granted a reprieve from his death sentence rather than risk having him return home again. Local elites engaged in a systematic effort to railroad a single male slave and violated the key tenets of Virginia's oyer and terminer courts to do so. And Virginia's political leaders orchestrated a riot in Richmond that threatened to storm the Governor's mansion to express their disapproval over the granting of a reprieve.[37] The slaves who committed these acts of violence had no idea of the impact their cases would have. Their actions revealed the deep fissures that threatened to tear Virginia's slave society apart. They speak to the ability of slave violence to have wide-ranging impacts beyond their initial confrontations.

Besides revealing the boundaries that the enslaved set on their oppression, physical confrontations had wide ranging implications. Most importantly, their impact extended far beyond the individual level. Barely a month after the death of Thomas Edwards, Johnson and Jim were dead—hanged by their necks at the King William County Courthouse with its historic brick façade. But the impact of their confrontation outlived them. Mrs. Edwards, Isaac and Warner Edwards, Thomas Shadwick, and other white men would never forget the search for Thomas Edwards's body. The discovery of the dismembered body, the bondsmen's blood-soaked clothes, and slowly unravelling horror at uncovering the truth of the situation would be hard to forget. The five justices of the peace who comprised the court of oyer and terminer likely never forgot the case of the two bondsmen who killed their master. Dinah, Obadiah, Jim's wife, and the other slaves who knew Johnson and Jim would remember the pair of enslaved men not only for their confrontation with their master, but for their place in the community. They were husbands, sons, comrades, and members of an enslaved community. Their violence was a story that the enslaved could pass on—the time two men fought back and killed their owners.

Johnson and Jim's violence had an impact well beyond the lives of those who knew them. In the days and weeks after the confrontation, articles appeared in local newspapers relaying the details of the confrontation. The story soon spread across the country as newspapers printed and reprinted accounts of Johnson and Jim's violence. The Norfolk, Virginia *Beacon* was appalled at the "most shocking spectacle" of the murder.[38] The *Ballston Spa Gazette* declared that Thomas Edwards was "BUTCHERED by his negroes with axes." The paper hoped that the details of the crime and others like it would "be the means of softening the passions of some, and deter them from committing a crime."[39] The *Boston Recorder* meanwhile hoped that "the curses of slavery will not be visited on our country: but that our repentance and its entire extinction will be speedy."[40] The story of Johnson and Jim reminded readers—in the North and South—that the enslaved were not content in their bondage and could turn the tide of violence back against their oppressors at any time.

NOTES

1. *National Gazette and Literary Register* (Philadelphia, PA), March 8, 1825.

2. *Commonwealth vs. Johnson & Jim*, James Pleasants Executive Papers 1822–1825, Accession 42046. Box 6, Folder 10. State Government Records Collection, The Library of Virginia, Richmond, Va. Henceforth, *Commonwealth vs. Johnson & Jim*, (LVA).

3. *Commonwealth vs. Johnson & Jim* (LVA).

4. *Commonwealth vs. Johnson & Jim* (LVA).

5. For more information on courts of oyer and terminer and slave trials in Virginia, see Peter Charles Hoffer and William B. Scott eds., *Criminal Proceedings in Colonial Virginia: Richmond County, 1710/11–1754, American Legal Records Series, Vol 10* (Athens: University of Georgia Press, 1984), xliv–lii; Daniel J. Flanigan, "Criminal Proceedings in Slave Trials in the Antebellum South," *Journal of Southern History* 40, No. 4 (November 1974): 543–545. For works on slave trials and

crime in Virginia see Philip J. Schwarz, *Twice Condemned: Slaves and the Criminal Laws of Virginia, 1705–1865* (Baton Rouge: Louisiana State University Press, 1988); Schwarz, *Slave Laws in Virginia* (Athens: University of Press, 1996).

6. *Commonwealth vs. Johnson & Jim* (LVA).

7. Thomas R.R. Cobb, *An Inquiry into the Law of Negro Slavery in the United States of America* (Philadelphia: T. & J.W. Johnson & Company, 1858), 233.

8. Douglas R. Egerton, *Gabriel's Rebellion: The Virginia Slave Conspiracies of 1800 and 1802* (Chapel Hill: University of North Carolina Press, 1993), 111–112. The execution of dozens of slaves in the aftermath of Gabriel's rebellion strained the commonwealth's coffers, leading to the law change that allowed condemned slaves to be sold out of Virginia with the money from the sale going back to the commonwealth.

9. *Commonwealth vs. Johnson & Jim* (LVA).

10. *Commonwealth vs. Johnson and Jim*, Virginia Auditor of Public Accounts, Records of Condemned Blacks Executed or Transported, 1823–1832. Misc. Reel 2252. Accession APA 756, State Records Collection, The Library of Virginia, Richmond, Virginia.

11. *Salem Gazette* (Salem, MA), March 11, 1825.

12. For the most famous and prominent example of this historical school see Ulrich B. Phillips, *American Negro Slavery: A Survey of the Supply, Employment and Control of Negro Labor as Determined by the Plantation Regime* (New York: D. Appleton and Company, 1918).

13. Kenneth M. Stampp, *The Peculiar Institution: Slavery in the Ante-Bellum South* (New York: Alfred A. Knopf, 1956).

14. Stanley M. Elkins, *Slavery: A Problem in American Institutional and Intellectual Life Second Edition* (Chicago: University of Chicago Press, 1968).

15. John W. Blassingame, *The Slave Community: Plantation Life in the Antebellum South Revised & Enlarged Edition* (New York: Oxford University, 1979), xii.

16. Thomas L. Webber, *Deep Like the Rivers: Education in the Slave Quarter Community, 1831–1865* (New York: W.W. Norton & Company, 1978), 261–262.

17. Peter Kolchin, "Reevaluating the Antebellum Slave Community: A Comparative Perspective," *Journal of American History* 70 (December 1983), 601.

18. Frederick Douglass, *Narrative of the Life of Fredrick Douglass: An American Slave* (1845: New York: Oxford University Press, 2009), 22.

19. For the use of slave autobiographies see William L. Andrews, *To Tell A Free Story: The First Century of Afro-American Autobiography, 1760–1865* (Urbana: University of Illinois Press, 1986).

20. John Hope Franklin and Loren Schweninger, *Runaway Slaves: Rebels on the Plantation* (New York: Oxford University Press, 1999), 209–233.

21. George P. Rawick, ed., *The American Slave: A Composite Autobiography Vol. 1–19* (Westport: Greenwood Press, 1972); Rawick ed., *The American Slave: A Composite Autobiography Supplement Series 1, Vol. 1–12* (Westport: Greenwood Press, 1977); Rawick ed., *The American Slave: A Composite Autobiography Supplement Series 2, Vol. 1–10* (Westport: Greenwood Press, 1979).

22. Christopher Chabris and Daniel Simons, *The Invisible Gorilla: How Our Intuitions Deceive Us* (New York: Broadway Books, 2009), 49.

23. On using the W.P.A. see John W. Blassingame, "Using the Testimony of Ex-Slaves: Approaches and Problems" *The Journal of Southern History* 41, No. 4 (November 1975): 473–492; C. Vann Woodward, "Review: History from Slave Sources," *The American Historical Review* 79, No. 2 (April 1974): 470–481; Paul D. Escott, *Slavery Remembered: A Record of Twentieth Century Slave Narratives* (Chapel Hill: University of North Carolina Press, 1979); Norman R. Yetman, "Ex-Slave Interviews and the Historiography of Slavery," *American Quarterly* 36, No. 2, (Summer 1984): 181–210; David Thomas Bailey, "A Divided Prism: Two Sources of Black Testimony on Slavery," *Journal of Southern History* 46, No. 3 (Aug., 1980): 381–404.

24. Woodward, "History from Slave Sources," 480.

25. Schwarz, *Twice Condemned*; Diane Miller Sommerville, *Rape and Race in the Nineteenth-Century South* (Chapel Hill: University of North Carolina Press, 2004); Ariela J. Gross, *Double Character: Slavery and Mastery in the Antebellum Southern Courtroom* (Princeton: Princeton University Press, 2000); Jeff Forret, *Race Relations at the Margins: Slaves and Poor Whites in the Antebellum Southern Countryside* (Baton Rouge: Louisiana State University Press, 2006).

26. For insight into the intersection of slavery and the law see Michael Stephen Hindus, *Prison and Planation: Crime, Justice, and Authority in Massachusetts and South Carolina, 1767–1878* (Chapel Hill: University of North Carolina Press, 1980); Mark V. Tushnet, *The American Law of Slavery, 1810–1860: Considerations of Humanity and Interest* (Princeton: Princeton University Press, 1981); Edward L. Ayers, *Vengeance and Justice: Crime and Punishment in the 19th Century American South* (New York: Oxford University Press, 1984); Thomas D. Morris, *Southern Slavery and the Law* (Chapel Hill: University of North Carolina Press, 1996); Paul Finkleman ed., *Slavery & the Law* (Madison: Madison House Publishers, 1997); Judith Kelleher Schafer, *Slavery, the Civil Law, and the Supreme Court of Louisiana* (Baton Rouge: Louisiana State University Press, 1997).

27. For broader histories of slave resistance in the United States see Herbert Aptheker, *American Negro Slave Revolts: 50th Anniversary Edition* (New York: International Publishers, 1993); Vincent Harding, *There Is a River: The Black Struggle for Freedom in America* (New York: Harcourt Brace Jovanovich, 1981); James Oakes, "The Political Significance of Slave Resistance." *History Workshop* 22 (1986): 89–107; Sylvia R. Frey, *Water from the Rock: Black Resistance in a Revolutionary Age* (Princeton: Princeton University Press, 1991); Saidiya V. Hartman, *Scenes of Subjection: Terror, Slavery, and Self-Making in Nineteenth-Century America* (New York: Oxford University Press, 1997); Walter C. Rucker, *The River Flows On: Black Resistance, Culture, and Identity Formation in Early America* (Baton Rouge: Louisiana State University Press, 2006).

28. Thomas J. Davis, *A Rumor of Revolt: The "Great Negro Plot" in Colonial New York* (New York: Free Press, 1985); Jill Lepore, *New York Burning: Liberty, Slavery, and Conspiracy in an Eighteenth-Century Manhattan* (New York: Alfred A. Knopf, 2005); Egerton, *Gabriel's Rebellion*; James Sidbury, *Ploughshares into Swords: Race, Rebellion, and Identity in Gabriel's Virginia, 1730–1810* (New York: Cambridge University Press, 1997); Douglas R. Egerton, *He Shall Go Out Free:*

The Lives of Denmark Vesey (Madison: Madison House, 1999); Michael P. Johnson, "Denmark Vesey and his Conspirators," *William and Mary Quarterly* 58 (October 2001): 913–976; "Forum: The Making of a Slave Conspiracy," *William and Mary Quarterly* 59 (January 2002): 135–202; Stephen B. Oates, *The Fires of Jubilee: Nat Turner's Fierce Rebellion* (New York: Harper & Row, 1975); Kenneth S. Greenberg, *Nat Turner: A Slave Rebellion in History and Memory* (New York: Oxford University Press, 2003); Scot A. French, *The Rebellious Slave: Nat Turner in American Memory* (Boston: Houghton Mifflin, 2004); Anthony E. Kaye, "Neighborhoods and Nat Turner: The Making of a Slave Rebel and the Unmaking of a Slave Rebellion," *Journal of the Early Republic* 27, No. 4 (2007): 705–720; Peter H. Wood, *Black Majority; Negroes in Colonial South Carolina from 1670 through the Stono Rebellion* (New York: Alfred A. Knopf, 1974), 308–326; John K. Thornton, "African Dimensions of the Stono Rebellion," *American Historical Review* 96 (October 1991): 1101–1113; Mark M. Smith, *Stono: Documenting and Interpreting a Southern Slave Revolt* (Columbia: University of South Carolina Press, 2005); Peter Charles Hoffer, *Cry Liberty: The Great Stono River Slave Rebellion of 1739* (New York: Oxford University Press, 2010); Daniel Rasmussen, *American Uprising: The Untold Story of America's Largest Slave Revolt* (New York: Harper, 2011); Winthrop D. Jordan, *Tumult and Silence at Second Creek: An Inquiry into a Civil War Slave Conspiracy* (Baton Rouge: Louisiana State University Press, 1993).

29. Peter Kolchin, *Unfree Labor: American Slavery and Russian Serfdom* (Cambridge: Belknap Press of Harvard University Press, 1987), 250–257.

30. Eugene D. Genovese, *From Rebellion to Revolution: Afro-American Slave Revolts in the Making of the Modern World* (Baton Rouge: Louisiana State University Press, 1979).

31. For historical analysis of day-to-day resistance see: Raymond A. Bauer and Alice H. Bauer, "Day-to-day Resistance to Slavery," *Journal of Negro History* 27, No. 4, (1942), 388–419; Stampp, *The Peculiar Institution*, 97–109; James Scott, *Weapons of the Weak: Everyday Forms of Peasant Resistance* (New Haven: Yale University Press, 1985); Stephanie M.H. Camp, *Closer to Freedom: Enslaved Women and Everyday Resistance in the Plantation South* (Chapel Hill: University of North Carolina Press, 2004).

32. Peter Kolchin, *American Slavery 1617–1877* (New York: Hill and Wang, 2003), 157.

33. See Douglass, *Narrative*; Harriet Jacobs, *Incidents in the Life of a Slave Girl*, eds. Nellie Y. McKay and Frances Smith Foster (1861: repr. New York: W.W. Norton & Company, 2001); Henry Box Brown, *Narrative of the Life of Henry Box Brown, Written by Himself* (Manchester, Lee and Glenn, 1851).

34. Charles L. Perdue Jr., Thomas E. Barden, & Robert K. Phillips eds., *Weevils in the Wheat: Interviews with Virginia Slaves* (Charlottesville: University Press of Virginia, 1976), 264.

35. See Stanley W. Campbell, *The Slave Catchers: Enforcement of the Fugitive Slave Law, 1850–1860* (Chapel Hill: University of North Carolina Press, 1970); Don E. Fehrenbacher, *The Slaveholding Republic: An Account of the United States Government's Relations to Slavery* (New York: Oxford University Press, 2001).

36. The literature on the development of slavery in Virginia is extensive, but major works include: Gerald W. Mullin, *Flight and Rebellion: Slave Resistance in*

Eighteenth-Century Virginia (New York: Oxford University Press, 1972); Edmund S. Morgan, *American Slavery, American Freedom: The Ordeal of Colonial Virginia* (New York: W.W. Norton & Company, 1975); T.H. Breen and Stephen Innes, *Mine Own Ground: Race and Freedom on Virginia's Eastern Shore* (New York: Oxford University Press, 1980); Rhys Isaac, *The Transformation of Virginia, 1740–1790* (Chapel Hill: Published for the Institute of Early American History and Culture, Williamsburg, Virginia by the University of North Carolina Press, 1982); Allan Kulikoff, *Tobacco and Slaves: The Development of Southern Cultures in the Chesapeake, 1680–1800* (Chapel Hill: Published for the Institute of Early American History and Culture, Williamsburg, Virginia by the University of North Carolina Press, 1986); Kathleen Brown, *Good Wives, Nasty Wenches, & Anxious Patriarchs: Gender, Race, and Power in Colonial Virginia* (Chapel Hill: Published for the Institute of Early American History and Culture, Williamsburg, Virginia by the University of North Carolina Press, 1996); Sally E. Hadden, *Slave Patrols: Law and Violence in Virginia and the Carolinas* (Cambridge: Harvard University Press, 2001); Anthony S. Parent, *Foul Means: The Formation of a Slave Society in Virginia, 1660–1740* (Chapel Hill: Published for the Omohundro Institute of Early American History and Culture, Williamsburg, Virginia, by the University of North Carolina Press, 2003); Joshua D. Rothman, *Notorious in the Neighborhood: Sex and Families Across the Color Line in Virginia, 1787–1861* (Chapel Hill: University of North Carolina Press, 2003).

37. William A. Link, "The Jordan Hatcher Case: Politics and 'A Spirit of Insubordination in Antebellum Virginia," *The Journal of Southern History* 64, No. 4 (November 1998): 615–648. See also Harrison M. Etheridge, "The Jordan Hatcher Affair of 1852: Cold Justice and Warm Compassion," *The Virginia Magazine of History and Biography* 84, No. 4 (October 1976): 446–463.

38. *Norfolk Beacon* (Norfolk, VA), March 3, 1825.

39. *Ballston Spa Gazette* (Ballston Spa, New York), March 29, 1825.

40. *Boston Recorder* (Boston, MA), March 9, 1825.

Chapter 1

Paternalism and Physical Confrontations

American slavery differed from its counterparts in the Western Hemisphere in two important ways. First, American slaves lived on smaller holdings compared to elsewhere in the Americas. In the United States, only one-fourth of all slaves lived on estates or plantations with fifty or more slaves. Half lived on holdings between ten and forty-nine slaves and the remaining one-fourth lived on holdings of fewer than ten slaves.[1] In 1860, the average holding in Virginia was just 18.8 slaves. In Jamaica, just prior to emancipation, 75 percent of slaves lived on holdings of more than fifty people. Second, American masters, with a few exceptions, lived with their slaves. In the Saint Domingue, where whites only accounted for 6 percent of the population at the time of the 1791 rebellion, the vast majority of masters lived abroad, leaving management of their plantations to hired employees.[2] In the United States, small slaveholdings and a resident master class meant that owners interacted with their slaves on a daily basis—giving them orders, overseeing their work, and punishing them as needed.

The frequent contact led slave owners to view and interact with their slaves through the lens of what historians have termed "paternalism." The use of the term has generated much debate.[3] But simply put, paternalism meant that masters involved themselves in and interfered with their slaves' private lives.[4] Slaveholder paternalism did not alleviate or lessen the horrors of enslavement. Rather it added another dimension to slavery as slaveholders inserted themselves into familial disputes, the naming of children, and other matters. Paternalism also led to slaveholders to hold an exaggerated view of themselves and the ways in which they intruded in the lives of the enslaved. Across antebellum Virginia, white slaveholders viewed slaves as part of their extended families. Legal scholar Thomas R. R. Cobb wrote, "The master is the head of his family. Next to wife and children, he cares for his slaves. He avenges their injuries, protects their persons, provides for their wants, and guides their labors. In return, he is revered and held as protector and master."[5]

Paternalism was a reciprocal relationship between masters and slaves. Masters were supposed to provide for their slaves and treat them humanely. The enslaved were expected to follow orders, be loyal to their owners, and work diligently.[6] In practice, however, this reciprocal relationship was much more complicated than it first seemed. Masters often failed to live up to their self-proclaimed ideals and duties. They provided food, clothing, and brought in ministers to preach to the enslaved. Owners set work quotas, whipped slaves, and supervised the slaves' labor. In practice, however, they inconsistently enforced rules, played favorites, and placed their self-interest ahead of their paternalistic obligations.

The enslaved and their owners, also, had very different understandings regarding masters' obligations in the master-slave relationship. For masters, paternalism was a wholly self-serving ideology. It justified their interference in the lives of their slaves while also requiring slaves to obey their masters. Slaves owed their masters obedience and loyalty. For their part, masters owed the enslaved very little beyond their continued existence. They were under no obligation to provide food, clothing, or other necessities. If masters chose to provide them, it was out of the goodness of their hearts. After all, masters did not acquiesce to the demands of slaves.

The enslaved, on the other hand, understood these necessities as obligations owed to them for their labor. The enslaved held up their end of the bargain and expected their owners to do the same. As Eugene Genovese has explained, "The slaves accepted the doctrine of reciprocity, but with a profound difference. To the idea of reciprocal duties, they added their own doctrine of reciprocal rights. To the tendency to make them creatures of another's will they counterposed a tendency to assert themselves as autonomous human beings."[7] The enslaved had little power to reject the ceaseless interference of their owners. As a result, they accepted it as a part of their existence. But in acceding to their reality, the enslaved extracted a heavy price demanding the recognition of their humanity and some measure of autonomy.

The enslaved managed to construct lives largely, but never totally, separate from their masters' interference. They married and created families. Although owners had to approve of marriages and sometimes named children against their parents' wishes. Owners also sold slaves away from their family members, splitting up families and even marriages. In response, bondspeople cultivated and practiced their own forms of Christianity that ran counter to the Christianity espoused by their masters.[8] They left home and visited family members without permission. They held dances and congregated in private spaces against the wishes of whites. Occasionally, they violently resisted. These actions were part of the constant negotiation and renegotiation of power between owners and the enslaved. As Peter Kolchin has explained, "Their resistance thus points both to a shared if never precisely defined understanding of what was acceptable and what was unacceptable within the general framework of a hated system, and to a conservative mentality under which slaves for the most part grudgingly made their peace with an oppressive reality but, when pushed too far, resisted behavior that violated that understanding."[9]

This chapter explores some of the circumstances that prompted the enslaved to resist. First, Virginia's slaves resisted when owners failed to live up to their paternalistic obligations. These failures struck at the very heart of slaves' efforts to carve out lives free of their owners' interference. Issues of punishment, the denial of food, and not being allowed to visit family members prompted Virginia's bondspeople to resist. Second, the involvement of overseers and hired-out owners undermined the paternalistic system of mutual obligations. Some slaves rejected the rights of overseers or hired-out owners to punish them at all, hoping to set limits on punishment. Others tried to take advantage of the tenuous power of overseers by claiming that their masters' orders superseded those of the overseer. When slaves engaged in confrontations, some owners and overseers kept a united front, while others blamed one another. Finally, despite the high-minded claims of whites, many owners failed to live up to or even acknowledge their paternalistic obligations to the enslaved. Instead, they whipped, starved, and maltreated their slaves at every turn. By refusing to recognize the humanity of their bondspeople, white owners ensured that their slaves would turn against them. With nothing left to lose, the enslaved turned the tide of violence back against their owners regardless of the outcome for themselves.

VIOLATIONS OF RIGHTS

Despite claims to the contrary, owners viewed providing the basic essentials, clothing and housing, not as an obligation, but as a sign of their generosity. Their slaves, on the other hand, saw these actions as masters were upholding their end of the paternalistic bargain in exchange for their slaves' labor. The enslaved rejected any efforts by whites to define these obligations as some form of kindness. As Eugene Genovese has observed, "Where the masters preferred to translate their own self-defined duties into privileges for their people—an utter absurdity of illogic of which the most servile slave could see through—the slaves understood duties to be duties."[10] For some slaves, these obligations extended even further. Not only were masters expected to provide basic necessities, they should not excessively whip their slaves. Nor should they deny the enslaved access to food or refuse to allow them to visit family members. The violation of these basic rights by masters prompted some slaves to violently resist their owners.

Some slaves rejected the discipline from any white person, even their owners. This discipline often came in the form of whippings, which could leave emotional and physical scars. Ishrael Massie, an ex-slave from Virginia, recalled that, "dey made ya take off all yo clothes—strip jes' like ya wuz bo'n an' beat on ya natural hide. Dis back of mine don' had a many, many lashin' an'—oh baby!—I jes had to take hit." Robert Ellett said that his master "was the meanest man out, but father wouldn't let him beat him. I've seen him time and again try to beat my father an' I always hear my father say, 'I'll die before I'll let you beat me!'"[11] In 1821, in Louisa County, Patrick, a slave belonging to Samuel Wade attacked his owner after Wade had whipped him. Cloe, one of Wade's slaves, testified that it had taken five people to whip Patrick. Patrick was resentful of the whipping and complained "that he was good negro when let alone, but if he was raised that he was the devil."[12]

Refusing to accept punishment from owners represented an important bulwark for some slaves against white domination in their lives. The enslaved recognized that whites targeted slaves who did not resist punishment for future whippings. As Frederick Douglass explained, "They prefer to whip those who are most easily whipped." Douglass had learned this lesson from firsthand experience. During his first six months with Edward Covey, "scarce a week passed without his whipping me. I was seldom free from a sore back. My awkwardness was almost always his excuse for whipping me."[13] After Douglass fought back, Covey never tried to whip him again. Slaves who were willing to accept and endure white discipline made themselves easy for targets for owners and overseers. Standing up to whites, Douglass argued had lasting ramifications for the enslaved, as the "slave who has the courage to stand up for himself against the overseer, although he may have many hard stripes at the first, becomes, in the end, a freeman."[14]

White slaveholders had to balance their desire to discipline their slaves while not pushing them too far and sparking resistance. Owners and overseers had some idea of who might or might not fight back—lending truth to Douglass's observation. Slaves who already accepted punishment would be less likely to resist. Although most owners favored administering too much punishment rather than too little. Too little, as the case of Andrew Bruce revealed, could end in tragedy. In 1843, George, a Fluvanna County slave, ambushed and killed Bruce, his master. George dragged his master's body from the road and hid it in some nearby woods. At George's trial, Hannah Bragg, one of Bruce's neighbors complained that Bruce "was a very kind and humane master and did not punish his servants as often as they deserved." Bruce's wife confirmed that he "frequently threatened to whip the servants, but rarely executed the threats." She revealed that George had made a habit of running away to avoid being punished. When George returned, Bruce would welcome him back rather than disciplining the runaway. Hannah Bragg was convinced that if Bruce had been a stronger master and wielded the whip a little more often his "end would have been a different one."[15]

While many of these confrontations wound up in Virginia's legal system, slaves engaging in physical confrontations were often not attempting to kill their owners or overseers. After all, the enslaved had other methods of killing whites that were less direct and easier to cover up. Poisonings and arson, for example, could rid slaves of troublesome masters without raising as much suspicion. Fires and death from intestinal ailments were not uncommon in antebellum Virginia. In their trials for assaulting and murdering their owners and overseers, the enslaved often claimed that they did not intend to kill. A petition in support of a pardon for Anthony, a slave belonging to William Bouldin, stressed the bondsman's regret at his violence. His jailor, Tarlton King, wrote that "he has ever appeared truly sorry for the crime he had committed and has often expressed himself in humble tones, disapproving his conduct."[16] After all, the penalty for violent crimes against whites—whether they be assault or murder—was death. Anthony, who had attacked a white man named William Hardin, was facing a date with a hangman's noose before Governor Pleasants granted him a pardon.[17]

The providing of slaves with enough food to survive was one of the principle obligations of slaveholder paternalism. In general, slaveholders lived up to their end of the bargain. Historical research has shown that antebellum slaves received more than enough food. In their analysis of slave diets, Robert William Fogel and Stanley L. Engerman found that "the slave diet was not only adequate, it actually exceeded modern (1964) recommended daily levels of the chief nutrients."[18] Deficiencies in slave diets—a lack of fresh vegetables and key vitamins and nutrients—mirrored a broader nineteenth-century ignorance of nutritional science. Just because the enslaved had enough food, however, did not mean that they were satisfied with the food provided by their masters. Frederick Douglass described how the slaves at Colonel Lloyd's farm received the same monthly allowance of "eight pounds of pork, or its equivalent in fish, and one bushel of corn meal."[19] This lack of variety did little to endear masters to their slaves. To add diversity to their meals, the enslaved supplemented their diets with seasonal vegetables, chickens, and seafood from nearby lakes and rivers.

Owners and overseers enjoyed a greater variety of foods and guarded against the theft of their food by their slaves. The enslaved, however, had no qualms about stealing food from their masters. They enjoyed fresh chicken and pig as much as their owners and felt that since they provided the bulk of the labor while raising and tending to the animals, they had just as much right as their owners to enjoy the spoils of nature. Incidents or accusations of theft occasionally boiled over into violence. In 1803, in Chesterfield County, Essex Elam, an overseer, engaged in a confrontation with Abraham, one of the slaves under his supervision. One morning Elam went to Abraham's house to order him into the fields to retrieve a scythe. While Abraham was retrieving the scythe, Elam entered the bondsman's house and found potatoes roasting in the fire. When Abraham returned, Elam accused him of stealing the potatoes. Abraham denied the theft and Elam "forcibly took the potatoes from him."[20] As a result, Abraham swung the scythe at his overseer's head. He then chased Elam into the overseer's house where he threatened Elam and his wife with an ax.

In 1829, in Princess Anne County, Parker, a slave belonging to Daniel Stone, killed his master's son, Thornton. On the day of the confrontation, Thornton had been antagonizing Parker with threats of punishment. The bondsman's anger finally boiled over when Thornton challenged Parker's desire to eat. Jacob, another slave, testified that "Parker said he was getting something to eat and Thornton Stone said go out, Parker said he would when he was ready."[21] Parker then went into the kitchen for some food. When he came out, Thornton continued to berate Parker. Fed up with Thornton's antagonistic behavior over his need for food, Parker attacked and strangled his master's son. In 1852, Molly, a slave, stabbed her overseer, John Magee during a dispute over food. One night, after Magee gave out the slaves' meal allowance, Molly complained that she had not received enough to eat. After Magee hit her with his hand, the overseer testified that she "called me a liar, and said you nor no white man should whip her to save your life. She said she meant to have the meal out of the house or lose the last drop of her blood."[22] Magee claimed that he had given Molly more food than his employer wished and that he had never had reason to whip her.

The lack of food was a common complaint by the enslaved, especially amongst young slaves. Frederick Douglass recalled while working on Colonel Lloyd's plantation that young slaves rarely received enough food. Douglass wrote, "The children were then called, like so many pigs, and like so many pigs they would come and devour the mush; some with oyster-shells, others with pieces of shingle, some with naked hands, and none with spoons. He that ate fastest got most; he that was strongest secured the best place; and few left the trough satisfied."[23] Other slaves noted that masters who provided them with enough food developed reputations for spoiling their slaves. Marriah Hines recalled that "we had plenty of food, never knowed what it was to want food bad enough to have to steal it like a whole lot of 'em." Hines noted that "'cause master was good and kind to us, some of the other white folks used to call him 'nigger lover.' He didn't pay dat no mind though."[24] In the eyes of many whites, too much food would spoil their slaves. As Solomon Northup explained, "It is for the interest of the master that the servant should not suffer in health from starvation, and it is also for his interest that he should not become gross from over-feeding."[25]

The enslaved, on the other hand, did not believe that food beyond dried pork and cornmeal was an extravagance. They considered it an important part of their survival and often supplemented their diets with food gathered from hunting and scavenging. Solomon Northup observed that "the weekly allowance of meal scarcely sufficed to satisfy us. It was customary with us, as it is with all in that region, where the allowance is exhausted before Saturday night, or is in such a state as to render it nauseous and disgusting, to hunt in the swamps for coon and opossum."[26] While hunting and growing vegetables supplemented slaves' diets, it also took away from time that could be spent elsewhere—relaxing, gambling, or even plotting escape. It seemed, from the slaves' perspective, that their masters were doing the bare minimum to uphold their end of the paternalistic bargain. Bondspeople, who believed they were living up to their obligations, resented white efforts to provide the barest amount of food possible. As a result, disputes over food could serve as lynchpins of slave violence.

While white slaveholders bragged about caring for the enslaved members of their families, they still broke apart slave families through sale. Slave sales were a frequent and emotionally scarring part of life under bondage. Virginia slaves resented the sale of their family members and vividly remembered the pain of separation. Martha Showvely, an ex-slave from Virginia, recalled how when she was nine years old, a slave trader took her and two of her cousins to Richmond to be sold. When she saw that her cousins were to be sold south, Showvely said, "I started cryin'. Massa Tinsley asked what I was cryin' for. I said I didn' want to leave my cousins. He said he didn' want dem an' den he carried me off." Samuel Chilton, another ex-slave from Virginia, remembered the cruelties of the slave trade, "I done seen 'em sel niggers sell 'em like cattle." He recalled that "you would see gangs of slaves chained together un, un setch a cryin' an' screaming you ain't nebbet heard like dem pitiful cries of dem po' slaves."[27]

As much as owners boasted of their generosity toward their slaves, they still refused to allow them to leave their homes and visit family members. In 1837, in Nottoway County, Abby, Betsy, and Lemons, slaves belonging to Frederick Foulkes, killed their master. Another slave testified at their trial that "his master was in the habit of keeping his negroes from going from home." Lemons, before his confrontation with Foulkes, had left the farm without permission. When he returned and presumably faced punishment for his actions, Lemons told another slave that "he was tired taking whipping for nothing."[28] In 1848, Simon, a Prince Edward County slave, engaged in a deadly physical confrontation with his hired-out master, Charles Scott. Simon had been angry with Scott because Simon "had been wanting to go home and he would not let him."²⁹ Jack, a slave residing in Henry County, engaged in a physical confrontation with his hired-out owner, John Barrow. Barrow had refused to allow Jack to visit a sick slave. Barrow worried that "the sick negro had the scarlet fever and that he, prisoner would be liable to catch it."³⁰ Jack ignored Barrow's orders and left anyway. The next day, Barrow confronted Jack and the two engaged in a physical confrontation. In September 1826, David, a slave belonging to Wright Griffin, slit his master's throat. Another of Griffin's slaves explained that she had heard David, "say that he would kill his master if he lived before the year was out, because he would not let him go to see his wife."³¹

On February 5, 1859, Jim, a slave belonging to William M. Lewis, attacked and beat John Thompson, his overseer. Early that Saturday morning, Thompson had ordered Jim to help some of the other slaves haul a load of fodder. Jim objected, pointing out that "it was his day to go home." Thompson acknowledged Jim's right to leave but wanted his help anyway. He promised Jim that if he helped "haul out a load of fodder you can have a mule to ride." Jim, however, wanted nothing to do with this plan. In an act of defiance, he reminded Thompson that he and Thompson's employer, Mr. Fairfax, had agreed that Jim could leave on Saturday morning without being obligated to work. An exasperated Thompson ordered Jim to get breakfast and "do what I tell you. I want no difficulty with you or something of this kind." Jim had similarly become irritated by the entire situation. He yelled at Thompson, "God damn you I will kill you right on the spot."³²

Jim then grabbed an axe and charged at his overseer. Thompson recalled that Jim "struck me three or four blows with the axe, I retreated some ten or fifteen steps from him and he threw the axe at me but missed me." When Jim attacked a second time, Thompson drew his pistol and fired four shots at the charging bondsman. Each bullet missed its intended target and Jim continued his attack with the ax. After Thompson cried out for help, his wife, Margaret, came to her husband's aid. Witnessing the attack, she begged Jim not to kill Thompson. An enraged Jim warned her, "don't you come here or I will kill you too." Margaret Thompson grabbed a nearby stick and as she turned to attack Jim, the bondsman "raised up off Mr. Thompson and struck me and knocked me down." Thanks to this brief distraction, John Thompson pulled himself off the ground and ran off to safety. Because of his wounds, Thompson complained at Jim's trial that "I bled considerably."³³

Visits to family members, sick slaves, and spouses were an important part of the world slaves tried to create outside of their masters' influence. Slaves who did not live with their family members but remained within walking distance presented challenges for slave owners. Masters did not like the idea of having their slaves leaving their property nor did they like the ties that slaves were creating away from their masters' supervision. Such visits off-farm or plantation could disrupt work schedules, create new demands by slaves for time to visit their loved ones, and give the enslaved reasons to run away. For slaves, such visits provided an opportunity to escape the drudgery of bondage. Married slave men who could visit their wives, as Emily West has explained, "were often spared witnessing their spouse's abuse, they extended their social world in regularly leaving their quarters, and they also had a break from the boredom of their everyday routine."[34] Slave owners who begrudgingly granted their slaves the ability to visit their loved ones over time saw this grant transformed into a right. Once granted, these rights were difficult to take away.

In the process of enslavement, bondspeople and their masters negotiated boundaries regarding behavior and privileges that achieved an uneasy peace. Typically described in terms of a spectrum of resistance and accommodation, these boundaries set limits on the excesses of slave owners' behavior in exchange for bondspeople's submission.[35] This dynamic varied across time and place in the history of American slavery but gave the enslaved a set of expectations regarding their behaviors. As long as whites did not cross those lines, then the uneasy peace would hold. When whites crossed those lines—as Jim felt John Thompson had done—bondsmen could respond violently. Jim refused to work because it would have undermined his ability to get home. It also set a dangerous precedent. If Thompson could demand his labor on Saturday, then he could make future demands on Jim's labor and interfere even further in the bondsman's life. Thompson acknowledged Jim's right to leave for home, but underestimated Jim's refusal to work. Thompson offered what he considered a reasonable accommodation—the use of the mule in exchange for Jim's labor. For Jim, however, any interference violated his right to go home.

Whippings, the denial of food, and the refusal to allow slaves to visit their loved ones were all areas of disagreement between bondspeople and their owners. Under the ideology of paternalism, owners should have punished their slaves according to set rules, given them ample food, and allowed them to visit family members. The realities of paternalism, however, were much different from the ideal. Slaveholders, through their constant interference in the lives of their bondspeople, unevenly applied the rules and lashed out at their slaves. Some enjoyed the power to beat to their slaves mercilessly. Some whites recognized that they need to provide their slaves food but did not want to give any more than necessary. Nor did they want to allow their slaves to leave their farms and plantations to visit family members lest they spent too much time away from their masters' supervision. The enslaved, however, viewed these activities as essential to their survival and to the construction of lives free from white influence. They resented whites for barely living up to their obligations. As a result, discord over punishment, food, and visits to friends and family could result in physical confrontations.

HIRED-OUT OWNERS AND OVERSEERS

Paternalism and the master-slave relationship became even more complicated when overseers and hired-out owners entered the picture. The addition of a third party into the master-slave relationship created what Jonathan D. Martin described as "divided mastery." As Martin has written, "hiring transactions were intrinsically and idiosyncratically triangular. Where they had been two people, now there were three, and the dynamics immediately changed."[36] Hired-out owners rented the labor of slaves for a specific period of time and did not have a long-term interest in the health and happiness of their slaves. Overseers generally cared more for fulfilling the requirements of their employers than caring about the obligations that masters and slaves owed one another. From the slaves' perspective, they sought to set limits on who had the right to punish them and even tried to take advantage of overseers. Confrontations also set owners and overseers against one another as they disagreed over who bore the responsibility for slaves' violence. Ultimately, the addition of overseers and hired-out owners into the master-slave relationship reduced it from a paternalistic bargain to an economic one.

Some enslaved men rejected the right of any white man who was not their master to administer punishments. Cromwell, a slave, worked in a blacksmith's shop in Pittsylvania county owned by his master, Samuel Tunstall, and another man named James M. Hall. One evening, Hall saw Cromwell and two of Tunstall's slaves fighting. The next morning after Cromwell came into work, Hall informed him that he would be punished for his behavior. Cromwell became increasingly angry and told Hall that he had no authority to whip him. The enslaved man demanded that his master, Tunstall, administer the punishment. When Hall tried to tie Cromwell's hands, the bondsman struck Hall in the head with a pair of heavy blacksmith's tongs. As the two men struggled, Hall called out to Lawson, another of Tunstall's slaves, to help him. Instead, "Lawson turned off and said he would have nothing to do with it."[37] During Cromwell's trial, Hall claimed Tunstall had granted him full authority to punish the slaves as he saw fit. Lawson and Cromwell, however, refused to recognize Hall's authority. As part of their relationship with Tunstall, the slaves recognized their master's right to punish them. That right did not extend to his business partner.

Solomon Northup similarly rejected the authority of his hired-out owner, John Tibeats, to discipline him. Northup believed that he had been a good and loyal worker, yet Tibeats continually disrespected and denigrated him. Northup wrote of his loathing for Tibeats: "He was my master, entitled by law to my flesh and blood, and to exercise over me such tyrannical control as his mean nature prompted; but there was no law that could prevent my looking upon him with intense contempt. I despised both his disposition and his intellect." Eventually Northup stood up to Tibeats and the two engaged in a brief physical confrontation. Tibeats ran off and returned with two other white men and tried to lynch Northup. Even though Northup survived the altercation, he recognized that his attitude would only lead to further trouble. He wrote, "I was conscious that I had subjected myself to unimaginable punishment. The reaction that followed my extreme ebullition of anger produced the most painful sensations of regret. An unfriended, helpless slave—what could I do, what could I say, to justify, in the remotest manner, the heinous act I had committed, of resenting a white man's contumely and abuse."[38]

Hiring out offered mixed prospects for Virginia's slaves. On the positive side, hired-out slaves had the opportunity to engage in different forms of labor and work under potentially kinder owners and overseers. By working in new circumstances, they could meet other slaves and expand their social networks. On the negative side, as the altercation between Jim and John Thompson revealed, slaves had to leave their families behind. Additionally, as Northup demonstrated, there was no guarantee hired-out owners would be kinder. Chapin, the overseer, saved Solomon Northup's life from Tibeats. Since Chapin worked for William Ford, Northup's owner, he had the responsibility to safeguard Northup's life. He told Tibeats, "My duty is to protect his interests, and that duty I shall perform. You are not responsible-you are a worthless fellow. Ford holds a mortgage on Platt of four hundred dollars. If you hang him he loses his debt. Until that is canceled you have no right to take his life."[39] Economic rather than paternalistic reasons saved Northup's life.

Overseers like Chapin occupied a nebulous middle ground in the masterslave relationship. As Chapin revealed, it was the overseer's job to protect his employer's interest and keep the slaves working. An advice writer in *De Bow's Review* explained that overseers had agreed "to carry out the orders of your employer, strictly, cheerfully, and to the best of your ability." The writer warned overseers that their duties would require their full attention, so they should not spend too much time drinking, entertaining guests, or away from their duties. When it came to disciplining the slaves, the author recommended that overseers "[b]e *firm,* and at the same time *gentle* in your control. Never display yourself before them in a passion; and even if inflicting the severest punishment, do so in a mild, cool manner, and it will produce a tenfold effect."[40] The author attempted to convey to overseers that they must control the slaves under their supervision, while keeping the interests of their employers in mind.[41]

As many overseers knew, advice from the pages of journals like *De Bow's Review* was self-serving rubbish. It presented the Platonic ideal of an overseer; slave owners wanted someone reliable, loyal, and willing to work for a pittance. All in service of performing the day-to-day mastery—whipping and supervising work—that slaveholders themselves had no desire to do. In addition to grappling with the demands from their employers, overseers had to establish and maintain authority over the slaves. The enslaved recognized the tenuous status of overseers and tried to exploit it for their own gains. Short of outright rebellion, slaves could not overthrow the system of bondage. But within the day-to-day interactions and management of their lives, bondsmen seized opportunities to assert more control over their own lives. The division of authority between a master and overseer provided one such opportunity. Slaves tried to play the two off one another, knowing that overseers needed bondspeople to work in order to keep their jobs. They might be willing to ease up on punishments and whippings in exchange for the slaves' labor.

Some bondsmen tried to negotiate their way out of punishment. In 1851, Silas Emory, an overseer, wanted to punish Hartwell, one of the slaves under his supervision, who had become "trifling and negligent about his work."[42] Hartwell ran off, fearful of punishment. When Emory tracked the bondsman down, Hartwell sought to avoid a whipping. He promised to return home if Emory agreed not to discipline him. After Emory rejected his request, Hartwell attacked him with a stick.

Other bondsmen tried to avoid punishment by shifting responsibility for their actions onto absent owners. Some overseers, however, had forged strong relationships with their employers, limiting the ability of slaves to exploit their divided mastery. In 1834, Aaron engaged in a confrontation with his overseer, William Harwood. One evening Harwood demanded to know why Aaron was working in a field away from the other slaves. Aaron replied that his master had ordered him to work there before leaving for Baltimore. Harwood, however, sensed that Aaron was lying and prepared to punish him. Aaron raised his hoe and swung it at Harwood's head. Harwood had worked for three years as the overseer for Aaron's master, John Minge. The two men had formed a strong partnership. Minge testified at Aaron's trial that "it was not his habit to authorize a negro to go to any work independently of the overseer." He had also affirmed Harwood's authority to punish the slaves in his absence. He had told his slaves that "all upon the farm were required to submit implicitly to the orders of the overseer."[43] The strong relationship between owner and overseer negated Aaron's efforts to exploit the division of his master's power.

In 1836, Wilson, a slave, attempted to take advantage of the divided mastery of his overseer, Reuben Bruce, and his owner, Joseph Bruce. For years, Reuben Bruce had managed his uncle Joseph's farm and his slaves. One March day, Rueben found Wilson working in the fields contrary to his orders. Wilson claimed that his master, Joseph Bruce, had ordered him to work there. Reuben rejected Wilson's explanation and prepared to punish him with a hickory stick. Wilson grabbed the stick out of Reuben's hands and pummeled him repeatedly with it. The two men battled back and forth until Reuben Bruce finally gained the upper hand. As he pressed forward with his desire to punish Wilson, Bruce told one of the other slaves that Wilson had been "obstinate and has struck me several times with the stick and I am determined to make him yield or one of us must die."[44] Wilson continued to half-heartedly resist, repeatedly claiming that he would not be whipped, but eventually gave in. Wilson had sought to use his master as an excuse to disobey the orders of his overseer. Reuben Bruce, however, would not tolerate any type of disobedience from the slaves under his control.

Not all masters and overseers, however, had such strong relationships and disagreed over who bore responsibility for confrontations. On March 30, 1845, Albert Jenkins stormed into the cabin of Edward, a slave belonging to his employer, Daniel Warwick. Despite repeated summonses, Edward had not come out of his cabin and prepared breakfast as the overseer demanded. On entering the cabin, Jenkins struck Edward with a cowhide whip in order to wake him up. Jenkins admitted during his testimony that Edward was hard of hearing and likely deaf, making it difficult for him to hear the yelling from outside the cabin. Jenkins noted that Edward "started up and seemed to manifest both surprise and torpor."[45] To rouse the sleepy slave to work, Jenkins slammed him against a wall and demanded rope to tie his hands. He then began whipping him with the cowhide. Edward screamed out demanding to know why he was being whipped. The enslaved man broke free, grabbed an ax, and swung at the overseer. He quickly gained the upper hand and Jenkins barely escaped with his life.

Jenkins and Edward's owner, Daniel Warwick, disagreed over who was responsible for Edward's violence. In response to the attack, Warwick sent Jenkins a letter and confirmed that Edward was indeed hard of hearing—making Jenkins's actions a gross overreaction to the entire situation. Warwick admitted that Edward had a temper but had been a good and loyal slave for almost fifteen years. The disagreement between Warwick and Jenkins highlighted the ambiguous relationship between owners and overseers. Jenkins wanted control over his labor force and to punish Edward for his failure to obey orders. Warwick had given up part of his mastery by hiring an overseer to compel his slaves to work. By losing control of the situation, Jenkins demonstrated his failures as an overseer. Through his own incompetence—not taking into account that Edward was mostly deaf—Jenkins had allowed the confrontation to escalate to the point where now Warwick was about to lose a valuable slave. The Amherst court of oyer and terminer sentenced Edward to hang. While Warwick received $470 in compensation, he could not get his slave back.[46]

Further highlighting the precarious position of overseers, their confrontations could leave them with permanent injuries and no hope for future employment. Ann Byrd, a female slaveholder in Louisa County, Virginia, recalled the confrontation between Nathan, one of her slaves, and Anderson Talley, her overseer. On May 26, 1825, Byrd left her house and headed toward the horse pen, about thirty steps away. She found Talley and Nathan engaged in a brutal struggle. She watched as Nathan struck Talley over the head with a fence stake. The blow left the overseer senseless. Talley's father, William, claimed he "thought his son would never recover." William claimed the wound left Anderson "unable to attend this court and occasionally delirious."[47] In 1856, Samuel Harris, an overseer, suffered various wounds from a confrontation with Peter, one of the slaves under his supervision. Harris recalled how Peter repeatedly struck him in the shoulders and head. Harris claimed he received a wound on his right arm "from which I have not yet recovered."[48]

As incidents of slave violence worked their way through the courts, the outcomes and efforts by masters to spare their slaves lives divided whites. Shadrach Vaughn, whose slave Dick had tried to kill his overseer, Robert Barlow, petitioned Governor James Monroe to commute Dick's sentence. Vaughn argued that testimony in the case proved that Dick's "intention was not to kill." Further, Vaughn claimed that Dick's youth and relative stupidity warranted sparing his life. He wrote to Monroe that Dick "is a young and rather a stupid negro."[49] Vaughn also believed that Barlow's quick recovery offered further proof of Dick's lack of intent to kill. Barlow, Vaughn claimed, had already returned to work as his overseer. A petition signed by numerous citizens supported Vaughn's request. Vaughn's efforts to commute Dick's sentence sparked a counter petition by a group of residents of Goochland County. In their petition, they claimed the current "situation of our Country from that class of people require public example to be made of those who shall be found guilty of similar crimes."[50] They requested that Governor Monroe allow the execution to go forward. Monroe, however, commuted Dick's sentence to transportation.

Owners also employed lawyers to protect their slaves from execution, even if they had attacked their overseers. In 1849, in Roanoke County, Charles, a slave belonging to William Johnson, engaged in a physical confrontation with his overseer, John Richardson. Charles had attacked Richardson after the overseer threatened to punish him. Four of the justices of the peace who convicted Charles of assault sent Governor John Floyd a petition noting that they had recommended Charles's sentence be reprieved to transportation, but the clerk had not recorded it on the trial transcript. Additionally, John Logan and Henry Blair, Charles' attorneys sent a lengthy petition to Governor Floyd arguing that Charles should not have been convicted assault with intent because he did not intend to kill Richardson. They wrote, "We submit that it is not sufficient that there shall have been a mere stroke with intent to kill on the Legislative would have used the word *strike* instead of the word *beat*, but that it must appear that there was a *beating* in contradistinction from a mere stroke."[51]

Overseers also tried to place their desires above those of their employers, but were not always successful. In 1856, a court of oyer and terminer in Buckingham County convicted Peter, a slave belonging to Daniel Mosley, of assaulting his overseer, Samuel Harris. One morning Harris had whipped Peter because he had argued with another slave. Later on that day when Harris went to inspect Peter's work in a barn, Peter attacked him with a winnowing fan. Harris recalled that Peter had a "disposition in him to get into a difficulty with me." After the confrontation, Peter was taken before a magistrate and whipped. Harris, however, was not satisfied. He testified that "I think the boy ought to be hung, that he attempted my life, and I want him hung."[52] Harris complained that he had not yet recovered from the wounds he sustained in the fight with Peter. The oyer and terminer court disagreed with Harris and sentenced Peter to be transported out of Virginia. After reviewing the case, Governor Henry Wise agreed. The court awarded Daniel Mosley $1,150 in compensation.

Owners were generally skeptical of overseers and their ability to manage their slaves properly.[53] Some like Rueben Bruce assumed managerial roles for older relatives before becoming slave owners themselves and knew how to handle the slaves under their command. Others like Albert Jenkins were of a small professional class of overseers. These overseers often came from lower class white families and working as an overseer offered a wage and an occupation. Some stayed with owners for long periods of time, but more often moved on to new employers after a few years. As a result, owners were often reluctant to completely cede their authority to their overseers and believed they understood the needs of their slaves better than their employees. As Peter Kolchin has written, "with boring repetitiveness, planters reviled their overseers for being greedy, dishonest, and lazy, mishandling the slaves, and showing a lack of proper respect for their employers."[54] As a result, owners often undercut their overseers' authority in front of the slaves to reassert their mastery. While these masters tried to reemphasize their paternalistic bond with their slaves, they also fostered a level of disrespect amongst the slaves toward their overseers.

Most bondsmen needed little help disparaging their overseers. Slave autobiographies and interviews with ex-slaves contained numerous complaints about the cruelty of overseers. Frederick Douglass famously described his hatred of the implausibly named overseer, Mr. Severe. Douglass wrote that "he was a cruel man. . . . He seemed to take pleasure in manifesting his fiendish barbarity." After Mr. Severe's death, Douglass viewed the new overseer, Mr. Hopkins as an improvement, mostly because he did not enjoy whipping slaves. Douglass wrote that Mr. Hopkins was a "very different man. He was less cruel, less profane, and made less noise, than Mr. Severe. His course was characterized by no extraordinary demonstrations of cruelty."[55] Ex-slaves had a low bar as to what traits made a good overseer. The better overseers, as Douglass noted, were ones who did not whip excessively or take pleasure in it. Solomon Northup wrote that "The requisite qualifications in an overseer are utter heartlessness, brutality and cruelty. It is his business to produce large crops, and if that is accomplished, no matter what amount of suffering it may have cost."[56] Economics, rather than paternalism, governed the relationship between the enslaved and their overseers.

FAILURE OF PATERNALISM

Pro-slavery advocates claimed that paternalism fostered and created a more humane system of labor than could be found elsewhere in the United States. George Fitzhugh, a Virginia slavery apologist, argued that Northern capitalists treated their wage workers worse than African-American slaves. He wrote that wage labor was "far more cruel than the Black Slave Trade, because it exacts more of its slaves, and neither protects nor governs them."[57] The testimony of ex-slaves and the history of physical confrontations contradicts Fitzhugh's claims of masters' protection and kindness. Virginia Shepherd remembered an overseer who killed a slave who would not be whipped. She explained, the overseer "cursed this particular nigger because he wasn't working to suit him. The nigger jumped on the overseer to fight him. The overseer just pulled out his gun and shot the slave."[58] When owners rejected their paternalistic obligations, they left their slaves with no other choice. The enslaved could only endure so much unrelenting cruelty before they struck back. In these cases, slaves graduated from spontaneous physical confrontation to premeditated murder. The only way to free themselves from white savagery was to kill—whether they could escape punishment or not.

On the morning of March 9, 1827, Davy and Billy, slaves belonging to John Hamlin, attempted to convince their fellow bondspeople to murder their master. Billy was angry with Hamlin because "Master took a pot of meat from me." Davy tried to recruit another male slave named Frank. He told Frank that they "intended to kill their master, and wanted him to assist them." When Frank refused, Davy warned that the time had come to take sides and if Frank "did not assist them, that they would lay him along side of him (their master)." Rather than threatening his fellow bondsmen, Billy tried to bribe them to participate in the murder. Billy promised Archer, another slave, some money and "a nice pair of pantaloons and a waistcoat" to help in killing Hamlin.⁵⁹ Archer agreed to join the conspiracy against his owner and reassured Billy that he would aid in killing Hamlin as long as Billy kept his promise.

On the evening of March 9, 1827, John Hamlin went down to the meadow where his slaves were working. He ordered Frank to retrieve the oxen and a cart. After Frank had turned away from his master, Frank heard Hamlin cry out, "Oh! Frank." The bondsman turned around and saw Lawney, another of Hamlin's slaves, running away. Frank, fearful that Davy had carried out his threat, fled as well. Frank's fears were realized as Billy, Archer, and several other slaves had crossed the meadow and approached their unsuspecting master who had been giving instructions to another slave, Nathan. Archer snuck up behind Hamlin and shoved him to the ground. Nathan grabbed Hamlin by the shoulders and held him down. Little Stephen and Billy rushed in and helped pin their master to the ground. After struggling to keep Hamlin's neck still, Davy, "took hold of his master's throat and choked him to death and stamped him on his neck after he was dead."⁶⁰ Billy and Archer climbed atop their master and choked him as well.

After killing Hamlin, the slaves struggled with how to dispose of their master's body. Billy suggested that "they should get his riding horse and carry him over the river in the big road and hang his feet in the stirrup, and turn the horse loose." He hoped that whoever found the body would assume that Hamlin died as the result of an accident. Nathan rejected that suggestion, arguing that someone would notice the blood dripping from Hamlin's mouth and discover their crime. After some more discussion, they agreed to burn Hamlin's body and remove any evidence of the murder. Big Stephen built a roaring fire and tossed the body into it. About three hours later, Archer told Cato that "they had burnt him his master so nearly up that his bones dropped apart."⁶¹ The next morning, the slaves brought their plows to the meadow and covered Hamlin's ashes and bones with soil. They also took his heart, which had survived the fire, and buried it in the field. Little did the slaves know that nothing they did would shift suspicion elsewhere.

After Hamlin had been missing for several days, Lew Jones, a neighborhood white man, organized a search and rounded up Hamlin's slaves. Jones and his neighbors began interrogating the slaves, suspecting they had killed their master. Billy quickly confessed to the crime. Frank showed Jones and the other men the location of Hamlin's bones as "they were mashed up into very small pieces and buried with the heart."⁶² A coroner's inquest concluded that the slaves "violently choked and suffocated the said John Hamlin to death."⁶³ All told, the Lunenburg County commonwealth attorney charged nine slaves: David, Archer, Billy, Nathan, Big Stephen, Tom, Sam, Little Stephen, and Robin, with their master's murder. The slaves stood trial ten days later and were found guilty. All nine were sentenced to hang on April

27, 1827. The court, however, recommended mercy for Robin and Little Stephen "on account of their tender years. The one (Robin) being only fifteen years, and the other Little Stephen only seventeen years of age."[64] Virginia Governor William B. Giles spared their young lives, but let the others hang.

The case garnered coverage in local newspapers. White Virginians were shocked and outraged at the murder. One paper claimed that the crime was "One of the most shocking acts of murder which stains the catalogue of crime in this section of the country."[65] Another newspaper article described John Hamlin as "an enterprising and intelligent farmer, whose death will be much regretted by that class of the community particularly, and by society generally."[66] According to the census of 1820, Hamlin owned twenty nine slaves.[67] In 1827, he owned at least nineteen.[68] He had a family of four sons and two daughters.[69] His holdings in slaves suggest that he was a man of some property and standing—at least among the white community. Hamlin's slaves had their own opinions about the character of this seemingly upstanding member of Virginia's slaveholding class.

Hamlin's slaves testified that their master governed his farm through violence and terror. As Frank demonstrated, the slaves threatened and feared one another. Frank ran off rather than wait and see if Davy carried out his threat to kill him if he did not aid in Hamlin's murder. Frank also recalled that "several times in the course of the two last years heard Archer, Billy and others the negroes of his master planning to kill him." Frank did not inform Hamlin of the threats because another of his slaves, Rachel, had once come to him with a similar warning. In response, Hamlin whipped her severely. He told Rachel that "if she or any of the other negroes ever told him such a thing again he would give them one thousand lashes." Hamlin claimed that "he was afraid of none of them- and if they choose to do, let them do it."[70] Unfortunately for John Hamlin, on March 9, 1827, his slaves put their threats into action.

Instead of recognizing the reciprocal relationship between masters and slaves, Hamlin refused to live up to his paternalistic obligations. Hamlin terrorized his slaves, interfered in their lives, and whipped them for reporting on another. He stole food from them and never recognized their humanity. He could have taken Rachel's warning as a sign that he needed to treat his slaves better. For as much as whites bragged about the loyalty of their bondspeople, they recognized that slaves could turn violent. Perhaps Hamlin had heard about the murder of Wright Griffin by one of his slaves in neighboring Brunswick County the year before. David, one of Griffin's slaves, had ambushed his master and slit his throat.[71] If he had, he likely dismissed such concerns. When whites were especially fearful of slave insurrections, they comforted themselves with the belief it was not their slaves who were violent but those belonging to other, worst masters. Hamlin likely believed as many masters did that his slaves would protect him rather than rise up in rebellion.[72]

Whites had difficulties recognizing or acknowledging when their fellow slaveholders failed to live up to their paternalistic obligations. Instead they blamed the slaves for being ungrateful and savage. In 1856, Nelly, an older slave, along with her daughter Betsey, and grandchildren James, Elias, and Ellen killed their master, George E. Green on Christmas Eve. Nelly explained to her interrogators that he "was a bad master and they were tired of living with him." On the night of the murder, Nelly led her family into the house and attacked Green with an ax. After he escaped from the house, the slaves chased him down and attacked him with "shovels, axe, and stick till they killed him."[73] When Green managed to briefly wrestle the ax away from Nelly, the five other slaves quickly overpowered their master and killed him. They dragged his body back to his house and set it on fire, hoping the flames would cover up their crime. Their efforts proved fruitless as white neighbors quickly put out the fire.

Under interrogation, Nelly and the other slaves shocked the whites investigating the crime. They vividly described Green's brutal treatment of them. Elias said Green "was such a bad master they could not live with him and concluded to kill him." James explained that the slaves had asked Green to sell them, but he had refused. When they confronted him, they asked him one last time to sell them away. Green refused and said, "they would all be hung for what they had done." Nelly told the assembled whites that Green "did not allow them enough to eat, did not allow them any privileges and said they should get in his corn during the holy days." P. Lipscomb, one of the neighborhood whites, was shocked by Nelly's statements. He told her that "Mr. Green was a mild good man. She said I knew nothing about him that he had taught school up there and treated the children so bad none of them liked him." Luther Lynn, one of Green's neighbors, claimed that he "never saw a more comfortable negro house" and he "considered Mr. Green as one of the best masters."[74]

While the enslaved themselves faced the death penalty for their actions, the implications of their violence did not go unnoticed. In cases like those involving John Hamlin and George Green, the offending slaves were generally executed. Governor Giles had spared the lives of Robin and Little Stephen on account of their ages. Governor Henry Wise, however, did not commute Elias and Ellis's sentences, even though they were fourteen years old. Whites in Virginia wanted to make examples of slaves who conspired and killed their masters in such brutal ways. These confrontations also stoked the fears of white slaveholders, who boasted of the superiority of slavery as a social system and of the loyalty of their slaves, but also lived in continuous fear of slave violence. Eugene Genovese has observed "That perpetual sense of insecurity existed at the same time, in the same place, and often in the same persons as the professed reliance on loyal slaves."[75] These incidents shook the foundation of white paternalism, but ultimately whites pushed their concerns aside rather than confront the reality in front of them; their loyal slaves could turn on them at any moment.

In response, whites made sure to demonstrate the costs of such actions to their slaves. As John Matthews, overseer for Miles King, sat on a stump while the slaves worked in the field, four of King's slaves seized the opportunity to kill him. Frank grabbed him by the neck and held him. As Matthews called for help, James, Edmund, and Jack, three other slaves belonging to King, ran over. Instead of aiding their overseer, James clubbed him over the head with a hoe. The slaves buried Matthews' body in a nearby ditch. Fearing it would be easily found, they then tossed it into a nearby river. Miles King returned home later that day and found his overseer missing. After several days, Matthews' body was found floating in the river. King interrogated his slaves and Billy, along with several other bondsmen, confessed to witnessing the murder. As a punishment for their crime, the justices who sat on the court of oyer and terminer directed the sheriff to "cause the heads of the said Frank and James to be severed from their bodies after they are executed and to be exposed to public view as a warning to others."[76]

The act of killing cruel owners and overseers left a lasting impression on the enslaved as well. On February 16, 1824, Humphrey and Thornton, slaves belonging to Edward Garland of Hanover County, Virginia murdered their overseer, George King. During the slaves' trial, witnesses revealed how the bondsmen had grown tired of King's cruelty and resolved to kill him at the next available opportunity. William Arnall, a white witness, claimed that Humphrey confessed to him that "he had agreed with the said Thornton on the sixteenth of the same month (the day the said murder was committed) that if the said George King came where they were at work, and found fault with what they had done, they would kill him." Jerry, another slave of Edward Garland, testified that "a week previous to the murder of the said King heard the prisoner [Humphrey] and the said Thornton say that if the said King whipped them, they would kill him." Garland Taylor, another white witness, claimed Humphrey explained that if King had not whipped them that day, he did not have long to live: "King would have been killed in the fork field, a field on the plantation where the said King lived, where the other negroes were at work."[77] Witness testimony made it clear that Humphrey and Thornton had reached their breaking point.

On February 16, 1824, Humphrey and Thornton decided to take matters into their own hands. As they were engaged in chopping down trees and turning them into rails, King came out to inspect their work. While King conversed with Thornton, Humphrey snuck up behind him and, "struck him with an axe and repeated the blow three times."[78] William Arnall testified that Humphrey admitted that "he struck the said King four licks on the head with an axe."[79] The blows knocked King to the ground. As he lay twitching in the dirt, Humphrey delivered a final killing blow. With King dead, the slaves returned to chopping and preparing the rails. They then left King's body behind and went home to feed the livestock. After the moon rose, Humphrey and Thornton journeyed back to the scene of the confrontation. Using some rope from King's pocket, they lashed him to one of the newly made rails and dumped the body deeper in the woods.

After George King failed to return home that night, his wife grew worried. The next morning, Mrs. King sent a slave woman to the home of Simeon Souther, a neighbor, and asked him to organize a search for her husband. Souther recruited the aid of William Arnall and several other white men and began their search in the quarters. There they discovered that Thornton and Humphrey were missing. King had told Souther earlier the previous night that he intended to go and inspect their work. With his suspicions aroused, Souther and the other white men set out for the woods. When they arrived, they found signs of a struggle. Quickly Souther spotted "a quantity of blood very near where the said prisoner and Thornton were cutting and malling."[80] He also found a piece of the rope that the slaves had used to transport King's body. William Arnall noticed a blood trail leading from the spot deeper into the woods. By this point, Souther was certain that Humphrey and Thornton had murdered their overseer. His suspicions were confirmed when the men followed the blood trail to King's body.

William Anderson, an ex-slave from Hanover County, described King's death in his 1857 autobiography. Anderson revealed the hatred that the slaves had for their overseer. He described King as "an awful tyrant—a monster among the negro race—whipping and driving both men and women, and cohabiting among the women, both married and single." King's cruelty, Anderson explained, pushed the neighborhood slaves to fight back. Anderson described how two slave brothers, Humphrey and Thornton "knocked him down with their axes and killed him." In describing King's death, Anderson could only explain the death of such a cruel man through supernatural means. He claimed that just before King died, "some little black thing or devil made his appearance and said, 'If he is not dead don't kill him.'"[81] Humphrey and Thornton, however, ignored the creature. As a result of their actions, Humphrey and Thornton were tried and convicted of King's murder. William Anderson saw them executed on April 1, 1824. King's cruel and inhumane behavior sparked the creation of neighborhood legends surrounding his death.

The failure of whites to live up the ideals of paternalism explains why enslaved Virginians killed their cruel owners. The slaves of John Hamlin, George Green, Miles King, and Edward Garland all could not bear the unrelenting violence unleashed by their owners and overseers. The constant punishment, denial of food, and maltreatment pushed the enslaved to risk their lives and kill whites. They had little alternative. Rachel had warned John Hamlin of the slaves' discontent. Nelly and her family had asked Green to sell them away. These masters missed the warning signs that their slaves might turn against them. The perverse power of paternalism meant that if owners wanted to perpetuate slavery, they should not exercise their mastery to its fullest. While slavery in the abstract denied the humanity of the enslaved, in reality recognizing the humanity of their slaves ensured years of service. Paternalism provided the enslaved a way to create and preserve semi-autonomous lives. When whites refused to live up to their end of the paternalistic bargain, the enslaved took matters into their own hands.

The residential nature of American slaveholders and the small size of American slaveholdings led to the development of an intense, personal relationship between masters and slaves. Masters took a deep and abiding interest in nearly all aspects of their slaves' lives. They monitored work, administered discipline, and interfered in slave families. Under the guise of paternalism, whites viewed their slaves as part of their families. Slaves owed their masters loyalty and obedience while masters owed them care and protection. Paternalism established a series of reciprocal obligations that the slaves took seriously. They agreed to work in exchange for the opportunity to raise families and lead semi-autonomous lives. Slaveholders, however, rarely lived up to their end of the bargain. In their daily interactions with their slaves, the right to punish their slaves as they pleased fed into their worst instincts. Even though owners and overseers established rules governing slave behavior, they often fell prey to their moods and prejudices. As a result, they spread dissatisfaction and discontent among their slaves, increasing the likelihood of resistance.

The enslaved rejected these violations of their expectations regarding their masters' behavior. They lashed out when owners and overseers punished them, denied them food, and intruded on their hard-won privileges like the right to go home. They fought against the right of owners and overseers to punish them and tried to take advantage of divided mastery in order to win better working conditions for themselves. They also revealed the limits of paternalism to mediate between different classes of whites. Masters' desire to hold onto their property overrode the interests of their overseers. Overseers also sought to assert their desires regardless of their employers wishes. Slaveholders who failed to acknowledge or live up to their paternalistic obligations pushed their slaves to violence. Unchecked power left the enslaved little choice but to resist. When owners refused to recognize their paternalistic obligations, their slaves no longer owed them anything. Their violence served as warning to other whites of the dangers of ignoring their paternalistic obligations. Within every seemingly loyal slave lurked the potential for great violence.

NOTES

1. Peter Kolchin, *American Slavery 1617–1877* (New York: Hill and Wang, 2003), 101.
2. Laurent Dubois, *Avengers of the New World: The Story of the Haitian Revolution* (Cambridge: Belknap Press of Harvard University Press, 2004), 30.
3. Eugene Genovese introduced slaveholder paternalism in *Roll, Jordan, Roll: The World the Slaves Made* (New York: Vintage Books, 1974), 3–7. The entire book is an elaboration on the paternalism thesis. See also Elizabeth Fox-Genovese, *Within the Plantation Household* (Chapel Hill: University of North Carolina Press, 1988); Willie Lee Rose, "The Domestication of Domestic Slavery," in *Slavery and Freedom*, ed. William W. Freehling (New York: Oxford University Press, 1982), 18–36; Drew Gilpin Faust, *James Henry Hammond and the Old South: A Design for Mastery* (Baton Rouge: Louisiana State University Press, 1982); Peter Kolchin, "Reevaluating the Antebellum Slave Community: A Comparative Perspective," *Journal of American History* 70 (December 1983): 579–601; Peter Kolchin, *Unfree Labor: American Slavery and Russian Serfdom* (Cambridge: Belknap Press of Harvard University Press, 1987); Kolchin, *American Slavery*.
4. Here I am following the definition laid out by Peter Kolchin, see Kolchin, *American Slavery*, 111.
5. Thomas R.R. Cobb, *An Inquiry Into the Law of Negro Slavery in the United States of America: To Which is Prefixed An Historical Sketch of Slavery* (Philadelphia: T. & J.W. Johnson & Co., 1858), ccxviii.
6. For more on reciprocity see Genovese, *Roll, Jordan, Roll*, 144.
7. Genovese, *Roll, Jordan, Roll*, 91.
8. The literature on African-American religion is extensive but begins with Albert J. Raboteau, *Slave Religion: The 'Invisible Institution' in the Antebellum South* (New York: Oxford University Press, 1978); see also Mechal Sobel, *Trabelin' on: The Slave Journey to an Afro-Baptist Faith* (Westport: Greenwood Press, 1979); John B. Boles ed., *Masters & Slaves in the House of the Lord: Race and Religion in the American South, 1740–1870* (Lexington: University Press of Kentucky, 1988); Paul E. Johnson, ed., *African-American Christianity: Essays in History* (Berkeley: University of California Press, 1994); Sylvia R. Frey and Betty Wood, *Come Shouting to Zion: African American Protestantism in the American South and British Caribbean to 1830* (Chapel Hill: University of North Carolina Press, 1998); Janet Duitsman Cornelius, *Slave Missions and the Black Church in the Antebellum South* (Columbia: University of South Carolina Press, 1999); Raboteau, *Canaan Land: A Religious History of African Americans* (New York: Oxford University Press, 2001); Allen Dwight Callahan, *The Talking Book: African Americans and the Bible* (New Haven: Yale University Press, 2006); Jason R. Young, *Rituals of Resistance: African Atlantic Religion in Kongo and the Lowcountry South in the Era of Slavery* (Baton Rouge: Louisiana State University Press, 2007).
9. Kolchin, *American Slavery*, 163.
10. Genovese, *Roll, Jordan, Roll*, 147.
11. Charles L. Perdue Jr., Thomas E. Barden, & Robert K. Phillips eds., *Weevils in the Wheat: Interviews with Virginia Slaves* (Charlottesville: University Press of Virginia, 1976), 206, 84.

12. *Commonwealth vs. Patrick,* Thomas Randolph Executive Papers, 1819–1822. Accession 41887. Box 4, Folder 9. State Records Collection, The Library of Virginia, Richmond, Virginia.

13. Frederick Douglass, *Narrative of the Life of Fredrick Douglass: An American Slave* (1845: New York: Oxford University Press, 1999), 59.

14. Frederick Douglass, *My Bondage, My Freedom: Part I. Life as a Slave. Part II Life as a Freeman* (New York: Miller, Orton, & Mulligan, 1855), 95.

15. *Commonwealth vs. George,* James McDowell Executive Papers, 1843–1845. Accession 43559. Box 2, Folder 7. State Records Collection, The Library of Virginia, Richmond, Virginia.

16. *Commonwealth vs. Anthony,* James Pleasants Executive Papers, 1822–1825. Accession 42046. Box 3, Folder 10. State Government Records Collection, The Library of Virginia, Richmond, Virginia.

17. Virginia Council of State Journals. December 26, 1823, p. 14. Misc. Reel 2993. Accession 35356. State Government Records Collection, The Library of Virginia, Richmond, Virginia.

18. Robert William Fogel and Stanley L. Engerman, *Time on the Cross: The Economics of American Negro Slavery* (Lanham: University Press of America, 1984), 115.

19. Douglass, *Narrative,* 21.

20. *Commonwealth vs. Abraham,* John Page Executive Papers, 1802–1805. Accession 41056. Box 2, Folder 5. State Records Collection, The Library of Virginia, Richmond, Virginia.

21. *Commonwealth vs. Parker,* William B. Giles Executive Papers, 1827–1830. Accession 42310. Box 7, Folder 8. State Records Collection, The Library of Virginia, Richmond, Virginia.

22. *Commonwealth vs. Molly,* Joseph Johnson Executive Papers, 1852–1855. Accession 44076. Box 2, Folder 6. The Library of Virginia. Richmond, Virginia.

23. Douglass, *Narrative,* 34

24. Perdue, *Weevils in Wheat,* 139–140.

25. Solomon Northup, *Twelve Years a Slave. Narrative of Solomon Northup, a Citizen of New-York, Kidnapped in Washington City in 1841, and Rescued in 1853, from a Cotton Plantation near the Red River, in Louisiana.* Ed. David Wilson (Auburn: Derby and Miller, 1853), 201.

26. Northup, *Twelve Years a Slave,* 200.

27. Perdue, *Weevils in Wheat,* 264, 71.

28. *Commonwealth vs. Abby, Betsy, and Lemons,* Wyndham Robertson Executive Papers, 1836–1837. Accession 43097. Box 3, Folder 5. State Records Collection, The Library of Virginia, Richmond, Virginia.

29. *Commonwealth vs. Simon, Simon, and John,* William Smith Executive Papers, 1846–1848. Accession 43708. Box 8, Folder 9. State Records Collection, The Library of Virginia, Richmond, Virginia.

30. *Commonwealth vs. Jack,* Joseph Johnson Executive Papers, 1852–1855. Accession 44076. Box 8, Folder 9. The Library of Virginia. Richmond, Virginia.

31. *Commonwealth vs. David,* John Tyler Executive Papers, 1825–1827. Accession 42267. Box 2, Folder 7. State Records Collection, The Library of Virginia, Richmond, Virginia. Henceforth, *Commonwealth vs. David* (LVA).

32. *Commonwealth vs. Jim*, Henry A. Wise Executive Papers, 1856–1859. Accession 36710. Box 17, Folder 3, Misc. Reel 4213. State Records Collection, The Library of Virginia, Richmond, Virginia. Henceforth *Commonwealth vs. Jim* (LVA).

33. *Commonwealth vs. Jim* (LVA).

34. Emily West, *Chains of Love: Antebellum Slave Couples in South Carolina* (Urbana: University of Illinois Press, 2004), 58.

35. See Genovese, *Roll, Jordan, Roll*, 597–598. Scholars have moved away from a resistance/accommodation dichotomy in favor of the recognizing the ways that enslaved people resisted with or without challenging the power structure of slavery. See also James C. Scott, *Weapons of the Weak: Everyday Forms of Peasant Resistance* (New Haven: Yale University Press, 1985); James C. Scott, *Domination and the Arts of Resistance: Hidden Transcripts* (New Haven: Yale University Press, 1990).

36. Jonathan D. Martin, *Divided Mastery: Slave Hiring in the American South* (Cambridge: Harvard University Press, 2004), 2.

37. *Commonwealth vs. Cromwell*, Joseph Johnson Executive Papers, 1852–1855. Accession 44076. Box 2, Folder 9. The Library of Virginia. Richmond, Virginia.

38. Northup, *Twelve Years a Slave*, 109, 113.

39. Northup, *Twelve Years a Slave*, 115–116.

40. *Duties of an Overseer, De Bow's Review*, Vol. 18, Issue 3 (March 1855): 339, 344.

41. On the lives of overseers see William K. Scarborough, *The Overseer: Plantation Management in the Old South* (Baton Rouge: Louisiana State University Press, 1966).

42. *Commonwealth vs. Hartwell*, John B. Floyd Executive Papers, 1849–1851. Accession 43924. Box 9, Folder 3. State Records Collection, The Library of Virginia, Richmond, Virginia.

43. *Commonwealth vs. Aaron*, Littleton Tazewell Executive Papers, 1834–1836. Accession 42998. Box 2, Folder 6. State Records Collection, The Library of Virginia, Richmond, Virginia.

44. *Commonwealth vs. Wilson*, Wyndham Robertson Executive Papers, 1836–1837. Accession 43097. Box 1, Folder 5. State Records Collection, The Library of Virginia, Richmond, Virginia.

45. *Commonwealth vs. Edward*, James McDowell Executive Papers, 1843–1845. Accession 43559. Box 6, Folder 4. State Records Collection, The Library of Virginia, Richmond, Virginia. Henceforth *Commonwealth vs. Edward* (LVA).

46. *Commonwealth vs. Edward* (LVA).

47. *Commonwealth vs. Nathan*, James Pleasants Executive Papers, 1822–1825. Accession 42046. Box 7, Folder 9. State Records Collection, The Library of Virginia, Richmond, Virginia.

48. *Commonwealth vs. Peter*, Henry A. Wise Executive Papers, 1856–1859. Accession 36710. Box 5, Folder 1. Misc. Reel 4198. State Records Collection, The Library of Virginia, Richmond, Virginia. Henceforth *Commonwealth vs. Peter* (LVA).

49. Shadrach Vaughn Letter, James Monroe Executive Papers, 1799–1802. Accession 40936. Box 7, Folder 3. Misc. Reel 5347. State Records Collection, The Library of Virginia, Richmond, Virginia.

50. Petition, James Monroe Executive Papers, 1799–1802. Accession 40936. Box 7, Folder 3. Misc. Reel 5347. State Records Collection, The Library of Virginia, Richmond, Virginia.

51. *Commonwealth vs. Charles,* John Floyd Executive Papers, 1830–1834. Accession 42665. Box 1, Folder 6. State Records Collection, The Library of Virginia, Richmond, Virginia.

52. *Commonwealth vs. Peter* (LVA).

53. Kolchin, *American Slavery,* 102–105; Genovese, *Roll, Jordan, Roll,* 12–22; Scarborough, *The Plantation Overseer.*

54. Kolchin, *American Slavery,* 104.

55. Douglass, *Narrative,* 22.

56. Northup, *Twelve Years a Slave,* 224.

57. George Fitzhugh, *Cannibals All! Or, Slaves Without Masters* (Richmond: A. Morris, 1857), 25.

58. Perdue et al., *Weevils in the Wheat,* 255.

59. *Commonwealth vs. Davy,* William B. Giles Executive Papers, 1827–1830. Accession 42310. Box 1, Folder 2. State Records Collection, The Library of Virginia, Richmond, Virginia. Henceforth *Commonwealth vs. Davy* (LVA).

60. *Commonwealth vs. Davy* (LVA).

61. *Commonwealth vs. Davy* (LVA).

62. *Commonwealth vs. Davy* (LVA).

63. *Inquest of John Hamlin,* Lunenburg County (Va) Coroners' Inquisitions, 1752–1924. Local Government Records Collection, Lunenburg County Court Records. The Library of Virginia, Richmond, Virginia.

64. *Commonwealth vs. Sam, Little Stephen, Tom, and Robin,* William B. Giles Executive Papers, 1827–1830. Accession 42310. Box 1, Folder 2. State Records Collection, The Library of Virginia, Richmond, Virginia.

65. *The Spectator* (New York City), April 6, 1827.

66. *The Spectator* (New York City), April 6, 1827.

67. Fourth Census of the United States, 1820, Virginia, Lunenburg, Lewiston, NARA Roll: M33_137; Page 170. Accessed on Ancestry.com on February 11, 2015.

68. *The Spectator* (New York City), April 6, 1827.

69. Fourth Census of the United States, 1820, Virginia, Lunenburg, Lewiston, NARA Roll: M33_137; Page 170. Accessed on Ancestry.com on February 11, 2015.

70. *Commonwealth vs. Davy* (LVA).

71. *Commonwealth vs. David* (LVA).

72. Genovese, *Roll, Jordan, Roll,* 615.

73. *Commonwealth vs. Nelly, Betsey, James, Elias, & Ellen,* Henry A. Wise Executive Papers, 1856–1859. Accession 36710. Box 6, Folder 2. Misc. Reel 4199. State Records Collection, The Library of Virginia, Richmond, Virginia. Henceforth *Commonwealth vs. Nelly et al* (LVA).

74. *Commonwealth vs. Nelly et al* (LVA).

75. Genovese, *Roll, Jordan, Roll,* 615–616.

76. *Commonwealth vs. Frank, James, Edmund, and Jack,* John Tyler Sr. Executive Papers, 1808–1811. Accession 41223. Box 2, Folder 4. State Records Collection, The Library of Virginia, Richmond, Virginia.

77. *Commonwealth vs. Humphrey*, James Pleasants Executive Papers 1822–1825, Accession 42046. Box 4, Folder 3. State Government Records Collection, The Library of Virginia, Richmond, Virginia. Henceforth, *Commonwealth vs. Humphrey* (LVA).

78. *Commonwealth vs. Thornton*, James Pleasants Executive Papers 1822–1825, Accession 42046. Box 4, Folder 3. State Government Records Collection, The Library of Virginia, Richmond, Virginia. Henceforth, *Commonwealth vs. Thornton* (LVA).

79. *Commonwealth vs. Humphrey* (LVA).

80. *Commonwealth vs. Thornton* (LVA).

81. William Anderson, *Life and Narrative of William J. Anderson, Twenty-four Years a Slave; Sold Eight Times! In Jail Sixty Times!! Whipped Three Hundred Times!!! or The Dark Deeds of American Slavery Revealed. Containing Scriptural Views of the Origin of the Black and of the White Man. Also, a Simple and Easy Plan to Abolish Slavery in the United States. Together with an Account of the Services of Colored Men in the Revolutionary War—Day and Date, and Interesting Facts* (Chicago: Daily Tribune Book and Printing Office), 50.

Chapter 2

Masculinity and Physical Confrontations

Slavery shaped the masculinities of African American and white Virginians. While some white conceptions of manhood differed along class lines, white Virginians generally shared similar ideas regarding their manhood. To be a man meant being independent, strong, and bold. Men commanded themselves, their wives, their families, their slaves, and even the world around them. Elite white men saw the world as needing to bend to their will. Poor and middling whites struggled to live up to these ideals, but nonetheless pursued them throughout their lives, seeking independence and prosperity for themselves. This emphasis on autonomy and aggressiveness emerged out of the world in which white Virginians lived, where slavery governed the economic, social, and political realms. Ideas of freedom and masculinity were therefore woven together. To define their manhood, white men also needed to point to its opposite. And slavery provided them a clear option—African American bondsmen. As Lorri Glover has written, white men "became men by personifying the antithesis of their slaves and became southern by protecting that institution."[1]

In the eyes of whites, the enslaved were not men at all. The process of enslavement had systematically stripped away any claims of African American men to manhood. After the moment of capture, bondsmen underwent a process of "natal alienation" as they found themselves forcibly removed from the culture and social relations in which they had grown up. The slave trade inserted these men into a new social order, where old distinctions of class and gender had no place. Whatever status they had previously held was gone, replaced by their new status as chattel.[2] Olaudah Equiano recalled how he was "trained up from my earliest years in the art of war; my daily exercise was shooting and throwing javelins; and my mother adorned me with emblems, after the manner of our greatest warriors." After being captured,

Equiano found himself in chains, moving across the West Africa and being sold from master to master. The aspiring warrior was now a supplicant, struggling to survive. Equiano's despair only increased after arriving in Virginia, where he described how "I had no person to speak to that I could understand. In this state I was constantly grieving and pining, and wishing for death rather than any thing else."[3]

White Virginians justified their denial of African American men's manhood by using varying and sometimes contradictory explanations. Some whites believed they needed to protect slave women and children from the savagery of slave men. Georgia planter Robert Collins wrote that "Negroes are by nature tyrannical in their dispositions; and if allowed, the stronger will abuse the weaker; husbands will often abuse their wives."[4] Others argued that the three stereotypical depictions of male slaves in southern literature demonstrated their lack of manhood. Sambo, the most prevalent stereotype, was submissive, loyal, and dishonest, always trying to pull a fast one by his master and fellow slaves. The child-like Sambo needed his master's firm hand to behave properly. Nat, on the other hand, represented the animal savagery of African-American males. Nat would run away, steal, and rape white women. He was beyond redemption—proof of the need to keep African Americans in bondage lest they run amok and destroy white society. Jack was the strong, silent type, content to work and obey his master, provided he was not harshly treated.[5] None of these depictions of African American men fit any definition of southern manhood. Real men were not abusive, dishonest, thieving, or submissive.

Enslaved men faced additional challenges beyond white stereotypes. In their day-to-day lives, as discussed in the previous chapter, owners meddled in the lives of enslaved families and undercut bondsmen's claims to manhood. Enslaved men had to seek their masters' approval for marriages. When owners punished bondsmen and their family members, they highlighted enslaved men's inability to protect their loved ones. Masters who issued food to their slaves undermined bondsmen's role as providers. Stripped of their roles as protector and provider, enslaved men had difficulty asserting manhood in their households. At work, owners, overseers, and other whites controlled the rhythms of the work day—setting quotas, work hours, supervising bondsmen's labor, and punishing them when they failed to live up to their expectations. Additionally, in African societies, field work was primarily women's work, heightening the loss of manhood amongst first generation bondsmen. On larger farms and plantations, enslaved men and women worked alongside one another, making it difficult for bondsmen to claim work as a male domain. No matter where enslaved men turned, the circumstances of slavery challenged their claims to manhood. As Darlene Clark Hine and Earnestine L. Jenkins wrote, "American manhood has always been contested ground, and the ground on which black men were forced to assert their masculine identity was slavery."[6]

Despite their circumstances, enslaved men still found ways to assert their masculinity. These assertions took on different forms depending on the geographic context. While slavery limited enslaved men's efforts to define their manhood, in spaces largely outside of white interference such as leisure activities, off-plantation socializing, and their escape attempts, they created and shaped their own views of masculinity.[7] During these activities, men interacted with one another outside the strict confines of enslavement. The bonds they formed with another represented an important bulwark against their masters' efforts to undermine their manhood. In the quarters and in their relations with their families, enslaved men tried to fulfill their roles as providers by working extra hours, hunting, or fishing. On the one hand, these efforts bolstered their claims to manliness by supplying their families with the necessities for survival. On the other hand, time spent fishing, hunting, or working was time not spent escaping or resisting their enslavement. In this way, when enslaved men asserted their masculinity, they undermined their own ability to be free.[8]

Violence was the one of the most important ways in which enslaved men demonstrated their manhood. This emphasis on violence was not unique to African American men. Rather violence was instrumental to manhood across racial and class lines in the antebellum South.[9] Violence took different forms amongst elite whites and poor or middling whites. Elite white men engaged in duels and violently upheld the social order by whipping their slaves and beating lower class men who challenged their authority. Lower and middling whites brawled and fought amongst one another, resolving their conflicts with knives in back alleys and gouging each other's eyes out on barroom floors. In disputes between slaves, slaves acted similar to poor whites. Brawls, knife fights, and other physical confrontations were common solutions to slave disputes. Even though whites interfered in altercations and punished the enslaved, bondsmen still used violence to resolve quarrels over food, family members, insults, and other issues.[10] Even with the threat of punishment, bondsmen still tried to claim their manhood in their interactions with their fellow slaves.[11]

Enslaved men, however, did not limit their violence and affirmations of their manhood to their fellow slaves. They also asserted and reasserted their masculinity to varying degrees in physical confrontations with their owners, overseers, and other whites. In some instances, bondsmen used violence to proclaim their masculinity and demonstrate their superiority over whites. The slaves who witnessed such confrontations recognized and appreciated the violence of their enslaved brethren and believed that the willingness to resist was a sign of their manhood. In other cases, when whites punished enslaved men and their families or raped wives or daughters, bondsmen responded violently to reassert their masculinity. Some men could not bear the indignity of seeing themselves or family members harmed. By resisting, enslaved men sought to restore some level of balance in their lives. They wanted their aggressors to feel the same pain that they themselves felt. These physical confrontations, however, came at a high cost. Men who defended themselves and their families or tried to assert their masculinity faced execution, brutal punishments or separation from their loved ones. Their willingness to engage in violence revealed the importance that bondsmen placed on proclaiming and preserving their manhood.

ASSERTING MASCULINITY

Enslaved men violently responded to challenges to their masculinity. In their autobiographies, ex-slaves linked their violence to their conceptions of manhood and extolled the virtues of resistance. In doing so, they created the archetype of the heroic slave. The heroic slave was a man who defended himself against white violence and by doing so proved his manhood. Additionally, his resistance warranted respect and admiration from his fellow bondsmen. In the day-to-day experience of slavery, however, examples of the heroic slave were few and far between. Rather when enslaved men asserted their masculinity in physical confrontations, they revealed the importance of the spoken word in their lives. They coupled verbal assertions of manliness with violence against whites. They also judged the character of their masters and overseers and refused to submit to men who failed to live up their standards of behavior. Enslaved men became enraged when whites of low character insulted them or used other provocative language. Rather than stay silent and thus admit the truth of the white men's words, enslaved men resisted. Ultimately, the emphasis on the spoken word, the judgment of the behavior of whites and the willingness to violently defend their manhood reflected the tenets of southern honor culture.[12]

After escaping bondage, ex-slaves repeatedly noted in their autobiographies the importance of violence in the assertion of their masculinity. As a young slave, Frederick Douglass engaged in a physical confrontation with his hired-out owner, Edward Covey. Douglass hated Covey, recalling how "Mr. Covey's *forte* consisted in his power to deceive. His life was devoted to planning and perpetuating the grossest deceptions." After months of beatings, Douglass finally fought back against Covey and defeated him in a confrontation. Douglass wrote that as a result of the altercation he had asserted his manliness and changed the course of his life. Douglass described how his victory over Covey "revived within me a sense of my own manhood." In describing the story for his readers, Douglass stressed that "you have seen how a man was made a slave; you shall see how a slave was made a man." Eventually, Douglass admitted, this rediscovered manhood encouraged him to escape from slavery.

Douglass, unlike most slaves who engaged in physical confrontations, managed to avoid punishment for his actions. He explained that if Covey had sent the 16-year-old boy to the whipping post for their confrontation, "his reputation would have been lost; so, to save his reputation, he suffered me to go unpunished."[13] Covey's own desire to protect his reputation—by extension his masculinity—spared Douglass the lash.

Harriet Jacobs similarly connected her uncle Benjamin's resistance to his master and his masculinity. She called him "The Slave who Dared to Feel like a Man." Jacobs described Benjamin as "a tall, handsome lad, strongly and gracefully made, and with a spirit too bold and daring for a slave." Benjamin's bold spirit had gotten him into trouble as he had resisted his master's efforts to whip him. Rather than accept a public whipping, Benjamin ran away, explaining that "he was no longer a boy, and every day made his yoke more galling." He, however, was eventually recaptured and imprisoned. When his mother appealed to him to beg his master for forgiveness, Benjamin replied, "No! I will never humble myself to him. I have worked for him for nothing all my life, and I am repaid with stripes and imprisonment. Here I will stay till I die, or till he sells me."[14] Instead, Benjamin rotted away in jail for months before being sold. Similar to Douglass, Benjamin willingness to resist eventually led him to successfully escape to the North.

Ex-slave John Thompson also linked the violence of Ben, a fellow bondsman, to the assertion of manhood. Unlike Douglass's case where Edward Covey sought to protect his reputation and spared Douglass from any more punishment, Ben's confrontation did not improve his lot in life. Ben had come into conflict with an overseer who wanted to assert his authority over the slaves under his supervision. Ben, however, believed "that one might as well die by hanging as whipping; so he resolved not to submit to be whipped by the overseer." Soon after, the two men engaged in a physical confrontation. Ben severely beat the overseer before fleeing to the woods. After Ben returned home, his owner nearly beat him to death. Afterwards Ben became increasingly bitter and angry. He lamented, "I wish I had killed the overseer, then I should have been hung, and an end put to my pain. If I have to do the like again, I will kill him and be hung at once!" Thompson admired Ben and his willingness to resist. He noted that "Ben was a brave fellow, nor did this flogging lessen his bravery in the least. Nor is Ben the only brave slave at the South; there are many there who would rather be shot than whipped by any man."[15] Ben's owner ordered the overseer never to whip Ben again and he was sent to a different part of the farm to work alone. While Ben was never punished again, his escape from the lash came at a high price.

Douglass, Jacobs, and Thompson presented themselves or their fellow bondsman as willing to violently resist their enslavement. They also explicitly linked violence to assertions of manhood. By doing so, antebellum authors created the literary trope of the "heroic slave" arguing that when faced with enslavement men had no choice but to fight back. Further, authors cited real-life slave rebels like Nat, Denmark Vesey, and Toussaint L'Overture as exemplars of this masculine ideal. All three had risked their lives and died for their freedom and that of their fellow bondsmen. As Rebecca Fraser has argued, "These links suggested that unless a man could claim his rights—the most fundamental of which was, by all accounts, freedom—he could not consider himself a man."[16] The ideal of the heroic slave, however, was a narrow view of enslaved men's masculinity since the vast majority of bondsmen did not physically resist their enslavement or run away to the North. Yet physical confrontations provided formerly enslaved authors with a powerful way of connecting to antebellum white audiences.

Authors like Frederick Douglass, Harriet Jacobs, and John Thompson also used enslaved men's violence to appeal to white Northern sympathies. They highlighted the real examples of violence that marked their lives to show the willingness of enslaved men to resist oppression. They hoped that their white Northern audiences would recognize that enslaved men were neither passive Sambos in need of civilization nor primitive brutes in need of the whip to restrain them from savagery. Instead African-American authors wanted to establish themselves firmly in the traditions of American masculinity and heroism. Douglass cast himself as a man fighting for his freedom. He explicitly linked his violence to rekindling his desires to escape. Jacobs described her uncle's violence in the same manner. Thompson similarly characterized Ben as a man willing to die in order to protect himself. His lasting image of Ben, defiant even in the face of such inhumane treatment, was meant to pull at the heartstrings of Northern readers. This portrait of African-American masculinity stressed connections and continuities with white understandings of masculinity, while also recognizing the limitations of enslaved men's lives.

Ex-slaves also used the heroic slave archetype to appeal to their brethren still in bondage and encouraged them to resist. Ex-slave and minister Henry Highland Garnet reminded slaves that "no oppressed people have ever secured their liberty without resistance." Like other African Americans, Garnet equated violence with an avenue for freedom. He stressed that slaves should "let your motto be RESISTANCE! RESISTANCE! RESISTANCE!"[17] David Walker made a similar appeal, arguing that "we can help ourselves; for, if we lay aside abject servility, and be determined to act like men, and not brutes--the murders among the whites would be afraid to show their cruel heads."[18] These arguments rested on the notion that enslaved men were not men at all. At least until they resisted their bondage. As ex-slave Lewis Clarke declared, "A SLAVE CAN'T BE A MAN!"[19] Walker wrote that whites knew that African-Americans were "too servile to assert our rights as men—or they would not fool with us as they do."[20] These calls for violent rebellion fit in the mainstream thinking regarding masculinity and America's revolutionary tradition. As Stanley Harrold has argued, "A republican tenet was that a man who submitted to oppression and thereby lost his manhood could regain it by struggling for his rights."[21]

The legacy of the revolution and the necessity of violence and freedom played an important role in the oratory of antebellum Southerners as well. The American Revolution provided a literary and oral template for southerners. While white southerners had many historical examples of violence to draw on, they most frequently fixated on the Revolution. There was no subject nearer and dearer to the hearts of Virginians. The sacrifices and leadership of brave men like George Washington, Thomas Jefferson, and Patrick Henry provided a model for men to copy. Independence came at a cost, but southerners willingly gave their lives in order to win their freedom. The founding generation provided a clear example of noble and masculine behavior in defense of the rights of men. As Dickson Bruce Jr. noted, "The purported willingness of patriots to risk all they had was noted as exemplary by many Southern orators."[22] When ex-slaves wrote of bondsmen's readiness to fight for their freedom, they, like their white counterparts, laid claim to a revolutionary tradition of violence and proved willing to struggle for their freedom.

While the writings and recollections of ex-slaves praised bondsmen's willingness to resort to violence, they also revealed the high price enslaved men paid to assert their manhood. William Wells Brown recalled the story of Randall, a physically imposing slave who had never been whipped by his owner or overseer. After Mr. Cook, the overseer schemed to whip Randall, the bondsman warned, "No man has laid hands on me, to whip me, for the last ten years, and I have long since come to the conclusion not to be whipped by any man living." Cook, however, soon succeeded in whipping Randall and attached a heavy ball and chain to his leg and compelled him to work in the fields alongside all the other slaves. While Brown's master was pleased with Cook, Brown still admired Randall. He described him as "six feet high, and well-proportioned, and known as a man of great strength and power. He was considered the most valuable and able-bodied slave on the plantation."[23] Even though Cook triumphed over Randall, Brown still respected him for his resistance.

John Thompson expressed similar admiration for Aaron, another slave who resisted the efforts of his owner to punish him. Mr. Wagar, the owner, grew tired of battling with Aaron over punishment so he decided to sell him. When slave traders arrived to take Aaron away, the bondsman resisted. Thompson recalled how Aaron "sprang from the scaffold, axe in hand, and commenced trying to cut his way through them; but, being defeated, he was knocked down, put in irons, taken to the drove yard, and beaten severely, but not until he had badly wounded two of his captors." Aaron eventually broke out of jail and remained free for a year before finding himself a new master. Thompson respected Aaron's bravery when he wrote that Aaron "never submitted to be flogged, unless compelled by superior force; and although he was often whipped, still it did not conquer his will, nor lessen his bravery."[24] While slaves like Ben and Aaron suffered brutal punishments, they won the respect and affection of their fellow bondsmen for their willingness to resist.

Bondsmen also admired slaves whose willingness to resist led to their deaths. Austin Steward recalled how a small group of slaves battled with patrollers trying to break up a slave dance. After the ensuing confrontation left several slaves dead, Steward attended their funeral. He recalled that "all moved on solemnly to the final resting-place of those brave men, whose descendants may yet be heard from, in defence of right and freedom."[25] Harry Smith remembered the courage of a slave named Jim Hayden. Smith described him as "the most powerful man, either white or black, that ever was known in the State of Kentucky." Jim came into conflict with his new overseer and "beat his brains out and beat the ground where they lay." Jim's new owner gathered up a posse of white men and they "riddled him with bullets, and then cut his heart out and placed it on a high pole in the field and his body was given to the hogs to devour."[26] Joseph William Carter similarly recalled the story of Jim Gardner, a slave blacksmith who resisted the efforts of his owner to punish him. During a confrontation, "Jim Gardner did not wait to feel the lash, he jumped right into the bunch of overseers and negro whippers and knifed two whippers and one overseer to death; then stuck the sharp knife into his arm and bled to death." Carter admired Jim's bravery noting that "suicide seemed the only hope for this man of strength. He could not humble himself to the brutal ordeal of being beaten by the slave whippers."[27]

In their day-to-day lives, enslaved men similarly linked violence with their masculinity in physical confrontations with their owners. In 1802, Cudgo and Randall, two Isle of Wight County slaves, attacked Reddick Goodwin, their master's son. Reddick had found Cudgo causing a disturbance in his father's kitchen and commanded him to leave. Later that day, Cudgo, angered by Reddick's actions, confronted the young white man and unleashed a "train of unqualified abuse and insult." When Reddick demanded Cudgo stop cursing, the bondsman refused, saying "he would be ordered by no white man."[28] Fearful for his life, Reddick decided that the only solution to the problem was to shoot Cudgo. Rather than solving the problem, the shot, which missed

Cudgo, only enraged the bondsman further. Cudgo's brother Randall soon joined the affray after hearing about the shot. The brothers then chased Reddick all the way back to his father's house, screaming and threatening him. As Reddick tried to retreat to the safety of an upstairs room, the bondsmen chased him up the stairs. In a desperate bid to escape, Reddick cudgeled Cudgo with the gun, breaking it into pieces all over the floor.

Reddick locked himself inside an upstairs room to spare himself Randall and Cudgo's wrath. Unleashing a torrent of curses and threats, the brothers attempted to batter down the door. After several minutes of failed efforts, Cudgo and Randall retreated outside and began pelting the window with bricks, hoping to injure Reddick. They then armed themselves with sticks and knives and attempted to storm the upstairs room again before their master intervened. Samuel Goodwin demanded to know why his slaves were trying to kill his son. Cudgo complained that Reddick had tried to shoot him and he "would be damned if he would not kill him for it." Randall told his master "in a threatening manner that he was a man, let any white man touch him, and he would do for him." Randall also said that "he had laid down his word sixteen years ago that if ever any white man shot him with powder and shot that he would shoot them with glass bottles and old nails, which would do their business in a few days."[29] Samuel Goodwin managed to calm his slaves and protect his son's life. Cudgo and Randall soon stood trial for attempting to kill Reddick.

Slaves who engaged in physical confrontations did not often explicitly connect their violence and their sense of masculinity. Yet Randall viewed Reddick's violence as a direct threat to his manhood. He had explicitly sworn that he would not let anyone shoot him or harm him or his brother. When confronted by Reddick, Randall lived up to his word. In a southern culture where manhood and honor depended on external evaluation by the community, words took on an especially powerful role. As Bertram Wyatt-Brown has written, "[t]he stress upon external, public factors in establishing personal worth conferred particular prominence on the spoken word and physical gesture as opposed to interior thinking or words and ideas conveyed through the medium of the page."[30] Since most slaves could not read or write, oral communication offered the best way to express their frustration and live up to their promises. As a result, only a well-built door in Samuel Goodwin's house managed to protect Reddick's life from the wrath of the two angry slaves.

Even enslaved women recognized the link between violence and masculinity. Jenny Clarkson, a slave from Nelson County, brutally murdered her master, Robert Allen, in September 1824. One evening Allen had gone out into the fields to supervise his slaves. He returned home "in perfect good humor, not in any manner angry."[31] Sometime later that night, Clarkson attacked Allen by striking him over the head. As one newspaper account reported, she "completely perforated his skull with a blow of some weapon. In this situation, his brains oozing from the gash, he lingered three days perfectly rational!"[32] Under interrogation, Jenny admitted that "she killed her master with an axe" and had once threatened Allen that if she was "a man she would murder her master."[33] Her threats and subsequent violence suggest that Clarkson, and other slave women, recognized the link between violence and manhood. While not a man, Clarkson had no problem adopting masculine ideas regarding violence.

In 1860, Winston, a slave of John Woods, attacked his overseer, Joseph Hoy, in another expression of enslaved men's masculinity. One morning early in March, Winston had gone down into a tobacco cellar and struck Hoy across the right side of his head with an ax. The confrontation emerged, as did many in antebellum Virginia, over the issue of punishment. The previous day Winston had threatened Joseph Hoy and declared that the overseer would never whip him again. Winston boasted that when he "was a boy when Mr. Hoy whipped him other time, but he was a man now . . . he warnt [sic] going to let anybody run over him but his master Dr. John Woods." Winston further warned that "if he put his bone on Hoy he would soon have him on his bed and in his grave."[34] Luther Hoy, Joseph's son, overheard the slave's threats and rushed to tell his father. As a result, Joseph Hoy confronted Winston and whipped him.

The attack in the basement emerged from Winston's growing sense of his own maturity and masculinity. For white men, awareness of manhood was part of the maturation process. As white men became adults and sought to claim their place in southern society, as Lori Glover has written, "they responded quickly and often violently to character aspersions, feared shame, and obsessed over communal evaluation of their conduct."[35] As a young man, Winston accepted punishment from whites. But now as an adult seeking to assert his manhood, Winston would not accept punishment from Joseph Hoy. In response to the violence of whites, the only way for enslaved men like Winston and Randall to prove their manhood was similarly through violence. Without the challenge from Reddick Goodwin and Joseph Hoy, Winston and Randall would not have had the opportunity to call themselves men.

Winston's claims also highlight the limits of enslaved men's claims to masculinity. White men's manhood could not tolerate punishment or violence from anyone. Winston, however, made one key exception—for his master John Woods. Why did Winston accommodate his manhood to his circumstances? First, he had little choice. John Woods had the right to punish, sell, or do with Winston as he pleased. Second, as the result of paternalism, slaves and masters knew one another intimately and could earn some level of respect from one another. Even as enslaved men loathed the system that held them in bondage, some accepted their masters' authority to punish them. This acceptance was a key part of conceptions of manhood. In order to determine their social standing, men figure out their status relative to other men—whose authority did bondsmen need to respect or whose did they not? As a result, some enslaved men tolerated punishment, but only at the hands of masters, not other whites.

In their autobiographies, ex-slaves recalled the hatred they felt for overseers, poor whites, and hired-out owners. Solomon Northup loathed every aspect of John Tibeats, his hired-out owner. He described Tibeats as "a small, crabbed, quick-tempered, spiteful man. He had no fixed residence that I ever heard of, but passed from one plantation to another, wherever he could find employment. He was without standing in the community, not esteemed by white men, nor even respected by slaves. He was ignorant, withal, and of a revengeful disposition."[36] Henry Clay Bruce expressed shame at the prospect of being punished by a poor white man. After Bruce ran away after a confrontation with his hired-out master David Hampton to avoid punishment, he admitted that "I would be ashamed of myself, even now, had I allowed that poor white man to whip me."[37]

The refusal to submit to the discipline of unworthy whites could result in deadly physical confrontations. Tom, a slave belonging to Wyatt Whitehead, killed his overseer, Richard Foster, following growing tensions between the two men. On the morning of September 18, 1825, Foster entered Whitehead's house and confronted Tom about a missing surcingle (a strap wrapped around the body of horse that helps pull farm equipment). The two men argued as Foster demanded to know what had happened to the surcingle. Tom replied that he knew nothing about it. As the overseer and bondsman continued to quarrel, Foster called Tom a liar and "picked up a small switch and gave him one lick." Tom, armed with a cane, struck Foster back. The two men brawled until Tom grabbed a hoe and clubbed Foster over the head, killing him. Tom quickly recoiled and picked up the overseer and said, "he hoped he was not dead, he did not intend it."[38]

The tension between Tom and Foster reached a fever pitch the day of the confrontation. That morning, Tom had complained to his mistress, Lucy Whitehead, about Foster's behavior. Whitehead was Foster's sister and Tom wanted her to know he had failed to properly tend to the tobacco and other crops. The bondsman complained to his mistress that if Foster "would keep sober he could do business, but he was always drunk."[39] At Tom's trial, Lucy Whitehead admitted her brother had been drunk the morning of the confrontation. Tom also criticized Foster for preventing him from reporting the overseer's drunkenness and incompetence to Wyatt Whitehead, his master. Tom had hoped that by informing his master of Foster's failings as overseer, Whitehead might fire him or at least lessen his responsibilities. Additionally, Tom wanted to make sure the blame lay where it belonged—with Foster—and not on the Whitehead slaves.

The tensions between slave and overseer had been simmering for months. Mat, another of Whitehead's slaves, recalled that he heard Tom call the overseer, "a mischievous contrary man." According to Mat, Tom said that if Foster "put his hands on him, he would kill him." The animosity ran both ways. Teiller, another slave, testified that during the confrontation Foster expressed his hatred for Tom. He claimed that Foster "said he had for a long time wanted to mash his damned mouth." Maria, a slave, recalled how one night before the murder, Foster had drunkenly threatened to kill Tom. Foster told Tom that "if he opened his mouth he would blow his brains out. Tom replied, 'I have done nothing.'"[40]

The confrontation between Tom and Richard Foster also revealed the importance bondsmen placed on protecting themselves from insults and attacks. Tom viewed himself as a hardworking and loyal bondsmen who sought the best possible outcome for himself and his owner. He likely recognized that his future and the future of those he cared about depended on a successful harvest. Richard Foster, through his drunkenness and general incompetence, put that future in danger. Additionally, in southern honor culture, since verbal communication was essential to judge a man's character, Tom could not simply walk away from his confrontation with Foster. If he did, then he was conceding the truth of Foster's claim—that Tom was a liar and no one, master or slave, could trust his word. To protect his manliness and his reputation, Tom had to fight back.

Insults also played a role in other physical confrontations as well. On October 9, 1827, Allen, a slave, engaged in a deadly confrontation with his master, Jonathan Smith. Their altercation arose over Allen's care of his master's horse. First, Allen had failed to bring the animal under control and injured it. Then when Allen did not bring out a halter to his master quickly enough, Smith tried to whip him. As the two men argued, Smith struck Allen several times, nearly knocking him to the ground. Allen began to fight back, and another slave heard Smith exclaim, "O! Allen do not do that." Allen fatally struck his master over the head with a club. Allen admitted to killing Smith, saying, "I wish to God I had kil'd [sic] him for I aimed to do it. He is such a rascal and has treated me so mean."[41] Jeff Forret has argued that when slaves used the word rascal they meant "someone judged dishonest, unprincipled, or mischievous, suggesting that in the quarters, slaves revered honesty, fairness, and trustworthiness."[42] Clearly Allen believed that violence was the only way to deal with Smith's continued rascality. Had Smith been a fair and honest master, Allen may have never resorted to violence at all.

Daniel, a slave belonging to Jacob Davis, viewed his murder of his overseer, John Allen, in a similar way. On an evening in May 1847, after a corn shucking, Jack, another of Davis's slaves, heard John Allen cry out for help because "there was a negro killing him." Jack ran toward the scream and discovered Allen's dead body. The pre-existing animosity between Daniel and Allen made the bondsman the prime suspect in the murder. Daniel also had disappeared into the woods immediately after the corn shucking and was not seen by his fellow slaves for several hours afterwards. When he returned, Daniel tried unsuccessfully to reassure his fellow slaves that he had nothing to do with the murder. He told them that "they need not think he did it for he would not have done for anything in the world."[43] Davis's other slaves, however, did not believe him. Neither did the white members of the community, who had Daniel arrested and thrown in the Halifax County jail.

After several days, Daniel admitted to killing his overseer. Daniel acknowledged he hated Allen and had sworn to kill him or die in the attempt. The previous week, Allen had whipped Daniel, and the slave claimed that the overseer continually mistreated him. Daniel explained that Allen "had whipped him as he thought without cause and he had determined to take satisfaction for it."[44] The idea of satisfaction implied a set of expectations that Daniel held regarding his treatment by the overseer. When Allen violated those expectations, Daniel killed him.

Insults revealed several other key components of how bondsmen constructed their masculinity. Insults were an important precursor to violence as they attacked the values and character traits that were essential to manhood. They denied the manhood of others by claiming the insulted person failed to live up to the standards of masculine behavior. They were also a way of establishing dominance as they placed the person issuing the insult above the insulted individual. As Kenneth Greenberg has argued, "Virtually all insults involved the imputation of 'slavelike' behavior—of being a coward, thief, liar, or something similar. . . . All insults were equal in the sense that they implied that someone had been reduced to slavish condition."[45] By calling Smith as a rascal, Allen inverted the master-slave relationship and elevated himself above his master. Tom had attempted to do the same thing to his overseer, Richard Foster. If whites like Smith and Foster were dishonest, unprincipled, and cruel, then Allen and Tom were the opposite of those things. Compared to their owners and overseers, bondsmen valued honesty and humane treatment as central to their conceptions of masculinity.

While enslaved men recognized and acknowledged one another's violence and praised themselves and others for their willingness to resist, there were serious limitations to the centrality of violence to manhood. Few bondsmen took the opportunity to engage in physical violence with whites. Certainly fewer than those who ran away or engaged in violence against other bondsmen. These confrontations afforded enslaved men an opportunity to resist their oppression and push back against the power of their masters and overseers. They also inspired other slaves with their willingness to fight and protect themselves. They won respect and admiration from their fellow bondspeople. On the other hand, whites often brutally punished enslaved men who resisted. They received severe whippings or even died as a result of their confrontations. The esteem of their fellow slaves, however, could not bring the dead back to life or undo the trauma unleashed by vengeful whites. While they held similar or even identical views to whites regarding manhood, enslaved men could never affirm it the way white men could. After all, as Edward Baptist has argued, "The denial of black manhood was central to white manhood, American nationalism, and class relations."[46] This complex legacy of enslaved men's resistance reveals the limits of their claims to masculinity.

REASSERTING MASCULINITY

Enslaved men's masculinity varied based on their circumstances and environment. In the quarters and amongst their families, bondsmen took upon themselves the role of providers and as heads of their households. While enslaved Virginians were slaves, they still largely followed the gender roles of the time. Men were expected to provide food and protect their family members. In homosocial environments like when men hunted, fished, or engaged in other similar activities, Sergio Lussana has argued that bondsmen "created an all-male subculture through which they constructed their own independent notions of masculinity, friendship, and resistance."[47] In their interactions with masters, overseers, and other whites, bondsmen largely hid their claims to masculinity beneath a mask of obedience. Bondsmen were expected to obey whites, tip their hats, avert their eyes, and engage in physical acts of deference.[48] Despite their outward signs of submission, enslaved men were deeply devoted to their conceptions of their manhood. When these conceptions came under attack—when whites raped or beat family members or shamed men in public—bondsmen fought back to reassert their masculinity. This violence revealed the importance that marriage, families, and personal pride held in enslaved men's masculinity.

Enslaved families were an important bulwark against the worst excesses of southern slavery. Husbands and wives reared children and, if they were lucky, saw them grow, marry, and have children of their own. If they were unlucky, they saw their fathers, mothers, spouses, and children sold away, whipped, beaten, or worse. The pain of these separations traumatized slaves. Solomon Northup recalled the desperation with which Eliza, a slave woman, tried to keep her family together, "She kept on begging and beseeching them, most piteously not to separate the three. Over and over again she told them how she loved her boy. A great many times she repeated her former promises—how very faithful and obedient she would be; how hard she would labor day and night, to the last moment of her life, if he would only buy them all together."[49] Her pleas, however, fell on deaf ears. Yet enslaved families also proved remarkably resilient. As John Blassingame has written, "However frequently the family was broken, it was primarily responsible for the slave's ability to survive on the plantation without becoming totally dependent on and submissive to his master."[50]

As a result, enslaved men engaged in physical confrontations to protect their families from punishment and sexual exploitation. This belief in familial protection mirrored the beliefs of the white southerners. In southern honor culture, attacking wives, mothers, sisters or daughters was akin to attacking the man himself. In response, white men responded quickly and violently lest their personal and family honor be permanently stained by such insults.[51] As historians have researched slave families, they have uncovered that bondsmen shared in this willingness to protect their family members. In disputes between slaves, men protected their wives and families, finding ways to claim their masculinity.[52] Enslaved men who engaged in physical confrontations straddled a tenuous line between two competing forces. On the one hand, they sought to assert their masculinity as heads of families and protectors. On the other, they tried to do so in a world that denied not only their role as heads of their families, but their manhood altogether.

Some enslaved men resorted to violence to avenge the rape of their wives. Manuel, a slave, brutally murdered Langford Harrison, a neighborhood white man, for raping his wife. On June 3, 1818, Manuel attacked Harrison on the road near William Coakly's Tavern in King George County, Virginia. Armed with a bayonet or similarly spiked weapon, Manuel repeatedly stabbed Harrison through the eyes, skull, and brain. Manuel had become enraged when he learned that "Harrison had had connection with his wife." The tensions between the two men had been simmering for some time. Manuel had feared that Harrison might kill him first and told another slave that he would "be damned if Harrison should not die before Saturday night."[53] Another enslaved man similarly killed Sam Watkins, a white man from Tennessee with a penchant for raping his female slaves. An ex-slave recalled that "one man said he stood it as long as he could and one morning he just stood outside and he [Watkins] got with his wife he just choked him to death." The slave understood the consequences for murdering Watkins; "He said he knew it was death, but it was death anyhow; so he just killed him. They hanged him."[54]

Josiah Henson's father became similarly violent in defense of his wife. Henson had few memories of his father, but "the only incident I can remember, which occurred while my mother continued on N.'s farm, was the appearance of my father one day, with his head bloody and his back lacerated." Henson described how his father's "right ear had been cut off close to his head, and he had received a hundred lashes on his back." Henson later learned that his father "beaten the overseer for a brutal assault on my mother, and this was his punishment." Henson described how before the punishment that his father was "a man of amiable temper, and of considerable energy of character." After the punishment, "my father became a different man, and was so morose, disobedient, and intractable, that Mr. N. determined to sell him. He accordingly parted with him, not long after, to his son, who lived in Alabama."[55] Henson's father paid a heavy price for trying to protect his wife.

Enslaved men also engaged in physical confrontations to avenge the punishment of their wives by whites. In November 1857, Peter, a slave from Adams County, Mississippi attacked his wife's owner, Wilson Spring. On a Sunday afternoon, after learning Spring had attacked his wife, Peter entered Spring's house and beat him while he laid in bed. Spring grabbed for his revolver as Peter repeatedly struck him over the head. Spring "tried to shoot Peter but he ran around the room and escaped." Spring then barricaded himself inside a slave cabin until help arrived. Stephen, another slave, testified that a year prior to the attack Peter had said "he was going to kill Spring because Spring had whipped his wife."[56] Phillip Evans, another slave from South Carolina, recalled how his Uncle Dennis attacked his overseer. The overseer had "insult[ed] my aunt and beat her. Uncle Dennis took it up, beat de overseer, and run off to de woods." Uncle Dennis escaped in the back of a wagon before being recaptured. Evans remembered how "they take him to de whippin' post of de town, tie his foots, make him put his hands in de stocks, pulled off his shirt, pull down his britches and whip him terrible."[57]

While slave marriages rested on tenuous foundations, enslaved men and women valued the love and emotional connections that stemmed from them. Enslaved couples offered one another comfort, support, and love, which were especially important when whippings, beatings, and untold cruelties were commonplace. By tending to one another's physical and psychological wounds, enslaved couples helped one another survive the horrors of slavery. The prevalence of slave marriage also demonstrated the resilience of the enslaved. As Emily West has explained, "Further, their ties of affection served as a means of resistance against oppression and illustrate how slaves of all generations were not demoralized by bondage."[58] Families also represented one area where the enslaved could create and cultivate a life at least partially separate from their owners unrelenting interference. Creating families provided African Americans a way to connect with one another outside of their relationship as chattel slaves. The depth of these emotional connections helps explain why enslaved men resorted to violence to avenge the rape and punishment of their wives.

Unlike in other instances where enslaved men attempted to assert their masculinity, white owners occasionally refused to punish bondsmen who fought to protect their wives. Turner Jacobs, an ex-slave from Mississippi, remembered how his father nearly killed an overseer. The overseer had ordered the slaves to dig a canal through the slave quarters. Jacobs explained that "My maw woan throwin' her dirt as high as de rest and de overseer knock her down and start lashin' her wid de whip." Jacobs's father, witnessing the punishment of his wife, became enraged. As Jacobs put it, "Hit made my paw so mad dat he started after him wid de shovel and I reckon he'd killed but some of de other darkies stop him. Dey knew what would happen if a nigger jump on a white man."[59] After hearing about the incident, Jacobs's owner fired the overseer rather than punish his father.

On other rare occasions, whites even allowed bondsmen to take punishments intended for their wives. Will Glass recalled how his grandfather Joe protected his grandmother from punishment. Glass explained that "just one time they whipped Grandfather Joe. That was because he wouldn't give his consent for them to whip his wife." Grandfather Joe demanded that his master whip him instead and leave his wife alone. As Will explained, Joe "was a good worker and they didn't want to kill him, so they strapped him and let her be like he said."[60]

These incidents revealed the extent to which some white southerners recognized enslaved men's masculinity and their role as protectors of their spouses. Familial protection was a key element of the southern masculine honor culture. In 1806, Andrew Jackson famously killed Charles Dickinson, a Tennessee attorney and plantation owner, in a duel. While the impetus for the duel had been an accusation of cheating during a horse race, the animosity between the two men stemmed from Jackson accusing Dickinson of insulting his wife Rachel.[61] This emphasis on familial defense, however, was not unique to white honor culture. African cultures and honor culture in general had long stressed the importance of protecting spouses. As Rebecca Fraser has argued, "whilst masters might have congratulated themselves on their seemingly invaluable lessons concerning proper conduct toward women in the slave quarters, enslaved men may have learnt these lessons of honour and integrity from within the slave quarters themselves."[62] Enslaved men's masculinity, then, was not merely a replica of white men's, rather it emerged out of the fusion between their cultural heritage, white supremacy, and the specific circumstances of their lives.

Enslaved men also engaged in physical confrontations in order to avenge the whippings of their children. On the morning of May 23, 1842, George, a slave belonging to John Holladay, encountered his overseer, Edmund Pendleton on his way to the fields. Pendleton demanded to know why George was late. George replied that he had tried to please his overseer and "would be damned if he tried hard to please him any longer." Without a pause, George struck Pendleton on the head with a hoe. As the two men struggled, Pendleton drew his knife. George exclaimed, "You damned Rascal to have the outdacious [sic] appearance to draw your knife upon me! I'll kill you now, I don't care where you go!"[63] Pendleton then ran toward the safety of Holladay's house. George, however, remained undeterred, chasing down the overseer and beating him repeatedly. Only Holladay's intervention stopped the attack.

The savagery of the attack shocked Holladay, who struggled to explain why George had turned so violent. During George's trial, Holladay explained to the court that "George maintained a general good character, had been considered a man more hasty than common." George had held a series of privileged positions for his current and previous masters. He had worked as the head man under his previous owner and Holladay had made him his carriage and wagon driver. On occasion, George even served as Holladay's personal valet. Slave owners generally awarded such privileged positions to slaves whose behavior conformed to white notions of slave docility rather than challenged them. Holladay had difficulty comprehending why such a well-behaved slave like George would resist. While his master had no idea why George turned violent, Pendleton explained to the court why George had tried to kill him. He testified that "four days before he had whipped a negro girl, the prisoner's daughter, for some neglect or misconduct." Since the punishment, George "had been very surly in his behavior and abrupt in his language."[64] While Pendleton seemingly identified the cause of George's violence, he still seemed shocked that George had resorted to violence.

In August 1849, Eddy, a slave belonging to John T. Kirby from Spartanburg District, South Carolina, engaged in a similar confrontation in defense of his son. Prior to the confrontation, Kirby had considered Eddy, whom he had owned for fifteen or sixteen years, "a good boy and a faithful servant except when under the influence of liquor." Eddy became "violent and boisterous" after Kirby began whipping his son. As Kirby was whipping him, Eddy cut his son loose and swore "he would kill his [Kirby's] son Augustus Kirby in two weeks if he was not killed." Later, Kirby gathered a group of neighborhood men and confronted Eddy. When Kirby demanded Eddy come out of his house, Eddy yelled, "Don't come near here or I will kill you."[65] As the confrontation escalated, Eddy emerged from the house and struck his master in the head with an ax. He was convicted of attempted murder and sentenced to hang.

In these instances where enslaved men avenged the whipping of their children, white southerners seemed shocked at the level of affection enslaved men had for their progeny. Some whites believed that bondsmen abused their wives and children and thus justified their undermining of enslaved men's role as fathers. The separation of slave families also led southerners and subsequent historians to conclude that fathers did not play a significant role in the development of their children. Yet the available evidence suggests that enslaved men were not the absent patriarchs depicted by twentieth century scholars.[66] They served as role models and providers. Enslaved men occupied gendered work spaces where they taught and bonded with their sons.[67] Through activities like hunting and taking on additional work, they provided food and resources for their families. In the aftermath of the Civil War, newly freed African Americans went to extraordinary lengths to reunite their families.[68] As Eugene Genovese has argued, "The slaves from their own experience had come to value a two-patent, male-centered household, no matter how much difficulty they had in realizing the ideal."[69] It is no surprise then that enslaved men engaged in physical confrontations to protect their children.

Siblings also fought back against whites who whipped their brothers and sisters. In October 1839, Harry, a slave belonging to John Allan, struck and killed his overseer, Isham Cheatham over the head with a piece of a wooden cart. One day while the slaves were working in the fields, Cheatham had begun punishing Harry, Jim's brother, in front of the other slaves. Jim had sassed the overseer and Cheatham wanted to make an example of him for "such impertinent language." As Cheatham disciplined Jim, Harry came up behind him and struck him on the head. After Cheatham crumpled to the ground, Harry ran off, fearful of the consequences of his actions. The other slaves carried the overseer back to their master's house where Cheatham died of his wounds. Harry remained at large for six days before turning himself in. When he returned home, Harry said that he "did not intend to kill Mr. Cheatham and was sorry for what he had done, and had come in to surrender himself that justice might be done." He confessed that he had struck Cheatham because "he was whipping his brother Jim."[70]

On even rarer occasions, a group of slaves bound together to protect a family member from punishment. On July 25, 1857, John H. Dodd, the overseer on the farm of William Boulware, was having trouble with Betty, one his employer's slaves. Betty claimed to be sick and unable to work. Dodd did not believe her and ordered Betty into the fields. That afternoon he found her back in her cabin and questioned her about why she was not at work. Betty, Dodd later testified, "gave me some of her slack jaw."[71] Dodd whipped her several times, causing her to run off. The following Monday morning, Dodd demanded Tom, the head man, fetch Betty from her cabin. He had waited all weekend to punish her for running off. Tom, however, refused. He asked that Dodd wait until his master, William Boulware, arrived. Dodd, undeterred, went into the fields where he found Betty already at work. As he prepared to punish her, Betty snatched the whip out of Dodd's hands and ran off.

Tom, alongside two other slaves Ben and Robert, convinced the overseer to allow them to speak with Betty. They persuaded her to accept punishment.

She was hesitant when Dodd told her he needed to tie her hands, but the slaves assured her it was for the best. As Dodd whipped Betty, he grew unsatisfied with the punishment. He began stripping Betty of her clothes to ensure the blows had their intended effect. By that point, Betty's brother Ben had had enough. Ben, along with Tom, Edmund, Moore, and Robert all raised their hoes and charged at the overseer. Dodd swore he heard the slaves yell out "kill him."[72] Dodd fled from the fields, but the slaves followed in close pursuit. He then ran to the home of Jackson Childrey, a neighbor and justice of the peace. By the time Childrey and Dodd returned to the fields, they slaves had all run away. They remained at large for two days before turning themselves in to their master.

Childrey, in his role as justice of the peace, investigated the attack and discovered that the slaves had only attacked Dodd because of his treatment of Betty. Under interrogation, Tom admitted that only wanted to "catch him [Dodd] and give him a whipping." Tom's honesty in describing the situation impressed his master. Boulware stated that Tom, whom he had owned his entire life, had said "it was no use to tell a lie about it, that they intended to whip Mr. Dodd."[73] Betty's brother Ben and Robert, another family member, admitted to attacking Dodd because they saw Betty being stripped naked and punished for refusing to work.

William Boulware was also frustrated with how Dodd treated Betty. He testified that "Betty is a half witted creature and excessively stupid, which fact I had communicated to Mr. Dodd, but which he seems to have forgotten." The Boulware family repeatedly questioned whether Betty had any good sense at all and had recently been ill. William Boulware testified that "She had been suffering for the last year with a disease of the womb, a disease of which men could not judge." After this incident, Boulware ordered Dodd to send for Mrs. Boulware to examine Betty and evaluate her fitness for work. The slaves also knew of Betty's illness, as Tom had told Dodd that instead of trying to punish her, he should wait for his master to come. Dodd recalled that Tom had told him that "it would be better for me and him too" if they waited until Boulware arrived.[74] In this case, Boulware sided with his slaves and their desires to protect Betty over the wishes of his overseer.

Enslaved men's masculinity extended to the protection of siblings and even sickly or weak slaves from punishments as well. As children, African-American slaves generally socialized together until the age of twelve or so. While their parents worked, enslaved children were supervised by older slaves no longer capable of working in the fields or by older children. By the age of eight or so, they began taking on responsibilities in their owners' and their parents' households by tending to gardens, watching younger children, and trapping small animals for food. At around the age of twelve, enslaved children assumed the work responsibilities of adults. On plantations, they joined work gangs and on smaller holdings, they took on greater work burdens. Until the first stirrings of sexual maturity, enslaved children wore similar clothing. As they became adults, however, they began wearing clothes appropriate to their sex. As a result, children raised together developed close bonds and even looked after one another. Despite the harsh realities of bondage that often pitted slaves against one another for food, tore their families apart by sale, or saw jealousies amongst each other erupt in violence, enslaved Virginians protected even the weakest among them.

Slave families were one of the few defenses bondsmen had against the brutality of bondage. When bondsmen tried to avenge rapes and punishments of their family members, their efforts came at a heavy price. All of the slaves discussed in this section were permanently separated from their families. The Commonwealth of Virginia executed Manuel and Harry for the murders of Langford Harrison and Isham Cheatham. George and the slaves involved in the confrontation with John Dodd were all sold to slave traders and carried out of Virginia. Eddy, in Spartanburg District, South Carolina, was hanged. The historical record is not clear on whether the Adams County Court spared Peter's life. Regardless of whether they were executed or transportation, by defending their family members, enslaved men were separated from them forever.

Slaves also displayed their commitment to protecting their masculinity when faced with public demonstrations of their inferior status or threats to their personal safety. On a November evening in 1809, Davy, slave of William Urton, killed John Tavener, a white man. That night, Davy and Tavener had attended a community corn shucking at the barn of Hezekiah Glascock in Fauquier County. James Fletcher, one of the white men present, recalled how late in the evening, he and Davy mounted their horses and prepared to leave the barn. Tavener, who was drunk, had "commenced playing tricks with their horses by putting a stick under their tails." Tavener's drunkenness upset the horses and annoyed Davy. A frustrated and slightly intoxicated Davy exclaimed, "If you want any thing with me come on by God." Tavener stopped pestering the horses and Fletcher and Davy rode off into the night. Shortly after leaving the corn shucking, Davy admitted that he may have made a mistake in speaking so harshly to a white man. He told Fletcher that "expected that the deceased would follow them."[75] Fletcher advised Davy to ignore the incident.

Davy was right to be concerned; Tavener was not so willing to forgive or forget the bondsman's harsh words. He ran out of the barn armed with a stick and confronted Fletcher and Davy. Fletcher continued to ride home, while Davy dismounted to confront Tavener. Their argument quickly escalated into a full-on brawl. Davy wrestled the stick out of Tavener's hands and beat him repeatedly with it. Davy then remounted his horse and rode off as two other slaves at the shucking found Tavener's wounded body. They carried him off to a nearby house where he died shortly thereafter.

Davy's actions seemed out of character. He had a good reputation amongst whites and blacks alike. His master, William Urton, claimed "Davy has always behaved himself in a peaceable and orderly way, that he is a slave of good character and temper, has always been perfectly obedient." James Fletcher similarly claimed that Davy had "a good character." The other slaves also viewed Davy positively. Peter, a slave of George Glascock, testified that "David is a slave of good character and temper and he never knew him engaged in fighting or quarreling before."[76]

Tavener's public drunken attempts to throw Davy off his horse revealed another component of enslaved men's masculinity—that they would not suffer public humiliation easily. In part, bondsmen endured unending humiliation. They were property, in some ways no different than a horse or hoe. They were subject to the whims of their owners. Everything they owned or had belonged to their masters. But bondsmen accommodated to this reality by modifying their manhood to mean that they would not suffer such humiliations by anyone other than their owners. But they were also cognizant that such public displays of their manhood could cause trouble. For a slave to brazenly challenge the character of a white man—no matter how drunk he was—was too much of a threat to the social order to go unnoticed. Davy recognized that his remarks to Tavener had crossed a line and could result in further trouble. As a result, bondsmen could not forcefully assert their masculinity unless they wanted to upset whites and run the risk of a violent response. The danger of violently claiming manhood represented another way in which slavery limited bondsmen's masculinity.

Besides using violence to protect and avenge wrongs committed against family members, bondsmen engaged in physical confrontations in response to the public shaming of their bodies. An examination of confrontations with whites in public spaces offers further evidence of slaves' claims to their masculinity. Napoleon, a slave of William Bryant, was convicted of assaulting Eldridge Meeks on a Lynchburg street in 1858. While walking home on the evening of June 5, Meeks "met prisoner and several other negro boys on the side walk opposite Kimmier's grocery." As the other slaves moved aside to allow Meeks to pass, Napoleon refused. Meeks testified that he "took him [Napoleon] by the arm and asked him to get out of the way, he said he wasn't in my way." Having physically manhandled Napoleon, Meeks continued walking down the street. He quickly noticed that someone was following him. After initially hastening his pace home, Meeks decided to slow down to see who was in pursuit. He testified that "just as I turned prisoner threw a stone striking me on the right side of my head, just above the ear." Meeks called out for help and Napoleon fled down the road. Meeks admitted, "I had never known or seen that I know of, the prisoner, when I asked the boy to get out of the way, I took hold of his arm just as I would a white man."⁷⁷

Lewis, a slave of Erastus Chandler, engaged in a physical confrontation in the street outside of the United States Hotel in Richmond in December 1860. A crowd of boys had gathered near the hotel and were throwing rocks at pigeons. William Shields, one of the boys, testified that he "threw at some pigeons in the street and struck the prisoner." An angry Lewis confronted the boys and demanded to know who had thrown the rock. Shields admitted he had "struck him, but he did not intend to do so." Lewis picked up a piece of a brick and threw it at Shields. He missed and instead hit John Shields, a seven-year-old boy. The brick wound up "knocking him senseless and inflicting a dreadful wound on his head." Several witnesses observed that the wound was bad enough that Shields was "bleeding very much."⁷⁸ Recognizing that he had severely wounded a white boy, Lewis fled down the street. Several white men who had been standing nearby pursued and captured him. A Hustings Court in Richmond convicted Lewis of assault and sentenced him to transportation.

On July 4, 1855, Richmond Edwards, a white man, spotted Juba, a slave, inside a tavern at the Black Water Depot in Isle of Wight County, Virginia. Edwards believed that Juba "was out of his place and ordered him out of the bar." When Juba refused to leave, Edwards "caned him out." About an hour later, Edwards left the tavern and walked across a rail road bridge into neighboring Southampton County. After he had crossed the bridge some sixty or seventy yards, Edwards "saw a negro come out of the bushes." Juba charged at him and Edwards "received a blow from some person with a stick which fell him to the ground- partly recovering he received a second and a third blow." The two men scuffled and Juba fell over onto Edwards. Edwards "recognized prisoner called him several times by his name Juba and asked him what he meant, prisoner gave no answer, but released himself and run off." A nearby white woman tried to interfere and Juba threatened to kill her. He then "commenced beating [the] witness again and how long he beat him or how many blows he gave him witness did not know, he became senseless."⁷⁹

The behavior of these slaves reveals how bondsmen defended their masculinity in public settings. Napoleon, Lewis, and Juba were driven to violence by public demonstrations of their inferiority by whites. Eldridge Meeks grabbed Napoleon by the arm and moved him out of the road while Napoleon was walking down the street with a group of fellow slaves. Lewis was minding his own business outside of the United States Hotel and Juba was trying to get drunk at a tavern on the Fourth of July. Meeks believed that slaves should yield the road to him, and Richmond Edwards believed it was not appropriate for slaves to drink in a tavern with whites. Rather than accept such physical attacks on their persons, the slaves decided to strike back. They refused to allow white men to insult them. Since these incidents occurred in public, the bondsmen felt compelled to act in defense of themselves. Their actions would show that they would not tolerate such attacks on their manhood or character.

This link between public perception and bodily protection had echoes in white southern conceptions of masculinity. White southerners viewed men's bodies as reflecting their inner character. This view of masculinity had long roots in history. As Bertram Wyatt-Brown has pointed out, "physical presence was no less a sign of worthiness in the Old South than it had been in ancient times."[80] Enslaved men, naturally, did not fit into this white southern masculinity. The behavior of male slaves—the following of orders, the lowering of eyes, the scars of whippings and other punishments—made it clear they were not fit to be called men. White southerners believed the control of enslaved men's bodies ensured their submission to the slave regime.

Despite the claims of southern whites, enslaved men valued their bodies and sought control over them. Ex-slave William Wells Brown linked his freedom with bodily autonomy. He wrote, "But with all this depression of heart, the thought that I should one day be free, and call my body my own, buoyed me up, and made my heart leap for joy."[81] Brown defined freedom, at least partly, as having control over his own body. Henry Bibb emphasized the destructive nature of slavery on the bodies and minds of slaves. As he put it, "It would indeed be astonishing to a christian man to stand in that prison one half hour and hear and see the contaminating influence of Southern slavery on the body and mind of man—you may there find almost every variety of character to look on."[82] Bondsmen recognized the importance of controlling and protecting their bodies from whites. They understood that this control represented one of the most important ways that whites held them in bondage.

Slaves also explained how slave owners' attempts to punish them—and harm or maim their bodies—could not destroy their willingness to resist. Like southern whites, their bodies reflected their inner character. After being ordered to strip by his master, James Watkins replied, "This I immediately did, then looking earnestly at him I told him my soul was happy, and although he might punish my body he could not harm my soul."[83] The enslaved believed that if their bodies could withstand the punishments of whites, then so could their spirits. Frederick Douglass similarly described how his time at Covey's had broken down his body and his spirit. Douglass wrote, "I started off to Covey's in the morning, (Saturday morning,) wearied in body and broken in spirit."[84] Douglass linked the status of his body to his valuation of himself. A physically weakened slave could not resist, spiritually or otherwise. As with southern whites, African American slaves linked their physical appearance with their outward physical character.

When bondsmen resisted whites after the rape or punishment of their family members or suffered personal humiliation, they sought to reassert their claims to masculinity. Enslaved men's manhood was malleable based on context. Among themselves or within the quarters, they were heads of household, family protectors, and men of merit. In their interactions with whites, they suppressed those values in order to survive their enslavement. In instances where whites undercut bondsmen's claims to manhood—by personally shaming them or harming their families—enslaved men fought back to reclaim their manhood. This violence came at a high price, as bondsmen risked death or separation from loved ones in order to prove their manliness. Yet their willingness to engage in such perilous behavior revealed just how important these values were to their sense of manhood and their sense of self.

White southerners could not tolerate resistance from enslaved men who were trying to assert their manhood. Such assertions struck directly at the heart of white manhood. The social and political power of white southerners rested on their exclusive claim to violence. As white men, they alone had the right to fight in defense of freedom and protect their family members and themselves from insult or attack. White men had the exclusive claim to the deference of their inferiors—women, children, and slaves. White men defined their manhood in contrast to the lack of manhood displayed by African-American men. No man, after all, would live as a slave, at the mercy of the whims of another man. This self-serving argument justified white rule in the South. As Edward Baptist has argued, "The absence of black manhood helped make white men into the active citizens who constituted a republic."[85] Such violence on behalf of enslaved men represented not only a threat to individual slaveowners, but to the entire institution of slavery itself.

Enslaved men, however, developed their own conceptions of masculinity. They were raised in the violent world of the master-slave relationship and violence kept them enslaved. In their own lives outside of the view of whites, enslaved men used violence to establish hierarchies and distinguish between themselves. They fought with one another to protect themselves and their families from harm. They fought over property, women, liquor, insults, and the usual things that men fight about. It is no surprise then that enslaved men created a form of masculinity rooted in violence. This masculinity, however, came a brutal cost. Slaves who attacked their owners or other whites wound up permanently separated from the families they sought to preserve. For all the praise of the "heroic" slave, only a few, like Frederick Douglass or Harriet Jacobs's uncle Benjamin, escaped to slavery. The rest faced death or brutal beatings for their resistance. Control over enslaved men's masculinity was not something white southerners would give up easily.

NOTES

1. Lorri Glover, *Southern Sons: Becoming Men in the New Nation* (Baltimore: Johns Hopkins University Press, 2007), 2.
2. Orland Patterson, *Slavery and Social Death: A Comparative Study* (Cambridge: Harvard University Press, 1982), 5.
3. Olaudah Equiano, *The Interesting Narrative and Other Writings* (New York: Penguin Books, 2003), 46, 62.
4. Robert Collins, *Essay on the Treatment and Management of Slaves: Written for the Seventh Annual Fair of the Southern Central Agricultural Society* (Boston: Eastburn's Press, 1853), 11.
5. John W. Blassingame, *The Slave Community: Plantation Life in the Antebellum South Revised & Enlarged Edition* (New York: Oxford University, 1979), 225, 224.
6. Darlene Clark Hine and Earnestine L. Jenkins, "Black Men's History: Towards a Gendered Perspective" in *A Question of Manhood: A Reader in U.S. Black Men's History and Masculinity Vol. 1*, ed. Darlene Clark Hine and Earnestine L. Jenkins (Bloomington: Indiana University Press, 1999), 1.
7. Sergio Lussana, *My Brother Slaves: Friendship, Masculinity, and Resistance in the Antebellum South* (Lexington: University Press of Kentucky, 2016), 18.
8. Rebecca Fraser, "Negotiating Manhood: Masculinity Amongst the Enslaved in the Upper South, 1830–1861," in *Black and White Masculinity in the American South*, ed. Sergio Lussana and Lydia Plath (Newcastle upon Tyne: Cambridge Scholars Publishing, 2009), 88.
9. This connection between manhood and violence was not universal. In the antebellum North, a new culture of masculinity—one of several in existence—stressed that restraint, rather than violence, characterized masculine behavior, see Amy S. Greenberg, *Manifest Manhood and the Antebellum American Empire* (Cambridge: Cambridge University Press, 2005).
10. Jeff Forret, *Slave Against Slave: Plantation Violence in the Old South* (Baton Rouge: Louisiana State University Press, 2015), 313.
11. James Oliver Horton and Lois E. Horton, "Violence, Protest, and Identity: Black Manhood in Antebellum America," in *A Question of Manhood*, 384.
12. Bertram Wyatt-Brown, *Southern Honor: Ethics and Behavior in the Old South* (New York: Oxford University Press, 1982); Kenneth S. Greenberg, *Honor & Slavery: Lies, Duels, Noses, Masks, Dressing as a Woman, Gifts, Strangers, Humanitarianism, Death, Slave Rebellions, The Proslavery Argument, Baseball, Hunting, and Gambling in the Old South* (Princeton: Princeton University Press, 1996); Elliott J. Gorn, "'Gouge and Bite, Pull Hair and Scratch': The Social Significance of Fighting in the Southern Backcountry," *American Historical Review* 90 (February 1985): 18–43.
13. Frederick Douglass, *Narrative of the Life of Fredrick Douglass: An American Slave* (1845: New York: Oxford University Press, 1999), 60, 68, 63, 69.
14. Harriet Jacobs, *Incidents in the Life of a Slave Girl*, eds. Nellie Y. McKay and Frances Smith Foster (1861: repr. New York: W.W. Norton & Company, 2001), 17, 18, 20–21, 22.

15. John Thompson, *The Life of John Thompson, a Fugitive Slave; Containing His History of 25 Years in Bondage, and His Providential Escape. Written by Himself* (Worcester: J. Thompson, 1856), 35, 37.

16. Fraser, "Negotiating Their Manhood," 78.

17. Henry Highland Garnet, "An Address to the Slaves of the United States of America. Rejected by the National Convention 1848," in *The Rise of Aggressive Abolitionism: Addresses to the Slaves*, ed. Stanley Harrold (Lexington: University Press of Kentucky, 2004), 188.

18. Peter P. Hinks ed., *David Walker's Appeal: To the Coloured Citizens of the World* (University Park: The Pennsylvania State University Press, 2000), 64–65.

19. Lewis Clarke, "'Leaves from a Slave's Journal of Life,' Published in Two Parts in National Anti-Slavery Standard, October 20, 27 (1842)," in *Slave Testimony: Two Centuries of Letters, Speeches, Interviews, and Autobiographies,* ed. John Blassingame (Baton Rouge: Louisiana State University Press, 1977), 152.

20. Hinks, *David Walker's Appeal*, 65.

21. Harrold, *The Rise of Aggressive Abolitionism*, 40.

22. Dickson D. Bruce Jr., *Violence and Culture in the Antebellum South* (Austin: University of Texas Press, 1979), 184–185.

23. William Wells Brown, *Narrative of William W. Brown, a Fugitive Slave, Written by Himself* (Boston: American Anti-Slavery Society, 1847), 19–20.

24. Thompson, *The Life of John Thompson*, 27, 26.

25. Austin Steward, *Twenty-two Years a Slave and Forty Years a Freeman; Embracing a Correspondence of Several Years, While President of Wilberforce Colony, London, Canada West* (Rochester: W. Alling, 1857), 33, 39.

26. Harry Smith, *Fifty Years of Slavery in the United States of America* (Grand Rapids: West Michigan, 1891), 135, 138.

27. George P. Rawick, ed., *The American Slave: A Composite Autobiography Indiana Narratives* Vol. 6 (Westport: Greenwood Press, 1972), 46. Henceforth Rawick, *Indiana Narratives,* Vol. 6, 46.

28. *Commonwealth vs. Randall,* James Monroe Executive Papers, 1799–1802. Accession 40936. Box 6, Folder 10, Misc. Reel 5345. State Records Collection, The Library of Virginia, Richmond, Virginia. Henceforth *Commonwealth vs. Randall* (LVA).

29. *Commonwealth vs. Randall* (LVA).

30. Wyatt-Brown, *Southern Honor*, 46–47.

31. *Commonwealth vs. Jenny Clarkson,* James Pleasants Executive Papers, 1822–1825. Accession 42046. Box 5, Folder 8. State Records Collection, The Library of Virginia, Richmond, Virginia. Henceforth *Commonwealth vs. Jenny Clarkson* (LVA).

32. *National Gazette and Literary Register* (Philadelphia, PA) September 18, 1824.

33. *Commonwealth vs. Jenny Clarkson* (LVA).

34. *Commonwealth vs. Winston,* John Letcher Executive Papers, 1859–1863. Accession 36787. Box 2, Folder 6, Misc. Reel 4707. State Records Collection, The Library of Virginia, Richmond, Virginia. Henceforth *Commonwealth vs. Winston* (LVA).

35. Glover, *Southern Sons*, 2.

36. Solomon Northup, *Twelve Years a Slave. Narrative of Solomon Northup, a Citizen of New-York, Kidnapped in Washington City in 1841, and Rescued in 1853, from a Cotton Plantation near the Red River, in Louisiana.* Ed. David Wilson (Auburn: Derby and Miller, 1853), 103.

37. Henry Clay Bruce, *The New Man: Twenty-Nine Years a Slave. Twenty-Nine Years a Free Man* (York: P. Anstdat & Sons, 1895), 66.

38. *Commonwealth vs. Tom*, John Tyler Executive Papers, 1825–1827. Accession 42267. Box 8, Folder 10. State Records Collection, The Library of Virginia, Richmond, Virginia. Henceforth, *Commonwealth vs. Tom* (LVA).

39. *Commonwealth vs. Tom* (LVA).

40. *Commonwealth vs. Tom* (LVA).

41. *Commonwealth vs. Allen*, William B. Giles Executive Papers, 1827–1830. Accession 42310. Box 2, Folder 9. State Records Collection, The Library of Virginia, Richmond, Virginia.

42. Jeff Forret, "Conflict and the 'Slave Community': Violence among Slaves in Upcountry South Carolina," *The Journal of Southern History* 74, No. 3 (August 2008): 580–581.

43. *Commonwealth vs. Daniel*, William Smith Executive Papers, 1846–1848. Accession 43708. Box 5, Folder 6. State Records Collection, The Library of Virginia, Richmond, Virginia. Henceforth *Commonwealth vs. Daniel* (LVA).

44. *Commonwealth vs. Daniel* (LVA).

45. Greenberg, *Honor & Slavery*, 62.

46. Edward E. Baptist, "The Absent Subject: African American Masculinity and Forced Migration to the Antebellum Plantation Frontier" in *Southern Manhood: Perspectives on Masculinity in the Old South*, ed. Craig Thompson Friend and Lorri Glover (Athens: University of Georgia Press, 2004), 137.

47. Lussana, *My Brother Slaves*, 18.

48. Greenberg, *Honor & Slavery*, 48.

49. Northup, *Twelve Years A Slave*, 81.

50. Blassingame, *Slave Community*, 151.

51. Wyatt-Brown, *Southern Honor*, 53.

52. Forret, *Slave Against Slave*, 288.

53. *Commonwealth vs. Manuel*, James P. Preston Executive Papers, 1816–1819. Accession 41737. Box 5, Folder 2. State Records Collection, The Library of Virginia, Richmond, Virginia.

54. Rawick, *Unwritten History of Slavery*, Vol. 18, 2.

55. Josiah Henson, *The Life of Josiah Henson, Formerly a Slave, Now an Inhabitant of Canada, As Narrated by Himself* (Boston: A. D. Phelps, 1849), 2–3.

56. *State vs. Peter*, Adams County Court Records, Group 1850, Box 27, File 60. Historic Natchez Foundation, Natchez, Mississippi.

57. Rawick, ed., *South Carolina*, Vol. 2, Part 2, 36.

58. Emily West, *Chains of Love: Antebellum Slave Couples in South Carolina* (Urbana: University of Illinois Press, 2004), 20.

59. George P. Rawick ed., *The American Slave: A Composite Autobiography Mississippi Narratives*, Supplement Series 1, Vol. 8, *Part. 3* (Westport: Greenwood Press, 1977), 116. Henceforth, Rawick, *Mississippi Narratives*, Sup. 1, Vol. 8, *Part 3*, 116.

60. Rawick, ed., *Arkansas Narratives,* Vol. 2, Part 3, 38–39.

61. See Robert V. Remini, *Andrew Jackson: The Course of American Empire, 1767–1821* (Baltimore: Johns Hopkins University Press, 1998), 125–143.

62. Fraser, "Negotiating Their Manhood," 85.

63. *Commonwealth vs. George,* John M. Gregory Executive Papers, 1842–1843. Accession 43537. Box 1, Folder 8. State Records Collection, The Library of Virginia, Richmond, Virginia. Henceforth *Commonwealth vs. George* (LVA).

64. *Commonwealth vs. George* (LVA).

65. *State vs. Eddy,* Spartanburg District, Court of Magistrates and Freeholders, Case #97. South Carolina Department of Archives and History. Columbia, South Carolina.

66. The myth of the absent father can be found in Kenneth M. Stampp, *The Peculiar Institution: Slavery in the Ante-Bellum South* (New York: Alfred A. Knopf, 1956), 340–349 and Daniel Patrick Moynihan's report on *The Negro Family: The Case for National Action* (Washington D.C.: Office of Policy Planning and Research, U.S. Department of Labor, 1965). Herbert Gutman, *The Black Family in Slavery and Freedom 1750–1925* (New York: Vintage Books, 1976) led the historiographical attack on this position.

67. Lussana, *My Brother Slaves,* 43–44.

68. Ira Berlin, Steven F. Miller, and Leslie S. Rowland, "Afro-American Families in the Transition from Slavery to Freedom," *Radical History Review* 42 (1988): 89–121.

69. Genovese, *Roll, Jordan, Roll,* 491–492.

70. *Commonwealth vs. Harry,* David Campbell Executive Papers, 1837–1840. Accession 4315. Box 7, Folder 1. State Records Collection, The Library of Virginia, Richmond, Virginia.

71. *Commonwealth vs. Ben, Tom, George, Robert, Moore, & Edmund,* Henry A. Wise Executive Papers, 1856–1859. Accession 36710. Box 9, Folder 2, Misc. Reel 4203. State Records Collection, The Library of Virginia, Richmond, Virginia. Henceforth *Commonwealth vs. Ben, et al.* (LVA).

72. *Commonwealth vs. Ben, et al.* (LVA).

73. *Commonwealth vs. Ben, et al.* (LVA).

74. *Commonwealth vs. Ben, et al.* (LVA).

75. *Commonwealth vs. David,* John Tyler Executive Papers, 1808–1811. Accession 41223. Box 3, Folder 11, Misc. Reel 6010. State Records Collection, The Library of Virginia, Richmond, Virginia. Henceforth *Commonwealth vs. David* (LVA).

76. *Commonwealth vs. David* (LVA).

77. *Commonwealth vs. Napoleon,* Henry A. Wise Executive Papers, 1856–1859. Accession 36710. Box 13, Folder 7, Misc. Reel 4209. State Records Collection, The Library of Virginia, Richmond, Virginia.

78. *Commonwealth vs. Lewis,* John Letcher Executive Papers, 1859–1863. Accession 36787. Box 6, Folder 8, Misc. Reel 4719. State Records Collection, The Library of Virginia, Richmond, Virginia.

79. *Commonwealth vs. Juba,* Joseph Johnson Executive Papers, 1852–1855. Accession 44076. Box 12, Folder 3. State Records Collection, The Library of Virginia, Richmond, Virginia.

80. Wyatt-Brown, *Southern Honor*, 48.

81. Brown, *Narrative*, 71.

82. Henry Bibb, *Narrative of the Life and Adventures of Henry Bibb, an American Slave, Written by Himself* (New York: The Author, 1849), 92.

83. James Watkins, *Narrative of the Life of James Watkins, Formerly a "Chattel" in Maryland, U. S.; Containing an Account of His Escape from Slavery, Together with an Appeal on Behalf of Three Millions of Such 'Pieces of Property,' Still Held Under the Standard of the Eagle* (Bolton: Kenyon and Abbatt, 1852), 20.

84. Douglass, *Narrative*, 66.

85. Baptist, "The Absent Subject" in *Southern Manhood*, 137.

Chapter 3

Resistance to Sexual Exploitation

The previous chapters demonstrated the corrosive impact of paternalism and how enslaved men asserted their claims to masculinity. Bondswomen, however, faced a unique set of circumstances specific to their gender that shaped their physical confrontations. The first was their position in the household under the supervision of their mistresses—to be discussed in the next chapter. The other was the near constant threat of sexual exploitation and rape from owners, overseers, and other white men. White men used their power to rape enslaved women and compel them into unwanted sexual liaisons.[1] This power stemmed from southern views on slavery, race, and gender and placed bondswomen in an especially precarious position. As Deborah Gray White has argued, "Black in a white society, slave in a free society, woman in a society ruled by men, female slaves had the least formal power and were perhaps the most vulnerable group of antebellum America."[2] As a result, bondswomen were especially susceptible to sexual exploitation by whites.[3]

Fannie Berry, an ex-slave, recalled the difficulties that Sukie, a fellow slave, faced in trying to prevent her master from sexually assaulting her. Berry explained that "ole Marsa was always tryin' to make Sukie his gal." One day, the master entered the kitchen where Sukie was boiling water and combining it with lye to make soap. He screamed at her and demanded that Sukie remove her dress. Sukie refused and her master "grabbed her an' pull it down off'n her shoulders. When he done dat, he fo'got 'bout whuppin' her, I guess, 'cause he grab hold of her an' try to pull her down on de flo'." Enraged at her master's actions, Sukie fought back and pushed him off of her. She then grabbed a hold of him and, as Berry colorfully described, "gave him a shove an' push his hindparts down in the hot pot o' soap." Berry's master then "got up holdin' his hindparts an' ran from de kitchen."[4] As a result of the confrontation and Sukie's continued refusal to submit to rape, her master sold her away.

Sukie's experiences were not unique in the history of slavery in Virginia. White men's rape and sexual exploitation of enslaved women was commonplace. When a white interviewer asked ex-slave Alice Marshall about her parentage, Marshall responded, "Well, I reckon I oughter to tell dat, but it ain' my shame. 'Twas my ole massa Jack Nightingale, mistiss' husband. He's my father. Chile, dat was ev'y day happenin's in dem days." May Satterfield described how masters would take their slave women "down in de woods an' use her all de time he wanted to, den send her back to work. Times nigger 'omen had chillum for de marster an' his sons and some times it was fo' de ovah seer."[5] White women, too, were aware of the sexual exploitation in their midst. In a famous quotation, the southern diarist Mary Chesnut observed, "any lady is ready to tell who is the father of all the mulatto children in everybody's household but their own. Those she seems to think drop from the clouds."[6]

Sukie, Marshall, Satterfield, and Chesnut revealed the reality of sexual abuse in the antebellum South. Sukie described the day-to-day threat of rape, endemic to enslaved women's lives. Marshall and Satterfield pointed to how white men routinely raped bondswomen and fathered children by them. Chesnut observed that white women recognized the pervasiveness of sexual exploitation, but, by denying that it occurred in their own households, refused to curb white men's sexual impulses. White women's refusal to act, coupled with their belief in their own racial superiority, made any sort of alliance along gender lines against white men impossible. In truth, little could stop white men from sexually abusing bondswomen. By the antebellum period, white views of African American women's sexuality, the immense value of women's bodies, and the reality of life under bondage had coalesced to justify white men's sexual exploitation. Since the future of American slavery rested on bondswomen's reproductive capacities, white men viewed bondswomen's resistance to rape differently than they did to other forms of slave violence. In physical confrontations with enslaved women regarding punishment, white men responded similarly to how they dealt with enslaved men. When it came to enslaved women's sexuality, however, whites marshaled all of their power to maintain their dominance. As a result, enslaved women's physical confrontations in response to sexual exploitation were rare and rarely successful.

In some physical confrontations—specifically ones that dealt with punishment, food, and overseers—bondswomen resisted in the same ways as men. On January 31, 1860, James Sherwood, overseer for William Croxton, a slave owner in Essex County, Virginia noticed that his employer was missing. Sherwood had last seen Croxton the previous morning as the two men went into the fields to work. Sherwood organized a search but found only his employer's horse and empty saddle. He spoke with Eliza and Ann, two of Croxton's slaves, who said their master had left the farm the day before but had not yet returned home. Unconvinced by their explanation, Sherwood led a group of white men to search for him. They soon found themselves at the farm's lye hopper.[7] They discovered "some bones which they believed to be the bones of a human being, that they also found a large pocket knife and a spectacle case."[8] A local doctor identified the bones as hand and thigh bones. Due to the warmth of the ashes, the men concluded that they belonged to Croxton and his body had only recently been consumed by the flames.

Sherwood and some of the white men searching for Croxton began interrogating the bondswomen. The questioning turned to torture after Eliza disrespected and sassed the white men interrogating her. Peter Toombs, one of the interrogators, testified that Eliza proved "very insolent to the witness and for which insolence he struck her two or three licks with a rope." Toombs placed Croxton's remains in front of Eliza and repeatedly beat her in order to elicit a confession. Ann claimed that Eliza delivered the first blow, while Eliza said that Ann had instigated the killing. William, one of Croxton's other slaves, later testified that Ann told him "that she intended to kill her master and burn him up because he had whipped her that day and sent her out of the house where she had been at work to work upon the farm."[9] The circumstances surrounding the death of William Croxton mirrored those seen in other instances of physical confrontations between enslaved men and their masters. Bondswomen also resented being whipped by their masters and proved willing to kill in order to avenge their punishments.

In the spring of 1836, Phoebe, a slave belonging to Carter Lumpkin, killed her master during a dispute over food and punishment. Their quarrel began one evening when Lumpkin dragged Phoebe into his house and demanded she move her bed so he could get some potatoes from the cellar. After Phoebe refused, Lumpkin tried to bribe her with alcohol. Phoebe gladly took it, but still refused to move her bed, sending her master off in a huff. Later that night, Lumpkin stormed into Phoebe's house, determined to get his potatoes. Frances, Lumpkin's wife, remembered that she "heard him at the house of the prisoner after midnight- and there appeared to be considerable noise as if the prisoner and deceased were quarrelling."[10] Carter Lumpkin never returned home that night. The next morning, Frances, found her husband's body about ninety yards from the house. Suspicion fell on Phoebe as white neighbors discovered near her doorstep a pile of bloody and burnt clothes and a bloodsoaked hoe with pieces of hair stuck in it.

The history of disagreements between Lumpkin and Phoebe extended far beyond potatoes. Frances Lumpkin recalled that Carter and Phoebe, "had a difference last fall and the deceased struck her when she resisted him and threw him down." Only with the aid of his wife did Carter Lumpkin manage to gain control of Phoebe and tie her up. Lumpkin "gave her a slight whipping after which the prisoner said the deceased should never whip her again." The animosity between slave and master did not end there. George Fay, a witness at Phoebe's trial revealed how she had "one of the most violent tempers of any negro he knows." Fay also claimed that Phoebe "was very disobedient to her master and frequently ran away." Although Fay conceded that some of the tensions came from Lumpkin's drinking, as he "sometimes got drunk and when so was difficult to please."[11] Like in the case of slave men, bondswomen resented the efforts of their owners to whip and punish them. Phoebe swore that her master would never whip her again and she kept her word.

On June 28, 1859, Rose, a slave belonging to Joseph Epperson, killed her overseer, John Deanor in a confrontation over punishment. That afternoon, Rose had gone to fetch a bucket of water for her fellow slaves, prompting chastisement from the overseer. Deanor yelled at Rose and demanded she return to work. He called her lazy and accused her of working less than the other slaves on the farm. When Rose backtalked the overseer, he flew into a rage. Deanor demanded to know "what sort of jaw is that you give me." Rose denied that she had intended to disrespect her overseer in any way. Her arguments did little to soothe his anger. He chided her, "you stinking bitch you I have a great mind to knock your brains out with this hoe."

Deanor then tried to strike Rose with a hoe while unleashing a torrent of profanities. In response, Rose raised her hoe and hit him on the head, causing a large wound. After being taken back to his employer's house, Deanor told Joseph Epperson about the confrontation and that "he wanted satisfaction." Epperson allowed Deanor to punish Rose for her insolence. The process of whipping Rose, however, coupled with the untreated head wound proved fatal. By the end of the punishment, Deanor had given Rose "a great many licks and exerted himself very much while whipping her." Billy, one of Epperson's slaves, recalled that Deanor "meant to have satisfaction if it cost him his life."[12] Despite Epperson's protestations that Deanor allow a doctor to examine his head wound, the overseer refused. As a result of his exertion and his fractured skull, Deanor died at around midnight that evening.

Like enslaved men's violence against labor exploitation, bondswomen could resist and win better treatment for themselves and their fellow slaves. Anna Williamson recalled when an overseer tried to punish her mother, Williamson's mother fought back. As Williamson explained, "A ridin' boss went to whoopin' her once and she tore every rag clothes he had on offen him." She gloated that "I heard ma say he went home strip stark naked." Williamson remembered, "I think they said he got turned off or quit, one."[13] Fannie Alexander recalled an incident where the slaves, who had grown accustomed to working without white supervision, banded together to fight off the efforts of their owner to install an overseer to supervise their labor. While working under the overseer, the slave women deliberately shirked their work. Alexander explained that "one day the overseer was going to whoop one of the women 'bout sompin or other." In response, "all the women started with the hoes to him and run him clear out of the field." Alexander stressed that "they would have killed him if he hadn't got out of the way." The overseer fled the farm and the master heeded the message from his slaves. The master "put one of the men on the place over the women. He was a colored foreman."[14] By installing a black driver, the master allowed his bondswomen to work without white supervision.

In these confrontations between white men and enslaved women that did not involve sexual assault, bondswomen's violence was identical to that of bondsmen. This type of resistance did not elicit the same vitriol from white men as when bondswomen resisted sexual assault because the terms of the resistance were different. Here enslaved women were resisting labor conditions and ill-treatment. Enslaved women had little other choice but to resort to violence in these instances because as Elizabeth Fox-Genovese has pointed out, "Slave women, like slave men, lived in a world in which no solid or independently guaranteed institutions mediated between their basic relations of gender and the masters power."[15] Since this violence did not have directly to do with control of enslaved women's sexuality, whites responded in the same way that they would to enslaved men. Eliza and Ann, Phoebe, and Rose all stood trial in oyer and terminer courts. While the death of a single overseer or master warranted strict punishment, this type of violence did not represent an existential danger to the future of slavery. The prospect of enslaved women gaining control of their sexuality, however, represented a threat that white men could not endure.

Throughout the spring and summer of 1830, Peggy, an enslaved woman from New Kent County, was attempting to avoid rape at the hands of her master, John Francis. Francis had repeatedly demanded that Peggy have sex with him and she had continually refused him. In response, Francis chained Peggy to a block and locked her inside his meal house, hoping to change her mind. Peggy, however, remained steadfast in her rejection. Over time, Francis became increasingly agitated. He demanded Peggy succumb to his desires and "if Peggy did not yield to his request in that he would beat her almost to death, that he would barely leave life in her, and would then send her to New Orleans." Still, Peggy refused to submit to her master, even after Francis threatened to have Jesse and Patrick, two of her fellow bondsmen, forcibly hold her down "to enable him to effect his object." Peggy discussed the ever-present threat of rape with the other slaves on the Francis property. Jesse, an enslaved man, recalled that Peggy "said she would not yield to his requests because the deceased was her father, and she could not do a thing of that sort with her father."[16]

At that point, Peggy could have acceded to Francis's wishes and become his concubine. But giving into his desires did not mean that she would guarantee herself a better life or even avoid being sold to New Orleans. Too many other enslaved women had suffered similar or worse fates. Solomon Northup described the life of Eliza, who had engaged in a sexual liaison with her master. He built her a house, fathered a child, and promised to emancipate Eliza and her daughter. They lived together for nine years where she was "with every comfort and luxury of life."[17] After the death of her master, his family took Eliza to Washington D.C. ostensibly to emancipate her. Instead they sold Eliza and her daughter, Emily, to a slave trader. Eliza was soon separated from her daughter in New Orleans and died not long after.

William Wells Brown recalled a similar incident between his master, Mr. Walker, and Cynthia, one of his slaves. On a boat trip to New Orleans, Brown overheard Walker propose to Cynthia that she enter into a relationship with him and he would "establish her as his housekeeper at his farm." If she refused, he would sell her "as a field hand on the worst plantation on the river. Neither threats nor bribes prevailed, however, and he retired, disappointed of his prey." The next morning, however, Cynthia consulted Brown and "Cynthia told me what had passed, and bewailed her sad fate with floods of tears. I comforted and encouraged her all I could; but I foresaw but too well what the result must be."[18] For a while, Walker kept his promise. But once he found a white wife, Walker sold Cynthia and her four children.

The cases of Peggy, Eliza, and Cynthia raise an important issue regarding whether enslaved women could consent to sexual liaisons with their masters. Enslaved women could not consent. They had no right to refuse their masters' sexual advances. They were property and legally required to obey. Additionally, enslaved women did not want these sexual encounters. They did, however, have some agency in how they responded to their masters' entreaties. Cynthia and Eliza chose to enter into a relationship with their masters and get better lives for themselves, at least temporarily. Peggy refused John Francis's demands and risked finding herself shipped to New Orleans. These choices were barely choices at all, but they were nonetheless part of the realities of bondswomen's lives and highlight their precarious position within the southern social order.

At first glance, John Francis appeared to be very much like the other white residents of New Kent County. He owned at least ten slaves and managed a prosperous farm. A closer examination of Francis's household revealed the horror that lay underneath the veneer of a country farmer. In 1830, Francis, then in his early fifties, lived without white companionship. His ten significantly younger slaves shared his household. They included a boy and girl under the age of ten, two boys and four girls between ten and twenty-three, and one man and one woman between twenty-four and thirty-five.[19] Even more disturbingly, in 1820, Francis had owned six slaves, all women, four of whom were under fourteen years old.[20] By 1830, Francis had fathered at least one slave child. Peggy, however, was probably not the only one. The realities of Francis's household suggest that he had long sexually abused his female slaves. The demographics of Francis's household made it likely that his desires toward Peggy stemmed from a long and brutal pattern of behavior.

John Francis's sexual exploitation of his slaves laid bare the power imbalance between white men and enslaved women. Francis used his status as a white, landowning man to demand sex from his slaves, demonstrating to all those around him just how powerful he was. Peggy, meanwhile, as an enslaved African American woman would pay a heavy price for resisting his advances. Francis created a continuing cycle of exploitation that benefited himself at the expense of enslaved women like Peggy. First, since Virginia's slave laws followed Roman traditions, any children born of these rapes were Francis's property since slave status followed the status of the mother. Francis's mixed-race children could serve a variety of purposes. He could sell them to other slaveholders and make a profit. He could also keep them on his farm and exploit their labor. If they were women, then he could keep them until they were mature enough for him to sexually exploit and repeat the cycle of rape and abuse. This was clearly his goal with Peggy. Her age is not identified in the court documents resulting from the case. But since historical research into demographics shows that enslaved women generally did not begin to have children until their late teens and early twenties, it is safe to assume that Peggy was one of the four girls between ten and twenty three listed in the census and had seen Francis's abuse and victimization of his bondswomen her entire life.[21]

As Francis demonstrated, control over the sexuality of enslaved women was crucial to the future of slavery. Not only did African American women provide physical labor for their masters, their offspring could be a source of ever-increasing wealth. Virginia's slave owners relied on the natural reproduction of the slave population since the end of American participation in the African Slave Trade in 1808. America received a relatively small percentage of slaves, approximately 3.6 percent of those who survived the Middle Passage, amounting to just over 388,000 Africans from the mid-1600s through 1860.[22] Unlike the slave societies in the rest of the Western Hemisphere, the American slave population had been naturally reproducing itself since the mid-eighteenth century. Historians have argued over different factors that led to this demographic boom including better access to food, higher proportions of women compared to elsewhere, the absence of tropical diseases, and the cultivation of less physically demanding crops. Whatever the specific cause, as Peter Kolchin has pointed out, "It is clear that for a variety of reasons American slaves had higher birth rates and lower mortality rates than those elsewhere in the Americas."[23]

America's limited participation in the Atlantic Slave Trade and the naturally reproducing slave population meant that white men like John Francis took a special interest in their bondswomen's sexual reproduction. Owners prized slave women who they believed would give birth to multiple children over the course of their lives. Slaveholders monitored their slaves' fertility and often discussed the reproductive capacities of their slaves amongst themselves in private conversations and published journals like *De Bow's Review*. Frederick Law Olmsted recalled an encounter with a planter who bragged that "his women were uncommonly good breeders; he did not suppose there was a lot of women anywhere that bred faster than his; he never heard of babies coming so fast as they did on his plantation." The selling of slave children, Olmsted stressed, offered a way for slave owners to pay off debts, acquire new land, or fund other business ventures. A southern friend of Olmsted's claimed that in the Upper South, "as much attention is paid to the breeding and growth of negroes as to that of horses and mules."[24]

Enslaved women's reproductive capacities were a key part of valuing them for sale. Potential owners closely examined bondswomen for physical clues that might indicate whether they would give birth to healthy children. During Solomon Northup's time in a New Orleans slave market, he noticed how serious buyers wanted to intimately inspect their potential human property. Northup wrote that "Sometimes a man or woman was taken back to the small house in the yard, stripped, and inspected more minutely."[25] William Johnson, an ex-slave from Virginia recalled that when slave women were sold, "bidders would come up and feel the women's legs—lift up their garments and examine their hips, feel their breast, and examine them to see if they could bear children." Fannie Berry, another ex-slave from Virginia, described how during the sale of Sukie, "de nigger traders 'zamined her an' pinched her an' den dey open her mouf, an' stuck dey fingers in to see how her teeth was." Sukie became angry and "pult up her dress an' tole ole nigger traders to look an' see if dey could fin' any teef down dere."[26]

Slave traders and purchasers paid the highest prices for attractive slave women who could serve as concubines. Robert Ellett, a former slave from Virginia noted that "In those days if you was a slave and had a good looking daughter, she was taken from you. They would put her in the big house where the young masters could have the run of her." Carol Anna Randall recalled how her master sold her sister, Marie, to a Richmond slave trader. Randall explained that "Marie was pretty, dat's why he took her to Richmond to sell her. You see, you could git a powerful lot of money in dose days for a pretty gal." Elizabeth Sparks noticed how her master showed favoritism toward the prettiest slaves. She recalled that "Old Massa done so much wrongness I couldn't tell yer all of it. Slave girl Betty Lilly always had good clothes an' all the priviliges. She wuz a favorite of his'n. But cain't tell all!"[27] Owners saw it as a point of pride to have the most sexually attractive bondswomen as their mistresses while also demonstrating their ability to sexually possess and control enslaved women.

In cities like New Orleans, Richmond, Charleston, and elsewhere across the South, African-American women with lighter complexions were sold in the "Fancy Trade"—the sale and purchase of enslaved women who were used as prostitutes and concubines.[28] Fancy girls fetched much higher prices than typical slaves. Lewis Clarke, an ex-slave, recalled that "I heard of some girls being sold in New Orleans for from $2,000 to $3,000. The common price of females is about from $500 to $700, when sold for plantation hands, for house hands, or for breeders."[29] Theophilus Freeman, a New Orleans slave trader, separated Emily, Eliza's daughter, from her mother. Freeman recognized Emily's potential value as a "Fancy Girl." He believed that "there were heaps and piles of money to be made of her, he said, when she was a few years older. There were men enough in New-Orleans who would give five thousand dollars for such an extra, handsome, fancy piece as Emily would be, rather than not get her." Emily's sexual potential meant that she was worth much more than one "of your thick-lipped, bullet-headed, cotton-picking niggers."[30]

The frequent exposure of the bodies of slave women during punishment also contributed to white understandings of their sexual promiscuity. Oliver Bell remembered when his master punished his mother, telling a WPA interviewer that "one day my mammy done sumpin en Ole Marsa made her pull her dress down 'roun' her waist en made her lay down cross de do' en he taken er leather strop en whooped her."[31] Celestia Avery stressed the connection between physical punishment and removing the clothes of female slaves. She remembered how her master punished her grandmother, Sylvia for praying. One morning she had begun her prayers and "the master heard her and became so angry he came to her cabin seized and pulled her clothes from her body and tied her to a young sapling. He whipped her so brutally that her body was raw all over." On another occasion, the overseer ordered Sylvia to remove her clothes before a punishment. The overseer commanded her "to take her clothes off when she reached the end of a row. She was to be whipped because she had not completed the required amount of hoeing for the day."[32]

Recognizing that avoiding rape at the hands of John Francis would be nearly impossible, on the evening of August 22, 1830, Peggy decided to take action. Francis had already chained her to a block and threatened to have Jesse and Patrick hold her down while he raped her. He also threatened to beat her and ship her off to New Orleans, permanently separating her from the life she had always known.

The prospect of being sold to New Orleans horrified slaves. William Wells Brown recalled working in the New Orleans slave market where he helped prepare the other slaves for sale before prospective owners. He remembered that "before the slaves were exhibited for sale, they were dressed and driven out into the yard. Some were set to dancing, some to jumping, some to singing, and some to playing cards. This was done to make them appear cheerful and happy. My business was to see that they were placed in those situations before the arrival of the purchasers, and I have often set them to dancing when their cheeks were wet with tears."[33] Brown and Solomon Northup, who was sold out of the New Orleans slave market, recalled in their autobiographies the horrors of the slave market, where traders paraded slaves in front of prospect owners in order to sell them for the highest possible price while ripping enslaved families apart, never to see their loved ones again.[34] Peggy had likely heard stories about New Orleans and wanted to avoid that fate at all costs.

So on the evening of August 22, 1830, Peggy enlisted the aid of Patrick and the pair broke into their master's house. Jesse, another of Francis's slaves, saw Patrick and Peggy come to the door armed with an ax and a stick. Jesse watched as Patrick and Peggy forcibly entered the house "and shortly after he heard a noise in the house and heard the deceased say 'O Lord have mercy.'" The two slaves had beaten their master to death. After killing Francis, Peggy and Patrick, with another slave, Caroline, briefly left the house. They returned carrying two quilts stuffed with straw. They lit the quilts on fire and left them inside the house. The flames soon began to devour the house and Francis's body.[35] Neighbors came rushing to help and soon extinguished the fire. The neighbors removed Francis's body from the ruins and found the ax and stick wounds all across his body. They quickly surmised that Francis's slaves had killed him and set the fire to cover up their crime.

On September 10, 1830, Peggy, Patrick, Caroline, and Franky, another of Francis's female slaves, stood trial at the New Kent County Courthouse for the murder of their master. During the brief trial, several of Francis's other slaves testified to seeing Peggy and Patrick enter their master's house and later set it ablaze. One witness, a twelve-to-thirteen-year-old slave girl named Sukey, told the justices that "Franky opened the door and kicked her master" and later she heard Francis scream for mercy. Jesse's testimony laid bare the horrifying reality of Francis's incestuous lust for his own daughter. Yet the admission shocked no one. Instead, members of the New Kent County community, white and black, all admitted to knowledge of Francis's desires. Hannah, Peggy's half-sister, recalled that "my mother always said that the deceased was Peggy's father and Peggy considered him her father." Hannah further stated that "I know the deceased wanted to cohabit with Peggy to which she objected and that was the cause of the difference between them. I know the deceased threatened Peggy to beat her almost to death and to send her off if she did not yeald to his wishes."[36]

The neighborhood whites and the magistrates investigating the case all knew of Francis's proclivities. Abner Ellyson, a white man and neighborhood resident, claimed that "it was currently reported in the neighborhood that the deceased was the father of Peggy and that he wished to have illicit intercourse with her." John W. Royster testified that "Peggy was generally said to be the daughter of John Francis her master, and heard, but did not know that Francis desired to cohabit with Peggy."[37] Royster and fellow magistrate William E. Clopton both lived within a mile of Francis's house.[38] Richard Burnett, Francis's neighbor who recovered the body from the flames, likely knew about Francis's behaviors considering they were related. In 1819, Burnett had married a woman named Rebecca Francis.[39] He also received compensation after the trial for the value of the slaves, inherited the Francis estate, and the two owned land together.[40] It would be difficult to believe that Burnett had no knowledge of Francis's sexual desires.

Francis's sexual exploitation of his bondswomen was neither surprising nor scandalous. By the antebellum era, centuries of intellectual developments regarding African American and gender roles justified white men's efforts to control enslaved women's sexuality. These ideologies also shifted the blame for sexual exploitation from the perpetrators to the victims. These views had coalesced into the image of African American women as Jezebels.[41] Jezebel was purely a sensual creature—undisciplined, rash, and solely fixated on sex. She stood in contrast to the ideal of white southern women. Southern ladies were pale, spoke softly, and did not show any signs of anger, passion, or other potentially explosive emotions.[42] The Jezebel archetype evolved over hundreds of years dating back to the first sustained European contact with African in the fifteenth and sixteenth centuries.[43] These ideas fused with the physical realities of life under slavery, where enslaved women's bodies were frequently exposed, to condemn all African-American women as controlled by their lust.

Even prior to sustained European contact with Africa beginning in the fifteenth and sixteenth centuries, Europeans had characterized Africans as licentious and overly sexual. In the famous travelogue, *The Travels of Sir John Mandeville*, the author described how "in Ethiopia, and in many other countries, the inhabitants lie all naked in rivers and waters, men and women together.... And the women have no shame of the men, but lie all together, side by side, till the heat has passed."[44] Armed with these assumptions, Englishmen found plenty of evidence to confirm their preexisting biases. When they actually visited Africa, African women's tribal dances, exposed skin, and polyamory led Europeans to reaffirm their belief that African women were obsessed with sex. As Winthrop Jordan has written, "Seizing upon and reconfirming these long-standing and apparently common notions about Africa, Elizabethan travelers and literati spoke very explicitly of Negroes as being especially sexual."[45] Through the spread of travel narratives, art, and other media, the association of Africans with rampant sexuality became ingrained in English cultural attitudes.[46]

Samuel Cartwright, one of the antebellum South's leading doctors who undertook extensive research into the culture, physiology, and supposed diseases that afflicted African Americans, gave the Jezebel archetype the veneer of scientific respectability. In his writings, Cartwright described how during a ritual dance, "the odor emitted from the men, intoxicated with pleasure, is often so powerful as to throw the negro women into paroxysms of unconsciousness, vulgo hysterics." Cartwright doubted that missionary efforts could rid African Americans of their inherent lust and savageness. Instead he argued that "nothing but compulsatory power can restrain uncivilized barbarians from polygamy, inebriety, and other sinful practices." Violence against African Americans, Cartwright argued, was the only way to raise them to the level of civilization. If left in their natural and degraded state, they would pose a threat to the safety and stability of white society. As Cartwright pointed out, "The plantation laws against polygamy, intoxicating drinks, and other besetting sings of the negro race in the savage state, are gradually and silently converting the African barbarian into a moral, rational, and civilized being."[47] Cartwright made no mention of how white rape fit into this civilizing campaign.

William Harper, chancellor of the University of South Carolina, however, argued that sexual exploitation was beneficial to enslaved women, especially compared to prostitutes in the North. He pointed out that fallen Northern women were "cut off from the hope of useful and profitable employment, and driven by necessity to further vice. Her misery, and the hopelessness of retrieving, render her desperate, until she sinks into every depth of depravity." White women in the North, reduced to prostitution had little way of finding their way back to respectability. Enslaved women, on the other hand, had no respectability to lose, since they were already racially and culturally inferior to whites. As Harper argued, "Her offspring is not a burden, but an acquisition to her owner; his support is provided for, and he brought up to usefulness."[48] Few southern whites subscribed to Harper's view, but his argument revealed the depth that white men went to rationalize their rape of African American women.

Thomas R.R. Cobb, the Southern legal theorist, argued that the rape of enslaved women was not a crime since they had no legal right to resist their master's advances. Cobb acknowledged that white men had sex with their slave women but laid the blame squarely at the feet of bondswomen. Cobb wrote that "An evil attributed to slavery, and frequently alluded to, is the want of chastity in female slaves, and a corresponding immorality in the white males." Cobb, however, steadfastly denied that whites ever abused their masterly authority. He boasted that "Every well-informed person at the South, however, knows that the exercise of such power for such a purpose is almost unknown." He claimed that the primary cause of mixed race children was "the natural lewdness of the negro." The origins of this behavior, he contended, were not a product of American slavery. Rather, Cobb wrote, "The free negro in Africa, in the West Indies, in America, exhibits the same disposition, perhaps not to the same degree when living in a Christian community."[49] Cobb's invocation of the Jezebel stereotype sparred whites of any of the responsibility for the rampant sexual exploitation that plagued the South.

European attitudes toward Africans and exposure of female African-American bodies in the southern United States, in the words of Deborah Gray White, "helped imprint the Jezebel image on the white mind."[50] As a result, white men like John Francis primarily viewed enslaved women through their sexuality. Whites assumed that slave women were obsessed with sex and wanted sexual liaisons with whites. By surrounding himself with enslaved women, Francis ensured himself access to a population of vulnerable sexual partners. Enslaved women meanwhile sought to control their bodies and their sexuality. They witnessed what happened to women who engaged—or refused to engage—in liaisons with white men. They, however, often had little choice in the matter. White men had the power of the law and cultural attitudes to justify their sexual exploitation—if they bothered to justify it at all. As a result, the reality of African-American slavery in the nineteenth century and ideology of the Jezebel archetype merged to create a world where enslaved women constantly fought for, but rarely succeeded in winning control over their own bodies and reproductive capacities.

When John Francis raged at Peggy, chained her to a block, threatened to beat her, and ship her to New Orleans, he expressed the frustrations of many white men who worried about losing control over bondswomen's sexuality. Centuries of cultural development regarding the role of mastery, African American women's promiscuity, and the realities of American slavery had justified rape. This ideology even suggested that white men might be doing bondswomen a favor by sexually abusing them. So when enslaved women resisted exploitation or were even suspected of doing so, white men became almost homicidally violent. Edwin Epps, Solomon Northup's owner, brutally whipped Patsey, one of his slaves, when he suspected she might be having sex with Mr. Shaw, a neighborhood white man. When Patsey returned home from a visit to the suspecting neighbor, Epps ordered Northup to tie her to the ground and whip her. Epps grew mad with passion, stomping on the ground and screaming as Northup whipped her. After Northup administered the brutal punishment, Epps grabbed the whip and continued until "She was terribly lacerated—I may say, without exaggeration, literally flayed." Epps's punishment nearly killed Patsey and left permanent psychological damage. Northrup recalled that after she recovered, Patsey "no longer moved with that buoyant and elastic step—there was not that mirthful sparkle in her eyes that formerly distinguished her."[51] The suspicion that Patsey might be trying to control her own sexuality sent Epps into a blind rage. Had she actually engaged in a relationship with her white neighbor, Epps may have killed her.

Harriet Jacobs's owner, Dr. Flint, became similarly furious when Jacobs entered into a relationship with another white man, Mr. Sands. Flint told her that she had ruined any chance of bettering her life by rejecting his advances. Flint chided her, "'You obstinate girl! I could grind your bones to powder! You have thrown yourself away on some worthless rascal. You are weak-minded, and have been easily persuaded by those who don't care a straw for you." Besides decrying Jacobs for falling for Sands's promises of an improved life, Flint pointed out how he could have violently compelled her to submit to him sexually: "I might have punished you in many ways. I might have had you whipped till you fell dead under the lash. But I wanted you to live; I would have bettered your condition. Others cannot do it. You are my slave.'"[52] In Flint's eyes, Jacobs's attempts to control her sexuality were condemnable.

After killing John Francis, Peggy had little hope of escaping with her life. The court of oyer and terminer convicted Peggy, Patrick, and Franky of murder and sentenced the three slaves to hang on October 29, 1830. The justices acquitted Caroline but did not provide a reason. The court, however, did recommend to Virginia Governor John Floyd that Franky's death sentence be reprieved to transportation. They suggested "mercy and commutation of her punishment unto transportation and if they should not think her worthy of mercy the Court recommends the said Franky for a respite of her sentence as she is pregnant until she may be delivered."[53] The court record made no mention of who the baby's father was.

Peggy's conviction and sentence mirrored the famous case of Celia, a slave from Missouri, who murdered her master after years of sexual abuse. Celia's owner, George Newsom, had purchased her in 1850 after the death of his wife. According Melton A. McLaurin, Newsom had bought Celia for sexual companionship.[54] Newsom wasted no time in raping Celia. At Celia's murder trial in 1855, Jefferson Jones, one of Newsom's neighbors, testified that he had heard Newsom had "forced her on the way home from Audrain County."[55] With that first rape, Newsom established a pattern of behavior that continued over the next five years. Newsom had even constructed a one story brick cabin, located fifty yards behind his own house for her. Newsom would leave the comfort of his home and white family for the privacy of Celia's cabin. There he likely fathered both of Celia's children.

By 1855, Celia found herself caught in a struggle between Newsom's claims over her body and sexuality and those of George, a male slave. Celia had begun a relationship with George while Newsom continued to rape her. Celia had become pregnant and did not know who had fathered the child. George, who could no longer bear sharing Celia sexually with another man, demanded that she stop having sex with Newsom, otherwise he would leave her. Despite the ample evidence to the contrary, George believed that Celia had the ability to stop Newsom's systemic sexual exploitation. George, either unwilling or unable to confront Newsom himself, put Celia in an untenable position. The liaison between owner and slave woman would not come to an end as easily as George hoped.

In June 1855, Celia acceded to George's wishes and attempted to convince Newsom to stop raping her. She threatened her master with physical violence if he ever tried to sexually exploit her again. On the evening of June 23, 1855, Newsom, undeterred by Celia's threat, went to her cabin. After entering the cabin, the exact nature of events is unclear.[56] According to testimony at Celia's trial, the two exchanged words and Newsom "was talking to her when she struck him. He did not raise his hand when she went to strike the first blow, but sunk down on a stool toward the floor. Threw his hands up when he sunk down. She struck him with left hand then right hand."[57] Celia struck Newsom several times fearing that she had not killed him with her first blow. Celia built up a roaring fire and placed Newsom's body in it. She hoped to destroy the body and any evidence of her involvement in the murder.

Like Peggy, Celia was put on trial for murder. Celia's trial, occurring in 1855 in Missouri amidst the tumult of the civil war in Kansas, garnered a significant amount of interest from the state's pro-slavery and anti-slavery factions. As McLaurin observed, "Proslavery Missourians would expect to see Celia hang; those less supportive of the institution would expect the court to treat her fairly, or at least in accordance with the law."[58] Because of the ban on slave testimony, neither Celia nor Peggy ever took the stand in their own defense. The legal ban on testimony prevented the judge in Celia's case and the justices of the peace in Peggy's case from ever having to directly confront the reality that enslaved were raped or threatened with rape. Since it was not legally possible to rape an enslaved women, the bondswomen could not raise the issue as a defense. Rather the question for the judges and justices overseeing these cases were simple—did these bondswomen kill their masters? The answers were an unequivocal yes. But the question then became should they receive the death penalty.

In both cases, higher authorities made the final decision on the fates of Peggy and Celia. On October 23, 1830, Virginia Governor John Floyd and his Executive Council discussed a petition requesting that Floyd commute the slaves' sentences to transportation. The petition had one hundred signatures and included the New Kent County sheriff, two justices of the peace, and a constable. The first signature belonged to John L. Poindexter, one of the five justices who presided over the trial. The petitioners claimed that "there are circumstances attending the case of the poor ignorant slaves although not sufficient to justify the act for which they were condemned yet in the opinion of the undersigners should mitigate the punishment." The petition also implied that further lurid details about Francis's relationship with his slaves had not entered the court record. The petitioners wrote that "The undersigners beg leave to refer your excellency for some circumstances connected with their offense and not entered on the record to John B. Christian Esq. (a member of the Executive Council) who defended the said slaves on their trial."[59] Nothing in the Governor's Executive Papers indicates precisely what this evidence may have been.

Celia's lawyers appealed her case to the Missouri Supreme Court. But the trial judge refused to stay her sentence pending an appeal. McLaurin explained that "it is more likely, however, that once a verdict was rendered the judge wished to dispose of the case as quickly as possible because of political tensions within the state resulting from the ongoing debates over slavery and Kansas." Facing a looming execution date and no word from the Supreme Court, Celia's supporters took desperate action. Five days before her execution date, Celia escaped from jail with the aid of an unknown number of supporters. The evidence, McLaurin notes, suggests that Celia "was hidden by those who engineered her escape until after the original execution date had passed, then returned to her captors."[60] In December 1855, however, the Supreme Court rejected her appeal and ordered that the execution go forward. And on the afternoon of December 21, 1855, the Fulton County authorities finally rid themselves of Celia's troublesome case for good as they hanged her at 2:30 in the afternoon.

Peggy's case, however, continued to present problems for Governor Floyd and his Executive Council. After receiving the petition from the leading members of New Kent County, Floyd commuted Peggy and Franky's death sentences, but left Patrick's in place. On October 28, 1830, a day before Patrick's execution, another petition arrived in Richmond pleading for Patrick's life as well. The petitioners claimed that Patrick was mentally disabled and should be spared the noose. Turner Christian, the New Kent County jailer, described Patrick as "scarcely one remove from an Idiot."[61] Floyd agreed to commute Patrick's sentence and, in December 1830, the State Auditor's Office paid out nine hundred dollars to Richard Burnett for the value of Peggy, Patrick, and Franky, closing the case for good.[62] In April 1831, slave traders carried Peggy, Patrick, and Franky out of Virginia to uncertain fates.[63] For all of her efforts to avoid being raped by her father, beaten, and sold to

New Orleans—Peggy could not escape sale southward. Nor likely, could she hope to avoid sexual exploitation in the future.

Francis's actions suggest why the white residents of New Kent County lobbied Governor Floyd to spare the lives of Peggy, Patrick, and Franky. Throughout Virginia and other states in the Antebellum South, petitioning on behalf of convicted slaves was a common practice. As historians such as Diane Miller Sommerville and Ariela Gross have demonstrated, whites interjected community judgments and customs into the legal arena through petitioning. These actions, Sommerville has argued, helped mitigate the harshness of southern rape laws.[64] The petitioners from New Kent County similarly sought to insert the judgment of the community into the case. The petition headed by John L. Poindexter did not seek to excuse Peggy from punishment for her crime. Rather it sought to soften it. The petitioners acknowledged the horror of murdering a white man and the necessity of punishing slave criminals. They believed, however, the horrifying circumstances of John Francis's household should convince the governor to spare Peggy's life. Similarly after Governor Floyd saved Peggy and Franky from the noose, white residents of New Kent County continued in their efforts to save Patrick as well. Peggy, they argued, had manipulated Patrick into helping her commit the murder. The execution of a mentally disabled man, in the judgment of the community, was neither fair nor just.

Francis's public lusting after his daughter flew in the face of southern traditions that tried to mask the widespread sexual abuse of female slaves. Harriet Jacobs speculated that concern about reputation and community punishment dissuaded her owner, Dr. Flint, from ever raping her. She explained, "Bad as are the laws and customs in a slaveholding community, the doctor, as a professional man, deemed it prudent to keep up some outward show of decency."[65] Francis, living without white companionship and surrounding himself with young slave women, seemingly had no such concerns. In his study of southern honor, Bertram Wyatt-Brown echoed Jacobs's sentiments when he wrote that "unrestrained promiscuity by men was by no means uniformly condoned, but discretion was the mark of a gentleman."[66] Francis's flaunting of his sexual exploitation of his slaves, likely generated some sympathy for Peggy and the others. But only enough to spare them their lives.

Celia's confrontation revealed how enslaved women could not always rely on their husbands for aid or sympathy in their struggles against sexual exploitation. Enslaved men's masculinity and desire to claim exclusivity to their women's sexuality led them to pressure or abandon bondswomen who tried or failed to resist. In Celia's case, George pressured her to confront Newsom. After escaping to freedom in the North, Henry Bibb condemned his wife, Malinda, for engaging in a sexual liaison with her new master. He wrote, "As she was then living with another man, I could no longer regard her as my wife. After all the sacrifices, sufferings, and risks which I had run, striving to rescue her from the grasp of slavery; every prospect and hope was cut off. She has ever since been regarded as theoretically and practically dead to me as a wife, for she was living in a state of adultery, according to the law of God and man."[67] As a husband, Bibb had exclusive claims over his wife's sexuality and her body. Now that Malinda had taken up with her master—likely against her will—Henry could no longer be married to her.

Bibb showed no sympathy for Malinda, who already spent a lifetime dealing with sexual exploitation. For their entire marriage Bibb was well aware that his status as a slave meant he would not have exclusive sexual access to his wife. During their marriage, a slave trader named Madison Garrison purchased Henry and Malinda. Garrison took Malinda "to a private house where he kept female slaves for the basest purposes." Garrison, Henry later wrote, "made a most disgraceful assault on her virtue, which she promptly repelled; and for which Garrison punished her with the lash, threatening her that if she did not submit that he would sell her child." After Malinda refused a second time, Garrison whipped her repeatedly. Additionally, Bibb recalled that when he asked permission to marry his wife Malinda from her master, "his answer was in the affirmative with but one condition, which I consider to be too vulgar to be written in this book."[68] Bibb's life experiences had taught him the fragility of slave women's control over their sexuality. Yet he had no problem blaming Malinda for acceding to her master's desires after he had escaped to freedom.

Nor could bondswomen rely on aid from white women. First, Southern notions of white southern women's sexuality stood in stark contrast to the Jezebel archetype. White women were expected to remain pure and modest before marriage and faithful during marriage.[69] White male honor culture, however, made the protection of women's sexuality a key responsibility for male family members. This position in Southern society afforded white women an elevated, but still subordinate position. In exchange for their virtue, white women received the protection of male relatives should they suffer any slight or insult. This reality made white women unlikely to help African American women avoid sexual exploitation. After all, white women shared the view of African American women as sexually promiscuous and were as likely to blame enslaved women for their husbands' behavior. As a result, enslaved women had little hope of receiving aid from white women in avoiding sexual exploitation by their masters.

White women were more likely to punish than aid slave women's efforts to resist the sexual demands of whites. Fannie Moore remembered how her owner's mother terrorized the slaves on their South Carolina plantation. The master's mother aided Hill, the overseer, in sexually exploiting the female slaves. Moore described Hill as, "mean as de devil." She explained that "on de Moore plantation Aunt Cheney, everybody call her Aunt Cheney, have two chillun by de overseeah." The owner's mother cajoled Aunt Cheney into a sexual liaison with Hill in the first place. She remembered how "Ole Granny call Aunt Cheney to de kitchen and make her take her clothes off den she beat her til she jest black an' blue."[70] Rather than endure further beatings, Aunt Cheney submitted to Hill's desires. The aid of the owner's mother made Aunt Cheney's efforts to resist nearly impossible.

Some white women even aided in the sexual abuse of slave women by their husbands. Jacob Mason, an ex-slave from North Carolina, highlighted the commonality of sexual exploitation by masters. He stressed, "At dat time it wus a hard job to find a marster dat didn't have women 'mong his slaves. Dat wus a ginerel thing 'mong de slave owners." Mason explained that his master "had no chilluns by white women. He had his sweethearts 'mong his slave women." He also told a story of a plantation mistress who refused to help protect a slave woman from sexual desires of her own husband. He explained that "one of de slave girls on a plantation near us went to her missus an tole her 'bout her marster forcing her to let him have sumthin to do wid her an her missus tole her, 'Well go on you belong to him.'"[71] Rather than aid the slave woman, the mistress helped doom her to further sexual exploitation.

White women sometimes took out their anger at their husbands' infidelity on enslaved women and their mixed-race children. Ryer Emmanuel, an ex-slave, described the scorn that her mistress had for a particularly light-skinned slave. Emmanuel described how "old Missus been mighty proud of her black chillum, but she sho been touches about dat yellow one." One day the Mistress's curiosity about the father of the child got the better of her and she asked the child who her father was. Emmanuel wrote, "De child never know no better en she tell her right out exactly de one her mammy had tell her was her papa. Lord, Miss Ross, she say, 'Well, get off my step. Get off en stay off dere cause you don' noways belong to me.'"[72] James Johnson described how his mother's birth of a light skinned child caused complications for his owners: "Mrs. Matair at once began accusing Colonel Matair as being the father of the child. Naturally the colonel denied, but Mrs. Matair kept harassing him about it until he finally agreed to his wife's desire and sold the child."[73] Other owners, however, refused to sell their slave children to appease their wives wounded feelings.

White mistresses also lashed out at slave women who were the targets of their husbands' sexual desire. Solomon Northup largely praised the character of his mistress, Mrs. Epps. He noted that she was "beautiful, accomplished, and usually good-humored." Northup also wrote that Mrs. Epps was also "possessed of the devil, jealousy." She envied the attention that Edwin Epps gave to Patsey, before he became suspicious of her visits to Mr. Shaw's. Mistress Epps repeatedly ordered Northup to whip Patsey while Mr. Epps was away from the farm. Northup recalled, "I would refuse, saying that I feared my master's displeasure, and several times ventured to remonstrate with her against the treatment Patsey received." Northup tried to protect Patsey from Mistress Epps and shift her anger toward her husband. He wrote that "I endeavored to impress her with the truth that the latter was not responsible for the acts of which she complained, but that she being a slave, and subject entirely to her master's will, he alone was answerable." Northup's pleading did little to assuage Mrs. Epps's jealously. When Edwin Epps beat Patsey for her alleged affair with Mr. Shaw, Northup remembered that "Mistress Epps stood on the piazza among her children, gazing on the scene with an air of heartless satisfaction."[74]

While southern views of white women's sexuality offered them an elevated position above enslaved women, they still were women in a patriarchal society. As a result, white men created a system that compelled white women to compete with black women for men's sexual affection. This competition created divisions between white and black women, negating the possibility of a gender-based alliance against white men. As Nell Irving Painter has explained, "the notion of a traffic in women is useful both literally and metaphorically with regard to American slave societies, in which white women saw themselves in competition for the attention of husbands whose black partners were present when called for and who were conceded no will of their own."[75] As a result of their anger, white women often lashed out at their husbands' victims rather than their husbands themselves. White men's behavior had wide ranging implications. Psychologically, they damaged themselves, their families, the enslaved, and by extension, all of southern society.

Some mistresses refused to help enslaved women because they themselves were afraid of their husbands. Virginia Hays Shepherd recalled the plight of Diana, a pretty house slave. Diana's owner "made demands on Diana just the same as if she had been his wife." Her master repeatedly sent Diana to the barn to shell corn and trapped her inside. Diana fought back, ran to the house, and pled with her mistress for help. Diana's mistress "sympathized with the girl, but couldn't help her, because she was afraid of her own husband. He would beat her if she tried to meddle."[76] After one attempted rape where Diana managed to fight off her master, he grew tired of her and brought her to Norfolk for sale. Diana, however, managed to convince a neighboring owner to purchase her, so she would not be sold away from her family. Diana's plight highlights how enslaved women found few allies powerful enough to aid in their efforts to avoid sexual exploitation.

Andrew Jackson described how his owners, George Wall and his wife, fought over Wall's attraction to Hannah, the enslaved cook. The minister's wife confronted him, saying, "You have been to the kitchen, to see Hannah." The preacher denied his wife's charge and accused her of lying. The wife responded, "Well I know you have, you brute; I have a great mind to cut my own throat!" Her husband replied, "O dear, I really wish you would." The wife, however, landed a final, devastating comeback, "Yes, I presume you do, so that you could run to the kitchen, as much as you please, to see Hannah." Andrew Jackson ascribed the behavior of his master and mistress to the cruelties of slavery as an institution. He believed that "if they had treated the slaves in a friendly manner, they would not have had such bad hearts towards one another."[77]

Enslaved women expressed bitterness at the response of white women to their plight. Harriett Jacobs resented her mistress, Mrs. Flint. Jacobs wrote that "Mrs. Flint, like many southern women, was totally deficient in energy. She had not strength to superintend her household affairs; but her nerves were so strong, that she could sit in her easy chair and see a woman whipped, till the blood trickled from every stroke of the lash."[78] Jacobs claimed that Mrs. Flint knew of her husband's lust for his slaves, but did little to stop him or help the slaves avoid him. Jacobs wrote that "Mrs. Flint possessed the key to her husband's character before I was born. She might have used this knowledge to counsel and to screen the young and the innocent among her slaves; but for them she had no sympathy. They were the objects of her constant suspicion and malevolence."[79] Jacobs's feelings toward her mistress were typical of enslaved women trying to avoid sexual exploitation. Enslaved women begrudged their mistresses' inability to see the pain their husbands caused to others.[80]

While Peggy had managed to kill her master and escape of her life, the commutation of her sentence did not mean that white Virginians sympathized with her. No one suggested pardoning Peggy for murdering her father and would-be rapist. Rather the whites involved in the case, merely felt that sparing her life was appropriate. During his interrogation of the slaves, justice of the peace John W. Royster claimed that the slaves "appeared to equivocate except Peggy." Royster asked her why she had killed Francis. Peggy answered that "she did not kill him, that she beat him with a stick, and that Patrick beat him with the axe." In one of the petitions asking for Patrick's pardon, Turner H. Christian, the New Kent County jailer, stressed that Peggy, not Patrick, orchestrated Francis's murder. He wrote to the Governor and Executive Council, "Peggy appears to be a girl of unusual intelligence and . . . . I believe that she was the mover and auther of the plot and conspiracy against the said John Francis which lead to his death." Christian further felt that "Patrick was used by the said Peggy merely as an instrument in executing her wicked design against her master."[81] White sympathy for Peggy's situation did not excuse her crime.

Rather Peggy's case revealed the power of the Jezebel archetype that victimized African American women. As a result, ex-bondswomen like Harriet

Jacobs and Elizabeth Keckley had to apologize for and appeal to their readers' sympathies to justify their efforts to control their sexuality. From a young age when she had observed Dr. Flint's treatment of his slave women, Jacobs knew the fate that awaited her if she became his concubine. She described how, "I knew that as soon as a new fancy took him, his victims were sold far off to get rid of them; especially if they had children. I had seen several women sold, with his babies at the breast. He never allowed his offspring by slaves to remain long in sight of himself and his wife."[82] As Nell Irving Painter pointed out, "Jacobs' character, Linda, becomes the literal embodiment of the slave as sexual prey in the testimony of slaves."[83] Jacobs's relationship with Sands and her resulting pregnancy allowed her to shield herself from rape at the hands of her master. The pregnancy, however, meant that Jacobs's child became Flint's property. While she avoided rape at the hands of her master, Jacobs could never fully free herself from his grasp until her escape from bondage.

Jacobs's beloved grandmother condemned her relationship with Sands and the resulting pregnancy. She chided Jacobs's behavior: "'O Linda! has it come to this? I had rather see you dead than to see you as you now are. You are a disgrace to your dead mother.'" Somehow, according to her grandmother, Jacobs's actions would have been less disgraceful if she had agreed to be Flint's concubine. When no one in her life understood her, Jacobs appealed to readers of her narrative to look beyond the prevailing ideas of slave women's sexuality and find pity. She reminded her largely Northern audience that:

> You never knew what it is to be a slave; to be entirely unprotected by law or custom; to have the laws reduce you to the condition of a chattel, entirely subject to the will of another. You never exhausted your ingenuity in avoiding the snares, and eluding the power of a hated tyrant; you never shuddered at the sound of his footsteps, and trembled within hearing of his voice.[84]

While Jacobs admitted that she had acted wrongly (and acceded to the conventions of female behavior in her time), she expressed no regret for her actions. In a world where white men like Flint and John Francis preyed upon vulnerable slave women, bondswomen had to do whatever was necessary to take control of their sexuality.

Elizabeth Keckley expressed shame at her inability to ward off sexual assault. So powerful was the condemnation of black women's sexuality that the victim of rape had to beg forgiveness from her Northern audience. She recalled that "I was regarded as fair-looking for one of my race, and for four years a white man—I spare the world his name—had base designs on me. I do not care to dwell upon this subject for it is one that is fraught with pain.

Suffice it to say, that he persecuted me for four years and I—I became a mother."[85] By describing the pain of sexual exploitation, Keckley revealed the horror of the life of an enslaved woman, but also acceded to a cultural that made the most vulnerable responsible for their own exploitation.

While some bondswomen used violence to resist rape, even women who resisted could not avoid sexual exploitation permanently. Jermain W. Loguen's mother, Cherry, had entered into a relationship with her master, David Logue, but resisted the efforts of anyone else to sexually exploit her. One day while at work at Logue's distillery, she resisted the sexual advances of a local planter. The planter "rushed upon her with the fury of a madman, and she then plied a blow upon his temple, which laid him, as was supposed, dead at her feet." Despite nearly killing a white man, Cherry managed to avoid punishment. As Loguen explained, "In the meantime Cherry was shielded from harm, partly by the shame of her violator—partly by her masters' sense of justice—more because they had a beastly affection for her as a family chattel—more still because they prized her as property—but most of all because she was the admitted mistress of David Logue."[86] In order to protect herself from punishment and further sexual exploitation, Cherry had to become her master's mistress. She had yielded control over her sexuality to one white man in exchange for protection from other white men.

Slave women were more likely to succeed in their confrontations and avoid sexual exploitation when they involved a third party powerful enough to protect them. Gus Feaster described how Wash Evans, an overseer on his master's plantation, "was a wicked man. He take 'vantage of all de slaves when he git half chance." Evans proved especially dangerous to the female slaves on the plantation, "Couse he 'vantage over all de darkies and fer dat reason he could sway everything his way, most all de time." One day the plantation mistress ordered Feaster's mother and another female slave to pick blackberries. Evans attempted to convince the women to surrender to his desires. The bondswomen pretended to submit, convincing the overseer to remove his clothes. Once the overseer had stripped, the bondswomen beat him up and left him the bushes. When the mistress found Evans beaten and lying in the blueberry bushes, she fired him.[87] By humiliating the overseer in front of his employer, Feaster's mother and the other woman managed to protect themselves and the other women on the plantation from sexual exploitation.

Louisa Picquet successfully avoided rape at the hands of her master thanks to the intercession of a boarding house owner, a passerby, and the local sheriff. Mr. Cook, Picquet's master, claimed to be sick and continually demanded that Picquet "come to his room that night, and take care of him." Picquet told Mrs. Bachelor, who ran the boarding house, of Cook's request. Bachelor and her sister told Picquet not to go to his room that night and they would tend to her master. The next morning, Picquet delivered Cook his breakfast, and as "he was kind a raising up out of the bed; then I began to cry; but before I had time to shut the door, a gentleman walk out of another room close by, picking his nails, and looking in the room as he passed on."[88] Cook ordered her out of the room to fetch salt, frustrated in his efforts to sexually assault her. He began whipping her to compel her into submission, Picquet recounted that "'He was very mad, and whipped me awfully. That was the worst whippin' I ever had.'"[89] Cook remained determined to sexually exploit Picquet up to the moment he was arrested by the local sheriff for failure to pay his outstanding debts. She was then sold away to a different master. Luck, a sympathetic white woman, and a master who did not pay his debts spared Picquet from sexual exploitation.

The intercession of whites protected a slave woman who resisted the sexual advances of a slave trader. Richard Macks, an ex-slave from Maryland, remembered one a slave woman who resisted the efforts of a slave trader to rape her. He described her as "a mulatto of fine stature and good looks" and that she "was of high spirits and determined disposition." One evening a trader took her to his room "to satisfy his bestial nature." Macks described how "she could not be coerced or forced, so she was attacked by him." In response, the slave woman "grabbed a knife and with it, she sterilized him and from the result of the injury he died the next day." Macks believed that the trader attempted to rape the slave woman as "the result of being goodlooking, for which many a poor girl in Charles County paid the price."[90] A Maryland court charged the slave woman with murder. She avoided execution when Union Army soldiers arrived and took her away to freedom. Without the intervention of the soldiers, she likely would have died for her crimes.

Slave women faced impossibly long odds when they attempted to resist sexual exploitation. Generations of white Europeans and their descendants in the Americas had cast Africans as sexual and sensuous—the opposite of how whites viewed themselves. Over centuries of slavery in the United States, these views coalesced into the Jezebel stereotype. Enslaved women found themselves condemned by an ideology that they had no role in shaping. Whites stripped them naked for punishment and sale. Bondswomen's work exposed their bodies to the leering eyes of their white masters and overseers. Whites also took an intense interest in enslaved women's fertility. They made the most private aspects of their slaves' lives a matter of public record. As Deborah Gray White has written, "If, in order to ease the burdens of slavery, they made themselves available, they only fulfilled the prophecy of their lustfulness, which in turn made it more difficult for other black women to reject the overtures made by white men."[91] So when enslaved women tried to resist sexual exploitation, they had little hope of success.

NOTES

1. When describing the sexual encounters between white men and enslaved women, the nomenclature can be difficult. Martha Hodes in describing encounters between white women and black men in the antebellum South prefers the term liaison rather than relationship, which incorporates a wide range of motivations and emotions, see Hodes, *White Women, Black Men: Illicit Sex in the 19th Century South* (New Haven: Yale University Press, 1997), 14. I use both terms and try to indicate the different levels of coercion present in sexual encounters between white men and black women.

2. Deborah Gray White, *Ar'n't I a Woman?: Female Slaves in the Plantation South* (New York: W.W. Norton & Company, Revised Edition, 1999), 15. For more on the experience on enslaved women in the Antebellum South see White, *Ar'n't I a Woman*; Jacqueline Jones, *Labor of Love, Labor of Sorrow: Black Women, Work, and the Family from Slavery to the Present* (New York: Basic Books, 1985); Elizabeth Fox-Genovese, *Within the Plantation Household: Black And White Women of the Old South* (Chapel Hill: University of North Carolina Press, 1988); David Barry Gaspar and Darlene Clark Hine eds., *More than Chattel: Black Women and Slavery in the Americas* (Bloomington: University of Indiana Press, 1996); Brenda Stevenson, *Life in Black and White: Family and Community in the Slave South* (New York: Oxford University Press, 1996); Patricia Morton, *Discovering the Women in Slavery: Emancipating Perspectives on the American Past* (Athens: University of Georgia Press, 1996); Stephanie M.H. Camp, *Closer to Freedom: Enslaved Women and Everyday Resistance in the Plantation South* (Chapel Hill: University of North Carolina Press, 2004); Jennifer L. Morgan, *Laboring Women: Reproduction and Gender in New World Slavery* (Philadelphia: University of Pennsylvania Press, 2004); Thavolia Glymph, *Out of the House of Bondage: The Transformation of the Plantation Household* (Cambridge: Cambridge University Press, 2008).

3. For more on the rape of African American slave women see: Darlene Clark Hine, "Rape and Inner Lives of Black Women: Thoughts on the Culture of Dissemblance," in *Hinesight: Black Women and the Re-Construction of American History*, ed. Darlene Clark Hine (Brooklyn: Carson Publishing Company, 1994), 37–48; Nell Irving Painter, *Soul Murder and Slavery* (Waco: Baylor University Press, 1995); Edward E. Baptist, "'Cuffy,' 'Fancy Maids,' and 'One-Eyed Men': Rape, Commodification, and the Domestic Slave Trade in the United States," *American Historical Review* CVI (December 2001), 1619–1650.

4. Charles L. Perdue Jr., Thomas E. Barden, & Robert K. Phillips eds., *Weevils in the Wheat: Interviews with Virginia Slaves* (Charlottesville: University Press of Virginia, 1976), 48–49.

5. Perdue, *Weevils in the Wheat*, 202, 245.

6. Mary B. Chesnut, quoted in White, *Ar'n't I a Woman?*, 40–41.

7. A lye hopper collects lye from ash. The ash is placed in large holding box and when it rains the water washes the lye down into a bucket that collects it. Lye has numerous household uses including for soap and stripping the hair off of dead pigs.

8. *Commonwealth vs. Eliza and Ann*, John Letcher Executive Papers, 1859–1863. Accession 36787. Box 2, Folder 3, Misc. Reel 4706. State Records Collection, The

84 Chapter 3

Library of Virginia, Richmond, Virginia. Henceforth, *Commonwealth vs. Eliza and Ann*, (LVA).

9. *Commonwealth vs. Eliza and Ann*, (LVA).

10. *Commonwealth vs. Phoebe,* Wyndham Robertson Executive Papers, 1836–1837. Accession 43097. Box 1, Folder 1. State Records Collection, The Library of Virginia, Richmond, Virginia. Henceforth *Commonwealth vs. Phoebe* (LVA).

11. *Commonwealth vs. Phoebe,* (LVA).

12. *Commonwealth vs. Rose,* John Letcher Executive Papers, 1859–1863. Accession 36787. Box 19, Folder 5, Misc. Reel 4216. State Records Collection, The Library of Virginia, Richmond, Virginia. Henceforth, *Commonwealth vs. Rose,* (LVA).

13. George P. Rawick ed., *The American Slave: A Composite Autobiography, Arkansas Narratives*, Vol. 11, *Part 7* (Westport: Greenwood Publishing Company, 1972), 193. Henceforth, Rawick, ed. Arkansas Narratives, Vol. 11, Part 7, 193.

14. Rawick, ed., *Arkansas Narratives,* Vol. 8, *Part 1*, 30.

15. Fox-Genovese, *Within the Plantation Household,* 299.

16. *Commonwealth vs. Peggy, Patrick, Franky, and Caroline,* John Floyd Executive Papers, 1830–1834. Accession 42665. Box 2, Folder 7. State Records Collection, The Library of Virginia, Richmond, Virginia. Henceforth cited as *Commonwealth vs. Peggy,* (Executive Papers).

17. Solomon Northup, *Twelve Years a Slave. Narrative of Solomon Northup, a Citizen of New-York, Kidnapped in Washington City in 1841, and Rescued in 1853, from a Cotton Plantation near the Red River, in Louisiana. Ed. David Wilson* (Auburn: Derby and Miller, 1853), 52.

18. William Wells Brown, *Narrative of William W. Brown, an American Slave. Written by Himself* (London: C. Gilpin, 1849), 47.

19. Fifth Census of the United States, 1830, Virginia, New Kent County; Series: M19; Roll: 192; Page: 24. Accessed on Ancestry.com, August 25, 2014.

20. Fourth Census of the United States, 1820, Virginia, New Kent County; NARA Roll: M33_133; Page: 202. Accessed on Ancestry.com, August 25, 2014.

21. James Trussell and Richard Steckel, "The Age of Slaves at Menarche and Their First Birth," *The Journal of Interdisciplinary History* 8, No. 3 (1978): 477–505.

22. "Estimates: Broad Embarkation Regions, North America," *Voyages: The Transatlantic Slave Trade Database,* http://www.slavevoyages.org/assessment/estimates (accessed: December 13, 2018).

23. Peter Kolchin, *American Slavery 1617–1877* (New York: Hill and Wang, 2003), 23.

24. Frederick Law Olmsted, *A Journey in the Seaboard Slave States with Remarks on the Economy* (New York: Mason Brothers, 1861), 57, 55.

25. Northup, *Twelve Years a Slave,* 80.

26. Perdue, *Weevils in the Wheat,* 166, 49.

27. Perdue, *Weevils in the Wheat,* 84, 236, 277.

28. See Baptist, "'Cuffy,' 'Fancy Maids,' and 'One-Eyed Men', 1619–1650; Walter Johnson, *Soul by Soul: Life Inside the Antebellum Slave Market* (Cambridge: Harvard University Press, 2001), 113–115, 153, 154.

29. Lewis Clarke, *Narrative of the Sufferings of Lewis Clarke: During a Captivity of More Than Twenty-Five Years, Among the Algerines of Kentucky, One of the*

So Called Christian States of America. Dictated by Himself (Boston: David H. Ela, 1845), 85.

30. Northup, *Twelve Years a Slave*, 86–87.

31. George P. Rawick, *The American Slave: A Composite Autobiography Alabama Narratives*, Supplementary Series 1, Vol. 1 (Westport: Greenwood Press, 1977), 56. Henceforth cited as Rawick, *Alabama Narratives,* Sup. 1, Vol. 1, 56.

32. Rawick ed., *Georgia Narratives,* Volume 13, *Part 1*, 25.

33. Brown, *Narrative of William W. Brown*, 44–45.

34. Northup, *Twelve Years a Slave*, 78–88.

35. *Commonwealth vs. Peggy,* (Executive Papers).

36. *Commonwealth vs. Peggy,* (Executive Papers).

37. *Commonwealth vs. Peggy,* (Executive Papers).

38. Joshua D. Rothman, *Notorious in the Neighborhood: Sex and Families Across the Color Line in Virginia, 1787–1861* (Chapel Hill: University of North Carolina Press, 2003), 284, en49.

39. Jordan R., Dodd, et al., *Early American Marriages: Virginia to 1850* (Bountiful, UT, Precision Indexing Publishers). Accessed on Ancestry.com, August 25, 2014.

40. *Commonwealth vs. Peggy, Patrick, Franky, and Caroline,* Virginia Auditor of Public Accounts, Records of Condemned Blacks Executed or Transported, 1823–1832. Misc. Reel 2252. Accession APA 756, State Records Collection, The Library of Virginia, Richmond, Virginia. Henceforth cited as *Commonwealth vs. Peggy* (State Auditor's Office). See also Rothman, *Notorious in the Neighborhood*, 284, en45.

41. White, *Ar'n't I a Woman?*, 28–29.

42. Fox-Genovese, *Within the Plantation Household*, 196–197.

43. For a discussion of the Jezebel stereotype see White, *Ar'n't I a Woman?*, 27–46; Fox-Genovese, *Within the Plantation Household*, 291–292.

44. *The Voyages and Travels of Sir John Mandeville* (London: Cassell & Company, Limited, 1886), 106.

45. Winthrop Jordan, *White Over Black: American Attitudes Towards the Negro, 1550–1812* (New York: W.W. Norton & Company, 1968), 34.

46. For a discussion of the evolution of European views on slave women's sexuality see, Jordan, *White Over Black*; Morgan, *Laboring Women.*

47. Samuel Cartwright, "Natural History of the Prognathous Species of Mankind," in E.N. Elliot, *Cotton is King, and Pro-slavery Arguments: Comprising the Writings of Hammond, Harper, Christy, Stringfellow, Hodge, Bledsoe, and Cartwright* (Augusta: Pritchard, Abbott & Loomis, 1860), 714–715.

48. William Harper, *Memoir on Slavery: Read Before the Society for Advancement of Learning of South Carolina at its Annual Meeting at Columbia* (Charleston: James S. Burges, 1838), 27–28.

49. Thomas R.R. Cobb, *An Inquiry into the Law of Negro Slavery in the United States of America* (Philadelphia: T. & J.W. Johnson & Company, 1858), ccxix.

50. White, *Ar'n't I a Woman?*, 34.

51. Northup, *Twelve Years a Slave*, 258–259.

52. Harriet Jacobs, *Incidents in the Life of a Slave Girl,* eds. Nellie Y. McKay, Frances Smith Foster (New York: W.W. Norton & Company, 2001), 50.

53. *Commonwealth vs. Peggy,* (Executive Papers).

54. Melton A. McLaurin, *Celia, A Slave* (Athens: University of Georgia Press, 1991), 18.

55. *Testimony of Jefferson Jones, State vs. Celia,* Testimony available at http://law2.umkc.edu/faculty/projects/ftrials/celia/jonestranscript.html

56. See McLaurin, *Celia,* 29–31.

57. *Testimony of Jefferson Jones, State vs. Celia,* found at: http://law2.umkc.edu/faculty/projects/ftrials/celia/jonestranscript.html.

58. McLaurin, *Celia,* 69.

59. *Commonwealth vs. Peggy,* (Executive Papers).

60. McLaurin, *Celia,* 103, 106.

61. Quote in Rothman, *Notorious in the Neighborhood,* 162.

62. *Commonwealth vs. Peggy,* (State Auditor's Office).

63. Rothman, *Notorious in the Neighborhood,* 163.

64. Diane Miller Sommerville, *Rape and Race in the Nineteenth-Century South* (Chapel Hill: The University of North Carolina Press, 2004), 7. See also Ariela J. Gross, *Double Character: Slavery and Mastery in the Antebellum Southern Courtroom* (Princeton: Princeton University Press, 2000).

65. Jacobs, *Incidents in the Life of a Slave Girl,* 27.

66. Bertram Wyatt-Brown, *Southern Honor: Ethics and Behavior in the Old South* (New York: Oxford University Press, 1982), 297.

67. Henry Bibb, *Narrative of the Life and Adventures of Henry Bibb, an American Slave, Written by Himself* (New York: The Author, 1849), 189.

68. Bibb, *Narrative,* 98, 40.

69. Fox-Genovese, *Within the Plantation Household,* 235.

70. Rawick, ed., *North Carolina Narratives,* Vol. 15, *Part 2,* 132.

71. Rawick, ed., *North Carolina Narratives,* Vol. 15, *Part 2,* 97–98.

72. Rawick ed., *South Carolina Narratives,* Vol. 14, *Part 2,* 14.

73. Rawick ed., *Florida Narratives,* Vol. 17, 95.

74. Northup, *Twelve Years a Slave,* 198, 254, 256.

75. Painter, *Soul Murder and Slavery,* 18.

76. Perdue, *Weevils in the Wheat,* 257.

77. Andrew Jackson, *Narrative and Writings of Andrew Jackson, of Kentucky; Containing an Account of His Birth, and Twenty-six Years of His Life While a Slave; His Escape; Five Years of Freedom, Together with Anecdotes Relating to Slavery; Journal of One Year's Travels. Sketches, etc* (Syracuse: Daily and Weekly Star, 1847), 24.

78. Jacobs, *Incidents in the Life of a Slave Girl,* 14.

79. Jacobs, *Incidents in the Life of a Slave Girl,* 28.

80. Painter, *Soul Murder and Slavery,* 18.

81. *Commonwealth vs. Peggy* (Executive Papers).

82. Jacobs, *Incidents in the Life of a Slave Girl,* 47.

83. Painter, *Soul Murder and Slavery,* 16.

84. Jacobs, *Incidents in the Life of a Slave Girl,* 47–48.

85. Elizabeth Keckley, *Behind the Scenes, or Thirty Years a Slave and Four Years in the White House* (New York: G.W. Carleton &. Co., 1868), 38–39.

86. Rev. J. W. Loguen, *The Rev. J. W. Loguen, as a Slave and as a Freeman. A Narrative of Real Life* (Syracuse: J.G.K. Truair & Company, 1859), 21–22.

87. Rawick, ed., *South Carolina Narratives*, Vol. 2, Part 2, 65–66.

88. Louisa Picquet and Hiram Mattison, *Louisa Picquet, the Octoroon, or, Inside Views of Southern Domestic Life* (New York: The Author, 1861), 10–11. The book is less an autobiography and more a verbatim interview conducted by Reverend Hiram Mattison who transcribed Picquet's answers and added his own comments.

89. Picquet and Mattison, *Louisa Picquet,* 12, 14–15.

90. Rawick, ed., *Maryland Narratives,* Vol. 16, 53.

91. White, *Ar'n't' I a Woman?*, 38.

Chapter 4

Enslaved Women's Violence and the Household

The social order of the antebellum South, Virginian Thomas Nelson Page wrote, "made the domestic virtues as common as light and air, and filled homes with purity and peace." This purity and peace in the home, however, did not appear magically out of thin air, no matter what Page's flowery language implied. Rather someone had to create and preserve it—the mistress. Page described her as "the most important personage about the home, the presence which pervaded the mansion, the centre of all that life, the queen of that realm." Her responsibilities included those of "mistress, manager, doctor, nurse, counsellor, seamstress, teacher, housekeeper, slave, all at once." To fulfill all of these duties, mistresses needed to be of remarkable or even superhuman character. Page spared no expense when he praised the household mistress as "a surprising creature—often delicate in frame, and of a nervous organization so sensitive as perhaps to be a great sufferer; but her force and character pervaded and directed everything, as unseen yet as unmistakably as the power of gravity controls the particles that constitute the earth."[1]

Mistresses could not perform their herculean tasks alone. They needed the help of their household slaves or "servants" as Page euphemistically described them. He wrote that the affection that whites held for their slaves meant that "they were never termed slaves except in legal documents." The most important slave in the household was the Mammy.[2] She helped her mistress care for the children and run the household. As Page explained, "The Mammy was the zealous, faithful, and efficient assistant of the mistress in all that pertained to the care and training of the children." Her devotion to her owners was so absolute that she had the power to discipline the children—white and black alike. The Mammy, Page contended, with her unimpeachable character, would never correct the children out of anger, only out of love. In return, whites spanning across generations loved their mammies and showered them with affection. Mammy, Page wrote, "If she was a slave, she at least was not a servant, but was an honored member of the family, universally beloved, universally cared for."[3]

Page's rendering of life in antebellum Virginia was complete and utter nonsense. He offered a postbellum eulogy for the slave South that grafted nineteenth century views of domesticity onto the interior life of southern households. In elite and middling slaveholding households, the full-time jobs of maid, cook, nurse, and seamstress did not fall upon the mistress's delicate shoulders. Instead female slaves performed much of the actual labor within the household while white women supervised them. Harriet Jacobs described how her Aunt Nancy kept her master's household running, "Aunt Nancy was housekeeper and waiting-maid in Dr. Flint's family. Indeed, she was the *factotum* of the household. Nothing went on well without her."[4] Aunt Nancy had to sleep on floor just outside of her mistress's bedroom in case she needed anything in the night, even a drink of water. The type of labor enslaved women performed depended on the size of their owners' household. In larger households, slave women could work in specialized positions like nurses or cooks. In smaller ones, enslaved women held a variety of positions—cook, maid, nurse—simultaneously. Bondswomen performed much of the labor that kept households running, regardless of their size.

This division of responsibility between enslaved women, who did much of the work, and mistresses, who oversaw and evaluated it, often led to conflict.[5] Mistresses whipped and beat enslaved women for even the lightest infractions. As a young girl, Henrietta King, an ex-slave from Virginia, ate a piece of her mistress's candy. In response, King recalled how her mistress "lif' me up by de legs, an' she stuck my haid under de bottom of her rocker, an' she rock forward so's to hol' my haid an' whup me some mo'." As a result of having her head held under the rocking chair, King recalled that "De next day I couldn' open my mouf an' I feel it an' dey warn't no bone in de lef' side at all." Elizabeth Sparks, another ex-slave from Virginia, recalled how her mistress's mother repeatedly beat Sparks' aunt. Sparks explained that "She uster make my aunt Caroline knit all day an' when she git so tired aftah dark that she'd git sleepy, she'd make her stan' up an' knit. She work her so hard that she'd go to sleep standin' up an' every time her haid nod an' her knees sag, the lady'd come down across her haid with a switch."[6]

Even prescriptive antebellum literature about white women's roles as domestic managers recognized the prevalence of violence in southern households. In 1828, Virginia Cary, a scion of a prestigious Virginia family, wrote *Letters on Female Character*, an advice book designed *"to train women for usefulness."* *Letters on Female Character* contained a wide range of instruction regarding religion, clothing, marriage, cultivating proper friendships, and domestic management. Cary also lamented the willingness of white women to resort to violence against their slaves. She wrote that "*Scolding* effectually destroys domestic peace, and it effectually disqualifies a woman for governing her family." Cary's euphemistic word choice shielded her readers from what scolding actually entailed. Something enslaved women, like Henrietta King and Elizabeth Sparks, knew all too well. Cary further believed that "there never was, and there never will be an instance of successful management where this expedient is resorted to by female rulers." Instead, she recommended that "gentleness is perfectly compatible with firmness; and I know by experience that both these qualities are indispensable in ruling a Virginia household."[7] Few mistresses, however, seemed to heed Cary's advice.

For their part, enslaved women resented their mistresses' and their efforts to discipline them. Harriet Jacobs contrasted her mistress's apathy toward work with her eagerness for whipping her slaves. Jacobs wrote that "Mrs. Flint, like many southern women, was totally deficient in energy. She had not strength to superintend her household affairs; but her nerves were so strong, that she could sit in her easy chair and see a woman whipped, till the blood trickled from every stroke of the lash."[8] Elizabeth Keckley recalled how her master had been "burdened with a helpless wife, a girl that he had married in the humble walks of life. She was morbidly sensitive, and imagined that I regarded her with contemptuous feelings because she was of poor parentage." As a result of her mistress's feelings as well as her owner's near poverty, Keckley explained, "I did the work of three servants, and yet I was scolded and regarded with distrust."[9] As the testimonies of white and black women revealed, there was nothing harmonious about life in antebellum southern households.

Unsurprisingly, enslaved women occasionally turned the tide of violence back against their mistresses. Physical confrontations between African American and white women bore some similarities and differences to other types of altercations. Similar to male slaves, bondswomen resisted their mistresses' efforts to punish them and their family members. Enslaved women naturally sought to avenge these punishments. In doing so, they revealed the limits of their mistresses' power in the household. While white skin afforded mistresses some level of privilege and protection, they were still women in a patriarchal society. As a result, bondswomen could occasionally avoid punishment or gain more control over their working conditions. Slave women's violence also stemmed from their resentment over performing the actual work of the household—cleaning, cooking, sewing, and so on—under the constant supervision of their mistresses. Even worse, bondswomen's labor upheld their mistresses' households and claims to a privileged position within it. Ultimately when enslaved women resisted, they rejected their mistresses' authority and by extension the notion of the southern household itself.

For their part, white women did not see their bondswomen's resistance as a rejection of the household. Rather they viewed it as further proof of African American women's racial inferiority. As Thavolia Glymph has explained, "the idea that black women were vessels of disorder and filth had become central to southern pro-slavery ideology and evolving notions of domesticity, more crucial to these concerns than all the vaunted notions about Jezebels and loyal mammies that came to occupy primacy of place in caricatures of black women in later years."[10] Since whites understood enslaved women's violence as a problem of household management, they found plenty of blame to go around. They blamed enslaved women for their poor character and savagery. They also blamed other owners for indulging their slaves or for punishing them too much. All of this victim blaming led white Virginians to rationalize away enslaved women's resistance. Ultimately, bondswomen resisted because they did not want to maintain their mistresses' households. Their violence also revealed the truth that lay beneath public declarations of household harmony. By handing the power to maintain their households over to enslaved women, white Virginians had also given their bondswomen the power to destroy them.

FAILING TO UNDERSTAND ENSLAVED WOMEN'S RESISTANCE

The household served as the organizing unit for southern society. On one level, the household was a physical piece of property belonging an owner, who had exclusive rights over it. These households existed within clearly defined spaces and could include a variety of physical structures like dwellings, barns, or gardens. Since the antebellum South evolved from agrarian roots, where survival depended on extracting value from the land, household owners also had rights to the labor of those who lived within the household. Southern households, then, had a social component as well. As Stephanie McCurry has explained regarding antebellum South Carolina, "households were the constituent units of society, organizing the majority of the population—slaves of both sexes and all ages and free women and children—in relations of legal and customary dependency to the propertied male head, whether yeoman or planter." This combination of spatial and social claims over land and labor were the organizing principles of the household and southern society as a whole. A successful man was one who was independent and owned his land. Ideas of masculinity and the household became so entwined for white men that, as McCurry wrote, "the household grounded their own claims to masterhood." [11]

The ideology of the household also played an important role in shaping the lives of white women. White women were supposed to be delicate and deferential. Yet they also had the task of keeping their households running efficiently. Running the household was a never ending task, beginning before dawn and ending well after sunset. In order to keep up, mistresses relied on the work of bondswomen. White women took supervisory roles for themselves and compelled enslaved women to perform the bulk of the physical labor for maintaining their households. White women had expectations regarding how enslaved women would and should work. Bondswomen, however, had their own ideas about the labor necessary to satisfy their mistresses' demands. These diverging views naturally led to conflict. Mistresses viewed their bondswomen as lazy and disobedient, while enslaved women rejected the right of their mistresses to punish them.

On one level, enslaved women, similar to bondsmen, engaged in confrontations over punishment. In April 1833, Mary, a slave from Virginia, attacked her mistress, Elizabeth Pond, after Pond sought to correct Mary's bad behavior. Pond had spoken to Mary about "some of her misconduct." Pond's testimony does not reveal precisely what she said to Mary. Whatever Pond's words, they provoked Mary into knocking her mistress to the ground and Mary "cursed her and said she meant to kill her."[12] After savagely beating and chocking Pond, Mary dragged her mistress over to a nearby well and attempted to toss her into it. Violet, a slave living in Spartanburg County, South Carolina in 1854, had a similar confrontation with her mistress, Polly Burgess. Finding Violet hanging about the kitchen and not performing her chores, Burgess ordered Violet "to go off on her own business or she would strike her." In response, Violet attacked her mistress and knocked her to the ground with an ax handle. The bondswoman struck her mistress several times before other members of the Burgess family intervened.[13]

Like their male counterparts, enslaved women also engaged in confrontations in order to avenge punishments or violence their mistresses had inflicted upon family members. In 1859, Caroline Adams ordered a young slave girl "to do the dishes and threatened to whip her." In response, the girl's mother, Dicey, grabbed her mistress by the throat and choked her. The incident was the latest in a series of confrontations between Dicey and Adams. Previously, Adams had struck Dicey and Dicey had cut her mistress with a knife.[14] Mary Armstrong, a former slave from Texas, recalled how she took revenge against her mistress who had beaten her nine-month-old sister to death. When she grew up, Armstrong went to live with her mistress's daughter. One day her old mistress visited and Armstrong took advantage. She told a W.P.A. interviewer how she "picked up a rock 'bout as big as half your fist an' hit her right in the eye an' busted the eyeball an' told her that was for whippin' my baby sister to death."[15]

When white Virginians tried to understand the causes of household confrontations, they often framed them as the result of bondswomen's poor character. Jane, a slave in Bedford County, killed her mistress, Elizabeth Musgrove, during a dispute over punishment. Jane had complained of a toothache and refused to go out into the fields to work. When Musgrove attempted to punish Jane, the bondswoman fought back, killing her mistress. One of the witnesses at Jane's trial testified that Jane was known to be "very insolent to Mrs. Musgrove whenever her master was from home."[16] In Powhatan County, another slave woman named Jane killed her mistress, Jarriger Beasley, during a dispute over punishment. On July 7, 1852, Beasley called for Jane to bring her an iron poker and then struck the slave woman with it. Jane snatched the poker away from her mistress, struck Beasley on the neck, and then choked her to death. One witness at Jane's trial speculated that Jane had grown tired of caring for her mistress. It was well known around the neighborhood that "Jane did not attend to her business faithfully and was insolent in manner and by words."[17] Beasley was between sixty and seventy years old, suffered from rheumatism, had lost the ability to walk, and could only use her right hand. She could only move around her house with Jane's help. Despite her infirmities, Beasley seemed to have had no problem disciplining Jane.

The use of words like "insolent" by white women to describe the behavior of slave women denied the dangers that lurked just beneath the veneer of the plantation household. These words reduced slave women's resistance to a problem of behavior and management. Whites contended that enslaved women merely needed to learn (from their mistresses) how to behave. And if they failed to follow their mistresses' instructions, whippings and other punishments would bring them to heel. By learning the ways of the household, African American women would learn the importance of hard work and discipline and begin the slow climb out of barbarity. White women's choice of language is highly revealing, as Thavolia Glymph has written, because "embedded within the camouflaging language of disorder and behavior is the story of the damage unruly household slaves did to mistress's worlds and the claims of southern domesticity."[18] As a result, white mistresses saw their bondswomen's behavior through the prism of southern domesticity instead of the reality of the situation—that bondwomen's resented their mistresses' efforts to punish them.

Since whites relied on the language of disorder and resistance to the household to understand enslaved women's violence, they were at a loss to explain why previously well-behaved slave women attacked their mistresses. On the morning of June 27, 1857, Thomas Hall returned home to find that his wife, Salina, had burned to death. Catharine, one of the household slaves, claimed she had gone out to fetch firewood and had last seen her mistress ironing. When Catharine returned home, she found Salina Hall lying on the floor, badly burned and dying. Salina, with her last few breaths, told Catharine to "give her love to Mr. Hall and tell him to pray for her."[19] Catharine's heart-wrenching story, however, failed to hold up to scrutiny. Hall's head had a number of sizeable wounds, unrelated to the burns that covered the rest of her body. Two neighborhood white women, who had come to the house in the aftermath of Hall's death, discovered a shovel with bits of blood and hair on it propped up against the door of the house. The women also noticed a small pool of blood on the floor nearby.

After questioning, Catharine admitted to murdering her mistress. She told one of her white interrogators that while she "was sitting down getting a splinter out of her foot, Mrs. Hall told her to get up and go and get wood." Catharine replied that she would retrieve the firewood as soon as she removed the splinter. Mrs. Hall then grabbed a cowhide and began whipping her. In response, Catharine "struck Mrs. Hall with the shovel, that she struck her twice before she fell." In a desperate effort to cover up her crime, Catharine grabbed the hot iron and used it to set fire to Hall's body. The admission came as a surprise to her master, Thomas Hall. He testified that his wife "never lodged any complaint to me that the girl had been disobedient." Hall revealed that he "never had any occasion to correct her since I had her." Catharine was about fifteen or sixteen years old and seemed "to be a right strong girl."[20] Based on Catharine's prior good behavior, Thomas Hall was utterly unable to explain why Catharine had killed his wife.

The case of Judy, an eight-year-old girl, accused of trying to kill her mistress further highlights the inability of whites to understand enslaved women's violence outside of the language of household disorder. On April 9, 1859, Judy attacked her mistress, Margaret Terrell, who was lying in bed recuperating from an illness. That morning William Terrell, Margaret's husband, had left the house with his brother-in-law, Charles Rogers, on a trip to nearby Charlottesville. After the two men had left, Margaret, who had been taking doses of opiates to help with pain associated with her illness, passed out. Awakened by a blow, Margaret Terrell saw her young slave girl attacking her with a pair of heavy fireplace tongs. When Terrell asked Judy what she was doing, the young girl answered that "she intended to kill me."[21]

The fight then escalated into a desperate and bloody brawl as Terrell attempted to wrestle the tongs out of Judy's hands. After trying to gouge out her mistress's eyes, Judy grabbed a shovel from the fireplace and struck Terrell several times, breaking four of her mistresses fingers. As a result of trying to deflect the blows, Terrell had "15 or 16 cuts on my head." Desperate to kill her mistress, Judy loaded the shovel with coal and ash from the fireplace and threw it on Terrell. Terrell recalled that Judy "threw the ashes all over my clothes and burnt my right knee—also my left arm in 4 or 5 places. She beat me with the tongs not only my head, but all along down my left arm, side, and leg."[22] Terrell unsuccessfully called out for her slave nurse, Caroline, who was working in the garden before passing out from her wounds. Only the arrival of Terrell's doctor, A.C. Wood, interrupted the attack and prevented Judy from killing her mistress.

The white authorities investigating the case were dumbfounded by Judy's behavior. Yet there was nothing unusual about having young girls at work in the household.[23] Children frequently performed small household chores. Additionally, as Elizabeth Fox-Genovese has pointed out, "It was widely believed that the best way to develop good house servants, who were notoriously difficult to come by, was to raise them." The investigators could not comprehend how an eight-year-old girl could be capable of such violence. Meanwhile, no one considered the violence that Judy had already been exposed to as a young girl. Within the household, as Fox-Genovese stressed, "slave girls received their first introduction to the conditions of their future lives. Even the youngest could become the object of the mistress's flash of anger."[24] O.G. Mitchell, a justice of the peace, interrogated Judy "supposing that she was instigated to this act."[25] Judy's mother and grandmother both belonged to the Terrells and seemed like natural suspects. Under interrogation, Judy denied that anyone else had encouraged her to attack her mistress.

White authorities could not understand Judy's violence since nothing in the young girl's character indicated a predisposition toward violence. Judy's trial, however, revealed that her motive was the same as most other women who resisted, the threat of punishment. Margaret Terrell testified that Judy primarily performed chores around the household and was "sprightly and intelligent." Terrell also described how Judy had a mischievous spirit. As a result, Terrell kept Judy in the bedroom where she could keep an eye on her. Despite her precociousness, the young slave girl had never previously shown an inclination for violence. Three or four days before the attack, Terrell had seen Judy steal something from her bedroom and threatened to whip her if she tried it again. For her part, Judy admitted that she attacked Terrell because "she was afraid she would whip her for stealing biscuit, and she wanted to take the advantage of her whilst she was weak."[26] Judy told her jailer, Samuel Harlow, that if given the opportunity she would try to kill her mistress again. As a result of Judy's testimony, an Albemarle court of oyer and terminer convicted her of attempted murder and sentenced her to hang.

Slave women's violence was a natural byproduct of the ideology that governed southern households. Enslaved women worked in households under their mistresses' direction. When slave women failed to live up to their mistresses' demands, white women punished them. They understood these behaviors by their slave women as a sign of their inferiority. As Thavolia Glymph has written, "Resistance could thus be construed, by turn, as a management problem and as incontrovertible evidence that black women were 'by nature' savage and uncivilized."[27] This rationalization, however, failed to grasp the true reasons for enslaved women's resistance. They rejected punishments from their mistresses, avenged the punishment of family members, and pushed back against their mistresses' authority. When slave women misbehaved, they undermined their mistress' claims to domesticity—a domesticity that justified white racial supremacy and white women's superior position within the household. It especially failed to explain why seemingly well-behaved slaves, like Judy and Catharine would attack their mistresses. This language of domesticity blinded whites to the real reason for their enslaved women's violence—they were resisting slavery itself.

TENSIONS WITHIN HOUSEHOLDS

Despite the claims of pro-slavery apologists who bragged about the harmony and stability of their households, southern households rested on a tenuous foundation. Tensions between owners and their slaves were commonplace across antebellum Virginia. For as much as white slaveholders wished otherwise, enslaved women had desires of their own that often conflicted with those of their mistresses. Yet disputes between mistresses and their bondswomen did not always stay that way. If pushed too far, enslaved women took out their anger on their masters and their children. Bondswomen also recognized that southern society circumscribed their mistresses' power. In certain instances, slave women took advantage of this reality to escape punishment or win better working circumstances for themselves. These confrontations also highlighted the fragility of poor white households especially when they depended on other wealthier whites to avenge slights leveled against them by enslaved women. Ultimately, these confrontations also revealed the power that enslaved women held over their owners' households.

On the morning of July 19, 1852, Nelly Scott, a slave residing in the household of Joseph Winston, ran into the streets of Richmond, raising an alarm. Her master, mistress, and their nine-month-old infant lay in their bedroom "weltering in their blood and butchered in the most horrible manner." Jane Williams, another of the Winston's slaves, had discovered the ghastly scene and alerted the rest of the household. As the slaves ran for help, neighbors entered the house and found that "Mrs. W. and her child were in the last struggles and agonies of death, and Mr. W. was writhing with the pains of his wounds, insensible from their effects, and also supposed to be dying." Mrs. Winston and the infant child died soon after the arrival of several doctors. City coroner R.T. Wicker immediately convened an inquest to investigate the attack on the Winstons. After examining the comatose Mr. Winston, Dr. James Bolton concluded that he "seemed to have been inflicted by two persons, one standing at the side, the other at the foot of the bed, or by one person in those two different positions."[28] Based on the circumstances of the attack, the investigators placed the Winston family slaves under arrest.

On the surface, the Winstons were a young and prosperous family. The twenty-nine-year old Virginia Winston had recently given birth to a daughter. Joseph Winston, aged twenty-seven and "a very respectable and esteemed merchant of Richmond," was a partner at the grocery firm of Nace and Winston with its office on Cary Street.[29] The firm frequently advertised its latest wares, from cotton to coffee, butter to buckwheat, and liquor to limestone, in the *Richmond Whig* and other newspapers.[30] The Winston house, located at the end of 7th Street, was only blocks from the Governor's mansion, Richmond City Hall, prominent churches, and the city's commercial center. Joseph Winston had opened the firm in 1848 and called "the attention of his friends and the public generally" that he would attempt to please his customers by selling goods "on reasonable terms." He boasted of "having had an experience of seven years, of the strict application to the business, feels assured that he can do them justice in his profession."[31]

About a month before the murder of Virginia Winston and the infant child, the firm had a placed an advertisement in the *Richmond Whig* that proved ominous. The ad called for "a German or Irish Woman, of good character, who understands Cooking, can secure an excellent situation in a small family."[32] Whether this advertisement was for Nace or Winston is unclear, but in retrospect it raised serious questions about the harmony of the Winston household. Joseph Winston owned several slaves and employed one of them, Nelly Scott, as the family cook. Why would he want to bring in a white woman for the cooking—one whom he would have to pay for her labor? Why might he want to take the cooking duties away from his slaves? Prior to the attack in July, one of the Winston children had died under mysterious circumstances. Perhaps Joseph and Virginia suspected that the child had been poisoned and decided to hire a cook to guard against the possibility of further trouble. By July, however, they had not hired anyone.

The brutal attack on the Winston family garnered an immense amount of attention and concern amongst the citizens of Richmond. The *Richmond Dispatch* reported that the entire city had been "thrown into a state of the most intense excitement by the news, that an entire family had been murdered near the City Spring."[33] The attack on the Winstons stoked the deepest fears of slaveholders. As the *Dispatch* explained, "The awful revelation that there were in their midst fiends capable of intruding into the sleeping chamber, and there in silence and in cold blood, slaying a whole family while asleep in their beds, unconscious of the approach of the uplifted hand of the murderer, was a fact terrible for contemplation."[34]

As newspapers covered every detail of the case, the coroner's inquest set to work investigating the Winston family slaves. They started with Jane

Williams, the maid and nurse, who had discovered the attack. While searching Jane's room, members of the inquest discovered a "large broad edged hatchet, with a small handle and stained with marks similar blood" hidden behind a chest.[35] They also found a blood-stained frock, a bloody chemise, and a roll of fake hair, approximately fourteen inches in length, belonging to Virginia Winston (why she had fake hair is unclear). When asked about the bloody clothes and hatchet, Jane explained that she had gone to the market early the previous day to buy some sirloin for soup. After using the hatchet to butcher the meat, she tossed it aside without bothering to clean it. The blood on her clothes, Jane explained, came from moving Mr. Winston's head onto the bed after she entered the bedroom. The members of the inquest did not believe Jane's story. Her husband John could not even confirm that she had made soup the day before.[36] Nor did anyone at the market remember seeing Jane.

As the investigators continued their work, they began to suspect that John Williams may have participated in the murders as well. The more the inquest learned about Jane and John Williams, the more they became convinced of their guilt. Nelly Scott, the family cook, testified that "Jane did not appear to be much affected by the death of Mr. and Mrs. Winston." Nelly also said that "Jane has said she did not like Mr. and Mrs. W." John Williams, meanwhile, had an unsavory reputation amongst his former employers. John Wortham, an overseer who had hired Williams the previous year, stated that he had "great trouble with him; threatened to whip him; he complained of too much work." When Wortham suggested that John Williams speak to his master about his displeasure, Williams refused and instead said "that he intended to put an end to it."[37] James Green told the inquest that he had hired John Williams from Joseph Winston for a short period of time. Green found John "turbulent and refractory, and that he would have whipped him for his insolent behavior if he had not been afraid of having his house burned by him." Green "regarded him as a dangerous man."[38] All of this testimony convinced the members of the inquest that John and Jane Williams's hatred of their owners led to the slaughter at the Winston household.

After the arrest of Jane and John Williams, investigators discovered that Jane and John Williams were having problems in their marriage. John told the inquest, "Last week my wife *ceased to sleep with me*." Instead, Jane slept on a small bed with her young daughter and refused to stop, despite John's insistence. Under interrogation, Jane confirmed that her relationship with her husband had grown worse. She testified, "Sometimes I would not sleep with him for a week. He was dissatisfied once or twice about it."[39] John Yarrington, a Richmond police officer guarding John Williams before he testified at the inquest, recalled how an unknown white man approached the two men. He told Yarrington that Jane Williams "was making a full confession." John

Williams meanwhile "appeared to be very much alarmed, and altered the position he had occupied a long time, and remarked that '*she did it.*'"[40] Later John Williams tried to walk back his damaging statement. He explained, "I believe that she ought to know of it. She goes into the house early and must have known something of it, if any one on the lot committed the murder."[41]

The inquest also revealed the animosity between the Williamses and the other Winston slaves. While being questioned, John and Jane attempted to divert investigators' suspicions to Anna, another of the family slaves. Jane Williams recalled how Anna "told me one day last week, that one night when it was raining, there was a gentleman talking to her through the window. She could not come out and the gentleman was very angry, and said that if it happened so again he would knock Winston in the head some of these times."[42] John Williams believed that "Anna knows something about the matter, because I have heard her say, that if any one interfered with her she would 'fix them.'" Anna, however, was not at the Winston home on the morning of July 19. Nelly Scott explained that Anna had run away two days earlier and "seemed to be very mad because of receiving a whipping from Mr. Winston." Nelly also admitted her dislike of Anna. The slave women had grown up together but Anna "did not like me" and after Anna had met a young man, "she afterwards became so very base." Nelly, however, did not believe Anna had harmed her owners.[43]

After being arrested by Richmond city authorities, Anna did not hesitate in laying the blame for the murders squarely at John and Jane's feet. She testified "I heard Jane say that she did not like Mrs. Winston and never would. It was not long ago when she said this. John told me he did not like master Joe, and never would." Anna portrayed Jane as single minded in her pursuit of revenge; "Jane says that she never forgets or forgives anything done to her." Anna also suggested that Jane's anger toward her master stemmed from an incident when Winston "threatened to sell her without her child." Anna further claimed that Jane "always had such bitter feelings towards Mrs. W. and her child." Anna accused Jane of poisoning one of the Winston children. She suspected John Williams "because he never liked Mr. Winston."[44] Despite the continued protestations of John and Jane Williams, Anna's testimony confirmed white suspicions regarding the estranged slave couple.

John Williams continually denied that he had anything to do with the murder of the Winstons. He testified before the coroner's inquest that "I like Mr. Winston very well . . . . I never made a threat against him; had no cause." John claimed that he never threatened the lives of his former employers. He explained, "Mr. Enders [his current employer] and overseer said that I was falsely accused." John tried to alleviate any concerns about his behavior on the morning of the murders. He testified that he "was waked by hearing a noise—my wife waked me, and called me by saying, 'I believe everyone in the house is dead.'" He then went downstairs and found "Nelly Scott hollowing, and asked her to stop." Joe Scott, Nelly's husband, complained that John had told Nelly "not to make so much noise" after the discovery of the crime. John explained that he wanted her to stop since he found "the noise was so distressing."[45] John Williams, however, failed to convince the members of the inquest of his innocence.

A week after her arrest, Jane Williams confessed to murdering Virginia Winston and the infant child. After meeting with Reverend Robert Ryland, the white pastor of the African Baptist Church where Jane was a member, she admitted her guilt. Ryland implored Jane to "make her peace with God, as she would undoubtedly be hung." In her confession, Jane admitted that she had attacked her master and killed her mistress and the Winston's infant daughter, but claimed she acted alone. Jane said her husband John was asleep in his bed and knew nothing of the crime. Jane later described to her jailor, Mr. Starke, how exactly she perpetrated the murders. She attacked Joseph Winston first, knocking him unconscious. She then "stepped around the bed, and commenced cutting into the head of Mrs. Winston."[46] After attacking the Winstons in their bed, Jane killed the infant child. At the urging of Reverend Ryland, Jane Williams accepted responsibility for her actions and the consequences that would surely follow. While Jane tried to exonerate John Williams of any role in the murders, white authorities refused to believe her.

On August 9, 1852, hours before Jane Williams faced her arraignment, citizens of Richmond packed themselves tightly into the courtroom. The *Richmond Dispatch* reported that "A deep and painful excitement pervaded the entire assembly." When Jane Williams entered the court room, she "appeared greatly discomposed, and was evidently laboring under the fear—which she had previously expressed—that she would be taken from the court house before the court adjourned, and publicly executed in the square."[47] When no lynch mob appeared to drag Jane away, the Hustings Court began its proceedings. John R. Gilmer, Jane's court appointed attorney, announced that his client intended to plead guilty to murdering Virginia Winston. When asked if she had anything to add before the court announced its sentence, Jane simply replied, "Nothing, sir." The court then sentenced Jane to hang on September 10, 1852. A newspaper account described Jane as receiving the news of her execution "with the utmost composure, not a muscle of her moving." [48]

John Williams stood trial a month later on September 14, 1852. The commonwealth attorney had delayed John's trial so a recovering Joseph Winston could testify.[49] The crowd that had gathered in the court room "loudly applauded the verdict, and some, it is said, threatened to seize him and hang him on the spot."[50] The justices sentenced John Williams to hang on October 22, 1852. The case, however, had already revealed the tensions that had violently torn the Winston household apart.

Jane Williams was not the only enslaved woman who took out her anger at her master and mistress on the family children. On September 28, 1812, James Tate of Augusta Country returned home to find Mary, his daughter, missing. He undertook a search of the house and surrounding area. About twenty yards from the still house, Tate found Mary in a puddle "lying on her face with her face in the water, the other part of her mostly out." After looking at the size of the puddle, Tate concluded that Mary could not have drowned in it—either purposely or accidentally. Additionally, her clothing reeked of stagnant water, while the puddle gave off no smell at all. Margaret Tate, James' mother, searched the property for the source of the smell. Inside the still house, she found a half empty hogshead of water that had been sitting idle for months.

James Tate, meanwhile, turned his suspicions toward Amey, one of his slaves. Amey had served as Mary's nurse when she was a baby and had frequent interactions with her. Tate also suspected that Amey had been violent toward his children. He claimed that "once that Mary's check was bruised as if pinched, the child said that Amey did it." He described Amey as being "of obstinate temper and more difficult to manage than any other he ever had to manage."[51] Three of the other family slaves suspected that Amey had killed the child as well. Sam testified that "Amey came out of the house in very bad humor one day and said to him, if her mistress did not care about whipping her, she would kill her too."[52]

When Amey stood trial for Mary's murder, the tensions within the household became apparent. Amey had resented the efforts of her mistress to discipline her and took her anger over her treatment out on Mary, repeatedly pinching and hurting her. Amey's role as Mary's nurse meant they frequently spent large amounts of time together and placed Amey under the constant supervision of her mistress. This situation especially fostered tensions, as Amey likely performed much of the household labor in addition to her nursing duties. Meanwhile, mistresses, like Margaret Tate (James Tate's wife was also named Margaret), had no problem disciplining slave women who failed to live up to their expectations. The Tates likely never considered the possibility that their slave woman would take out her anger not against them, but against their daughter, who could not fight back.

On August 10, 1838, Lucinda and Andrew, two slaves belonging to George Mayse, murdered Mary and Margaret, Mayse's two daughters, as they walked home from school. Lucinda and Andrew coaxed Caroline, Lucinda's daughter, into luring the children to a nearby blackberry patch. Once Caroline brought them there, Andrew "seized Mary, and Lucinda coming up, took hold of Mary by the head, and stood behind her, whilst Andrew stood on one side and cut her throat with a new-looking shoeknife." Margaret ran off, but Andrew captured her and slit her throat as well. The three slaves then returned home, leaving the girls' bodies in the blackberry patch. Lucinda threatened Caroline that "she would be hung if she told any thing about it."[53] When the girls failed to return home, the Mayse family sought the help of their neighbors to undertake a search. While Lucinda tried to send the searchers off in the wrong direction, Caroline directed them toward the blackberry patch. George and Sarah Mayse quickly found the bodies of their eight and nine-year-old daughters nearby.

The trial of Lucinda and Andrew in a rural Bath County, Virginia court of oyer and terminer revealed the tensions that existed within the Mayse household. In 1830, George Mayse owned seven slaves and by 1840 he had increased his holding to twenty. By all accounts, he was a prosperous farmer, but had trouble controlling his slaves.[54] A few days before the girls' murders, George Mayse had attempted to whip Lucinda, but she had run away before he could punish her. Andrew also loathed his owner. Sarah Mayse testified that "Andrew had also made threats, and said he would do something to make his master sell him, for he would not live with him." In an attempt to assert his masterly authority and make his slaves more obedient, George Mayse had recently purchased a new whip. He had not yet used it, but "placed it so that they might see it, in order to alarm them and make them behave better." Sarah Mayse testified that Lucinda and Andrew "were both much incensed against their master, and both of them had made threats." Lucinda had been particularly vociferous about her hatred for her master. She had "declared that neither her master nor any other man should ever whip her—if they did, there would be murder committed for she had as soon die one death as another."[55] George Mayse's efforts at controlling his household backfired, prompting his slaves to take their anger out on his daughters.

Besides revealing the tensions between slaves and owners within households, bondswomen's violence also exposed the limits of white women's power especially in relation to their husbands. In some circumstances, husbands undercut their wives' authority over the household by refusing to punish enslaved women for their violence. After marrying, Mark Lowery's new wife came into conflict with Selina Jordan, one of the household slaves. Jordan's daughter Josie recalled that "the Mistress was trying to make mammy hurry up with the work and she hit mammy with the broom stick." Jordan fought back and Mrs. Lowery insisted that Lowery punish her. Lowery, however, refused. Dissatisfied with her husband's refusal to act, Mrs. Lowery summoned several of her male family members to whip Jordan for her. Lowery, however, refused to allow to them to discipline his slaves. He told his in-laws "[w]hip your own slaves. . . . Mine have work and if they're beat up they can't do a days work."[56] Lowery cared more about keeping his slaves working than upholding his wife's control over the household.

Other slaves avoided punishment and won better lives for themselves by resisting their mistresses. Fannie, an enslaved women, engaged in a brutal confrontation with her mistress over punishment. After Mrs. Jennings struck her, Fannie flew into a rage, attacking her mistress and tearing off all of her clothing. Jennings barely escaped with her life but was determined to see Fannie punished for her behavior. Rather than try to punish Fannie herself, Jennings sent a pair of men to do it. Fannie again refused to submit, savagely fighting off both men. After the second failed attempt at punishment, Mrs. Jennings told Fannie, "I'll have to send you away. You won't be whipped, and I'm afraid you'll get killed. They have to knock you down like a beef."[57] As a result, Mrs. Jennings agreed to allow Fannie and her husband to hire themselves out in Memphis rather than risk the continued disruption to the Jennings household.

While white women wielded considerable power within the household, the difference between their power and that of masters offered some opportunities for bondswomen to take advantage. In the antebellum era, mistresses' political authority in the South flowed from their husbands. White southern women had to navigate different and sometimes contradictory gender roles. In their relationships with their husbands and when presenting themselves to southern society, mistresses had to uphold ideas of women's domesticity and gentility. According to these societal expectations, mistresses civilized their naturally inferior slave women through caring and education. While in reality, violence ruled the day in the household. As Thavolia Glymph has explained, white women "regularly contravened notions of white female gentility that undergird ideologies of race and class and southern domesticity, slipping in and out of the costume of the soft, gentle 'southern lady.'"[58] Within this shifting between submissiveness to their husbands and dominance over the slaves, gaps in authority and power emerged. Just as slave men sought to exploit the diverging interests of owners, overseers, and hired employers, bondswomen similarly recognized that the power of their mistresses rested on uneven ground. Mark Lowery's new wife wanted to establish her authority over Selina Jordan, but her husband had no interest in upholding her claims to power. Lowery wanted his slaves working and his wife would have to find some other way to assert control over the household.

In the case of Fannie, it was clear that her mistress could not manage her, so Mrs. Jennings passed the responsibility off to someone else. Hiring the bondswoman out allowed Jennings to maintain her right to profit off Fannie's labor, but she gave up the responsibility of trying to transform her into a pliant and obedient slave. Cornelia Jennings, Fannie's daughter, remembered that in the year that her mother was away, "there was no excitement around the place."[59] While Cornelia considered her mother's actions as prompting "excitement" on the farm, Jennings understood them as undermining her household. Fannie's persistent resistance was more than just the actions of an unruly or undisciplined slave. In her unwillingness to follow orders, Fannie rejected her mistress's authority to discipline her and by extension the ideology of the household that justified her mistress's status. Mrs. Jennings attempted to punish Fannie on several occasions in order to assert control over her bondswoman and restore order to her household. When Fannie proved unwilling to submit to her rightful place, the Jennings decided to remove her from the household entirely.

Disputes between bondswomen and whites also revealed class tensions between white households. On March 15, 1857, John Davenport, an overseer for Peter Watkins, engaged in a brutal confrontation with Milly, one of the slaves under his supervision. Davenport's wife, Martha, had spotted Milly milking the Davenport's cow. When Martha confronted the enslaved woman, Milly answered that "she did not milk her cow and repeated in a short manner that she did not milk her, witness's *old cow*." Martha Davenport became upset and demanded that Milly "not dispute her word."[60] Martha then followed Milly back to her mistress and demanded that she be disciplined for her disrespect. Mrs. Watkins assured her that Milly would be punished.

John Davenport did not hear about the incident until the following morning and did not appreciate his wife being referred to as an "old cow." He tracked Milly down and tried to punish her. When Davenport grabbed her by the collar, Milly tried to bite him. The overseer then struck her with his fist, prompting Milly to lower her head and charge into his chest. As the two continued to struggle, Milly drew a knife and stabbed Davenport repeatedly, leaving behind extensive injuries that required a month's convalescence.

John Davenport's willingness to avenge his wife revealed the tenuous stature of poor white households in Virginia's slave society. By confronting Milly, Davenport had hoped that "correcting her would give him satisfaction." Davenport's use of the word satisfaction highlights how he understood Milly's rudeness toward his wife in terms of honor culture and how she had disrespected his household. Milly had insulted his wife, her status within the household, and by extension Davenport himself. As Davenport explained, "He felt it a duty he owed to his wife to correct Milly for her treatment to her." This was a role that only he could fulfill, as Martha Davenport reported that "She was not satisfied that Mrs. Watkins would have Milly corrected, as she replied in a very *short manner* 'Mrs. Davenport I will have Milly corrected.'"[61] Martha Davenport resented Mrs. Watkins' condescending tone and suspected that she had no desire to see Milly punished for her misbehavior. If white women of different classes would not support each other in maintaining their households, then it fell upon John Davenport to correct the recalcitrant slave woman and uphold the honor of his household.

The confrontation also revealed the tensions between poor whites and slaves. Slaves contrasted the class status of their owners and with the poor whites frequently employed as overseers, patrollers, and other hired hands. Slaves' animosities toward poor whites were understandable. Poor white women, like Martha Davenport, engaged in similar labors as their black counterparts. John Davenport had worked for seven years as Watkins' overseer and was responsible for much of the day-to-day operation of the farm, including dispensing discipline, making him a natural target for slave violence and animosity. Milly had no problem taking out her anger on the Davenports. She repeatedly sassed Martha Davenport and knifed her husband. After being accused of hiding a knife on her person, Milly proudly proclaimed, "'I brought it in my hand' and damn him I will show him who he fools with." William Pharis, a neighborhood resident, had intervened during Milly's confrontation with Davenport. He called her an "insignificant hussy." Milly, armed with a quick wit, replied that she "was no more of a hussy than he . . . was."[62] Pharis, with the aid of several white neighbors, subdued Milly and had her arrested, but not before she tried to bite him as well.

Antebellum southern households were rife with tensions between white owners and their slaves. White mistresses relied on enslaved women to perform the labor that allowed the household to function. Enslaved women, meanwhile, had their own desires that often diverged from those of their owners. For some slaveholders like Joseph Winston, George Mayse, and James Tate, these tensions resulted in violence that shattered their families. Enslaved women also exploited their mistresses' limited power to win better working conditions for themselves. Slaves like Fannie Jennings and Selina Jordan exploited the desires of their masters not to lose their slaves' labor. They avoided punishment or even gained some control over the nature of their labor. These altercations also revealed the tenuous nature of poor white households. John Davenport attempted to avenge Milly's insult against his wife. Instead he encountered an uncooperative mistress and required a month's recovery from his wounds. In the end, these confrontations revealed how enslaved women had the power to destroy their owners' households.

RATIONALIZING AWAY ENSLAVED WOMEN'S VIOLENCE

In antebellum Virginia, murder and conflict in the household attracted the attention of the press and ordinary white Virginians. Newspapers filled their pages with descriptions of the murders and assaults and kept the public updated on the trials of accused slaves. These descriptions also provided white Virginians insights into the circumstances and motives that led enslaved women to attack their mistresses. These speculations performed an important societal function. Instead of confronting the reality that the system of slavery itself had caused bondswomen's violence, whites rationalized away enslaved women's resistance as a failure of household management. These newspapers, trial records, ministers, and other leading figures placed the blame for enslaved women's violence on their vile or irredeemable character. Additionally, they chided masters for either being too indulgent of their slaves or for whipping too much. Newspapers reported on the executions of the enslaved to reassure their readers that the legal system would punish violent slaves and uphold white rule. Ultimately, it was much easier to blame enslaved women's violence on a few "bad" slaves than reexamine the social order that had driven them to violence in the first place.

On September 10, 1852, Jane Williams, clad entirely in white, rode in an open wagon from the Richmond jail to the place of her execution. Local newspapers estimated that approximately six thousand people gathered to witness her hanging. The crowd contained a collection of "all sexes, colors and ages." Reverend Robert Ryland, Jane's minister, offered a prayer on her behalf. He also asked her whether anyone had been aware of or participated in the murder of Virginia Winston and her infant child or the assault on Joseph Winston. Jane replied, "no one," refusing to implicate her husband John one last time. At 10:46 a.m., the executioner pulled a chair out from under Jane's feet. The *Richmond Dispatch* hoped that "her merited and summary execution will operate as a warning to the fractious portion of our negro population."[63] Jane's body was then taken from the scaffold and buried nearby. At long last, the people of Richmond could rest easy; Jane Williams, the slave murderess, had met her fate.

The brutal nature of Jane's crime and her refusal to identify John as a co-conspirator angered the white community. The *Richmond Dispatch* reflected the attitudes of Richmond's white community toward Jane and her execution. The paper lamented, "Never before in this city, perhaps, did religious ceremonies of so serious and impressive a character, fall upon more unwilling ears. The thick-crowding thoughts of the diabolical murder of two innocent, guileless beings, committed by Jane with the coolness and deliberation of a fiend, rendered unimpressive, cold and tedious, those ceremonies."[64] Newspapers also made sure to highlight Jane's evil character. Before her execution, one newspaper had described her as a "yellow woman, about medium height, with one eye and a most diabolical visage." The paper claimed that she "met her fate with the same stolid, besotted indifference which she manifested in taking the lives of others."[65] Another described her "one of the most vile wretches that ever disgraced humanity."[66]

Even in death however, Jane Williams continued to plague Richmond's white community. Reverend Ryland revealed that Jane had also confessed to poisoning one of the Winston children weeks before the attack on the rest of the family. Jane had asked that Ryland keep the confession a secret because she feared "that a mob would seize and destroy her."[67]

A little more than a month later, on the morning of October 22, 1852, Reverend Jeremiah Jeter, a local Baptist minister and missionary, travelled with John Williams on the way to his execution. A small crowd consisting mostly of African Americans, much smaller than had occasioned the death of Jane Williams, had gathered at the gallows. As Williams ascended the steps, the *Richmond Dispatch* expressed shock at Williams's appearance, "When first committed, his complexion was of a dark dingy brown; when placed in the hangman's cart . . . his face was nearly of the light color of a mulatto or quadroon." The paper attributed the change to fear, noting that Williams "exhibited marked trepidation, and trembled at times, violently."[68]

Williams briefly addressed the crowd. He informed the gathered citizenry, "Gentlemen—I desire to inform you that the charge alleged against me I am innocent of. I feel myself innocent of the crime." Williams hoped to speak to the crowd for longer, but the City Sergeant interrupted him. The *Dispatch* declared that "there would have been a manifest impropriety in allowing him to address the crowd of negroes around him, to the perversion of their minds under the circumstances." At about 10:30 a.m. the executioner pulled a black cap down over Williams's face. He stepped onto a chair situated atop a wagon. Once the executioner fixed the rope around Williams' neck, "the wagon drove off, and Williams was launched into eternity."[69]

From the beginning of the investigation and until after John and Jane Williams had been executed, white Virginians sought to uncover the slaves' motive. They concluded that the married couple were a pair of vengeful and ungrateful slaves. According to the *Richmond Dispatch*, Jane said "she had been ill-treated by Mr. and Mrs. Winston and had been brooding over her bloody revenge for some time. The devil, she stated, had such possession of her that morning, that she believed she could have went further than she did, if necessary."[70] John Williams confessed that Jane "had threatened to murder them because they intended to send her to the country, and that he remonstrated with her."[71] The *Richmond Enquirer* offered a different interpretation. The paper claimed that John and Jane "desired to be sold, but Mr. W. . . . refused to sell them—hence their dissatisfaction, and hence, it is thought, their too fatal revenge."[72] Whether their specific motive, the Williamses, the Richmond papers suggested, hated the Winstons and wanted them dead.

The newspaper coverage of the case also placed some of the blame for the slaves' violence on their master, Joseph Winston. Winston had purchased John Williams in South Carolina and brought him back to Richmond to be with Jane. The *Richmond Enquirer* viewed Winston's purchase of John as a sign of his generosity and good character. The paper made a clear juxtaposition between Winston's kindness and John and Jane's ingratitude. The paper wrote that "Mr. Winston purchased Jane's husband at Charleston, where he had been sold and had him brought back to this city, to please her."[73] What some saw as betrayal by the Williamses of their kind master, others saw proof of Winston's poor mastery. A pamphlet produced in aftermath of the case by John D. Hammersley, which sought to take advantage of the publicity that the case had garnered, blamed Joseph Winston for the deaths of his wife and daughter.[74] The pamphlet claimed that "it is notorious with all who were acquainted with Mr. Winston and his wife, that John and Jane Williams, and all the negroes of the family of Mr. W., were the most indulged in the city of Richmond."[75] If only Winston had not spoiled his slaves so much, Hammersley argued, then Jane and John Williams would not have murdered his wife and daughter.

Leaders of Richmond's religious community, meanwhile, sought to remind whites of their masterly duties and remind enslaved African Americans of their subordinate place in Virginia's households. In a eulogy for Virginia Winston delivered by Reverend T.V. Moore of the First Presbyterian Church on July 25, 1852, Moore placed the blame for the crime on the failure of whites to civilize their slaves. The minister believed that the cause of the rising crime rate amongst the slaves could be "found in the want of adequate moral instruction, the abandonment of them during part of their time to causes of corruption that are at work, and the growing relaxation of that system of firm restraint that such a state of facts imperatively demands." On July 25, 1852, Reverend Robert Ryland, Jane's minister and the minister of the African Baptist Church, reminded his parishioners of their place in Virginia's slave society. He told them, "God has given this country to the white people. They are the law-makers—the masters—the superiors. The people of color are the subjects—the servants—and even when not in bondage, the inferiors." He warned that crimes like the attack on the Winston family "will increase the strictness of discipline to which you are subject in the family, in the factory, on the farm."[76]

The sensational level of violence, the crime's location within the capital of Virginia, and the circumstances of the murders all helped popularize Jane Williams's case. Whatever Jane's specific motive, the tensions between Jane, John, and the Winstons led to the violence that tore the household apart. In July 1852, Jane had reached her breaking point and, possibly with the aid of her husband, killed three members of the Winston family and eventually killed the fourth. Joseph Winston died in 1880 of an epileptic fit, brought on by the wounds he sustained in the assault.[77] The case reminded the citizens of Richmond of the potential danger that lurked in their homes. Their seemingly happy slaves, who served their food, carved their meat, and tended to their houses, could turn on them at any moment. Instead of confronting this threat white Virginians rationalized it away, insisting that it was Jane's sinister character that prompted her violence or the laxness of Joseph Winston's discipline or some other reason—not that she was resisting her enslavement.

In other confrontations, Virginia newspapers similarly blamed masters for failing to properly manage their households. Following the death of Mary and Margaret Mayse, the Stanton, Virginia *Spectator* blamed the bad character of the slaves on George Mayse's failure to run a strict household. The paper claimed that "the ill temper of the woman had been greatly excited by something which had occurred in the family, and thus cruelly and savagely, it would seem, has she wreaked her vengeance."[78] The *Richmond Enquirer* reported that the lax discipline of George Mayse, likely caused his slaves' violence. The paper claimed that "the family had been very indulgent towards the slaves." The lack of masterly authority, "operated upon such too malignant and reckless spirits, so as to produce the perpetration of two of the most cold blooded and atrocious murders which the present day has produced. It thrills the blood of every humane person, to see two such tender and helpless innocents fall victims to the demon-like passions of two such fiends."[79] In making these claims, the paper placed the responsibility for the death of Margaret and Mary Mayse squarely on their father.

Similar failures of mastery plagued the household of Basil Hall. In December 1857, Jenny, one of the family slaves, murdered her mistress, Elizabeth Hall, by repeatedly tossing her into a fireplace. Hall died of her wounds later that night, but not before giving a deposition that helped ensure Jenny's execution. Earlier that day, before settling down for a nap, Hall had ordered Jenny to fetch water from the spring and Selina, another household slave, to begin making dinner. When she awoke, Hall asked why Selina was not cooking dinner, and Jenny answered that "she had sent her to the spring, I asked her why she had done that contrary to my orders." Hall wrote in her deposition that Jenny responded with "some of her insolence and I slapped her in the mouth."[80] Jenny, meanwhile, began adding wood to the fireplace against her mistress's orders. After Hall tried to pull the wood out of the fireplace, the two women came to blows. Jenny grabbed hold of her mistress, put Hall's head between her knees, and pushed her into the fire. As Hall smoldered in the fireplace, Jenny blocked the door to prevent her from escaping.

Hall pulled herself out of the fireplace and tore off her flaming clothes. Jenny then grabbed ahold of her and threw her into the fireplace a second time. Hall managed to pull herself from the flames again. As Jenny approached her mistress, Hall promised the bondswoman that she would never whip her again and offered her money and her freedom if she would cease her attack. Undeterred, Jenny threw her half-dead mistress into the fireplace for a third time. Jenny then grabbed a pile of nearby clothes and threw them into the fire on top of Hall's head. Amazingly, Hall dragged herself out of the fireplace once again. She doused herself with a bucket of water and climbed out of a nearby window. Jenny desperately grabbed at her mistress's legs and tried to drag her back inside the house. Hall somehow managed to free herself and called out for help. William, one of Hall's slaves, heard his mistress's screams and came over to help. Jenny yelled to him to go and fetch his master, Basil Hall, because "Mistress was almost burned to death." Elizabeth Hall begged William to stay because she was "afraid if he left me she would murder me."[81]

Jenny's initial seeming submission to her master and mistress pointed to another problem that plagued antebellum Virginian households. Some bondswomen undermined their mistresses by deliberately disobeying or reinterpreting their orders. Jenny had followed her mistress's orders, but not to Hall's satisfaction, leading to the escalation of the situation. As Elizabeth Fox-Genovese has written, "When servants compounded sauciness and subtle disrespect with a studied cheerful resistance to accomplishing the task at hand, the mistress could rapidly find herself losing control—of herself as well as her servant."[82] Mistresses could easily lose control over the work rhythms of their households, prompting them to take whatever means necessary to reassert their will. Bondswomen were notorious amongst their mistresses for their laziness, inefficiency, and inability to properly manage the household. When confronted with this reality, mistresses turned to violence as way to retake command. Only in Elizabeth Hall's case, it led to her death.

Jenny's anger, which had been building throughout the day, led her to brutally kill her mistress. But violence was nothing new in the Hall household. They had a reputation in the community for being strict owners. As the *Washington Star* reported, Hall and his family "were considered by respectable persons in the neighborhood, as being hard on servants." Shortly before Elizabeth Hall's death, her husband "had a portion of his farm building burned by some of his own servants."[83] The newspaper report suggested that, unlike George Mayse or Joseph Winston who had been too lax with their slaves, Basil Hall had been too strict. The prior actions of his slaves meant that Hall should have eased off on the lash rather than risk his slaves burning something more than the farm building.

The case of Judy, the Albemarle slave girl, sentenced to hang for attacking her mistress similarly plagued white Virginians. They could not understand Judy's motives or easily rationalize them away. Nor could they ignore the crime she had committed. Throughout Judy's trial, no one questioned the propriety of charging the eight-year-old slave girl with a capital crime. Yet no one could fully believe that she was capable of such a crime either. Despite this confusion, an Albemarle court of oyer and terminer convicted Judy of assault and sentenced her to hang. After passing the death sentence, at least one member of the court began to have doubts about the appropriateness of executing the young girl. As Egbert Watson, Judy's attorney, wrote to Virginia Governor Henry Wise, "One of the justices comprising the court was opposed to the sentence and it was so announced from the bench, but he finally acquiesced, upon the express condition that there should be a recommendation for mercy."[84] Yet without interference from the governor, Judy was set to hang on November 4, 1859.

Eventually, local and international pressure prompted Governor Wise to spare Judy's life. As Judy's attorney, Watson attempted to persuade Wise to commute her sentence to transportation. He cited Judy's age as the primary reason for the granting of mercy. Watson wrote, "I sent the application solely upon the ground that the prisoner is too young and too ignorant to have been conscious of the crime she was committing." He acknowledged that the law granted the state the power to execute an eight-year-old but could not find evidence of such an execution dating back three hundred years in English legal history. In the United States, Watson argued, "it is believed *no one under twelve years of age has ever been executed*. It would be a *blot* upon our state and wholly at war with the present state of civilization (to say nothing of religion) to execute a child *nine* years of age."[85] Watson attached a petition from white residents of Albemarle citing Judy's age as a justification for asking for a reprieve of the sentence to transportation. John Moffat, a Presbyterian minister in Montreal, sent a letter pleading with Wise to spare the young girl's life. The prospect of execution, he wrote, "outrages every principle of humanity and justice and is nothing less than a legal murder."[86]

Without the language of the household to understand Judy's violence, whites defaulted to the tenets of slave law, leaving behind a confusing case history. After reviewing Judy's case, Governor Wise commuted her sentence citing "her *infancy*, being less than 9 years of age when the offence was committed."[87] Instead, Wise sentenced Judy to spend her life laboring on the public works. Despite her age, neither Watson nor the petitioners from Albemarle county sought to grant the eight-year-old a pardon for her crime. Even though Watson acknowledged that Judy lacked the mental maturity to understand the implications of her actions. Instead he merely argued that executing an eight-year-old would set a dangerous legal precedent. Watson acknowledged that the petitioners from Albemarle preferred that the governor spare the girl's life but were not entirely opposed to her execution. Throughout the entire case, no one involved, from the Terells to the justices of the peace to Egbert Watson, Judy's attorney, to Governor Wise, objected to putting her on trial in the first place. Only when it seemed like she would hang did anyone bother to question the propriety of their actions. Even the Governor's commutation of the sentence was hardly merciful. Judy's life would be spent working as a slave of the state rather than being executed.

From the perspective of enslaved women, their violence represented an opportunity to strike back against their owners and the ideology of the household. When whites sought to understand their bondswomen's actions, they viewed them as a failure of household management. Enslaved women who attacked or killed their mistresses were evil or lacked character. Clearly their masters and mistresses had failed to discipline them properly. These rationalizations also placed the responsibility for that violence on the individuals involved. Whites could then avoid questioning the broader causes of enslaved women's violence and the slave society that had placed enslaved women in these situations in the first place. It was easier for white Virginians to write off these cases of enslaved women's violence as aberrational rather than question Virginia's social, political, and racial order. Which was easier to believe? That Joseph Winston was a lenient master and Jane Williams a wicked slave or that antebellum Virginians lived in an inherently violent society where enslaved African American women resented having to perform the labor that upheld their owners' households?

The household served as the basis for the southern social order. In the patriarchal antebellum South, men were the heads of the household, but women had the responsibility to keep them running. Among whites who owned slaves, however, bondswomen generally performed the labor that kept their mistresses' households functioning. Nineteenth-century ideas of domesticity placed tremendous burdens onto white women. They had to remain submissive to their husbands, be gentle and kindly, keep the house clean and everyone clothed and fed. African American women had their own ideas about how they should be spending their time and it rarely included sweeping floors, cooking meals, and tending to someone else's children. Southern domesticity encouraged enslaved women to see their mistresses' desires as their own. When bondswomen failed to place their mistresses' needs above their own, they undercut their mistresses' claims to domesticity.[88] As a result, white women understood their enslaved women's resistance to laboring in the household through the lens of domesticity. This reality also placed white and African American women into conflict.

Since southern households stood for order and civilization, whites viewed enslaved women's resistance as signs of their inferiority and depravity. While prescriptive literature like Virginia Cary's *Letters on Female Character* suggested that mistresses had the responsibility to gently instruct their slave women on how to work, mistresses used violence to keep their enslaved women in line. Bondswomen's refusal to work according to their owners' demands justified their mistresses' violence. Enslaved women, on the other hand, wanted to avoid being whipped, protect their family members from punishment, or to express their displeasure with their enslavement. They resented the efforts of their mistresses to punish or "civilize" them. They resented having the responsibility of maintaining their mistresses' households.

By placing the burden of upholding the household onto slave women, white women lifted the burdens of domestic labor off themselves. For enslaved women, however, the responsibility to uphold the household provided the opportunity to destroy it. Whites governed through physical, emotional, and psychological violence. Occasionally enslaved women fought back. Whites, however, often rationalized away their resistance to the household (and enslavement) as a management problem. These rationalizations bolstered white views of enslaved women as lazy, undisciplined, and naturally inferior. They also missed what lay at the heart of enslaved women's resistance. A rejection of their enslavement and the ideology of the household that dictated their day-to-day lives. White Virginians went to great lengths to dismiss the real causes of enslaved women's violence. They criticized the inadequacies of masters who failed to keep their slaves in line or contended that some slave women were too savage to be civilized. Ultimately, however, enslaved women's violence revealed that southern households, by relying on the labor of enslaved women, rested on a shaky foundation.

NOTES

1. Thomas Nelson Page, *Social Life in Old Virginia Before the War* (New York: Charles Scribner's Sons, 1897), 109, 34, 37–38, 35–36, 7.

2. For the cultural evolution of the Mammy ideal see Micki McElya, *Clinging to Mammy: The Faithful Slave in Twentieth Century America* (Cambridge: Harvard University Press, 2007).

3. Page, *Social Life in Old Virginia*, 109, 59.

4. Harriet Jacobs, *Incidents in the Life of a Slave Girl*, eds. Nellie Y. McKay and Frances Smith Foster (1861: repr. New York: W.W. Norton & Company, 2001), 113. A factotum is someone responsible for performing labor.

5. For claims of alliances between slave women and their mistresses see Ann Firor Scott, *The Southern Lady: From Pedestal to Politics, 1830–1930 25th Anniversary Edition* (Charlottesville: University of Virginia Press, 1995); Catherine Clinton, *The Plantation Mistress: Woman's World in the Old South* (New York: Pantheon Books, 1982); Leslie A. Schwalm, *A Hard Fight for We: Women's Transition from Slavery to Freedom in South Carolina* (Urbana: University of Illinois Press, 1997); Brenda Stevenson, *Life in Black and White: Family and Community in the Slave South* (New York: Oxford University Press, 1996). For more on the relationship between white and black women in the Antebellum South see Mary Ellison, "Resistance to Oppression: Black Women's Response to Slavery in the United States." *Slavery and Abolition* 4 (May 1983): 56–63; Carol K. Bleser, "Southern Planter Wives and Slavery" in *The Meaning of South Carolina History: Essays in Honor of George C. Rodgers Jr.*,

ed. David R. Chestnut and Clyde N. Wilson (Columbia: University of South Carolina Press, 1991), 104–120; Virginia Bernhard, Betty Brandon, Elizabeth Fox-Genovese, and Theda Purdue eds., *Southern Women: Histories and Identities* (Columbia: University of Missouri Press, 1992); Patricia Morton ed., *Discovering Women in Slavery: Emancipating Perspectives on the American Past* (Athens: University of Georgia Press, 1996); Marli F. Weiner, *Mistresses and Slaves: Plantation Women in South Carolina, 1830–1880* (Urbana: University of Illinois Press, 1998); Kirsten E. Wood, *Masterful Women: Slaveholding Widows from the American Revolution through the Civil War* (Chapel Hill: University of North Carolina Press, 2004).

6. Charles L. Perdue Jr., Thomas E. Barden, & Robert K. Phillips eds., *Weevils in the Wheat: Interviews with Virginia Slaves* (Charlottesville: University Press of Virginia, 1976), 191, 275.

7. Virginia Cary, *Letters on Female Character: Addressed to a Young Lady on the Death of Her Mother* (Richmond: A. Works, 1828), vii, 216. Italics in original.

8. Jacobs, *Incidents in the Life of a Slave Girl*, 14.

9. Elizabeth Keckley, *Behind the Scenes Or Thirty Years a Slave, and Four Years in the White House* (1868: repr. New York: Oxford University Press, 1988), 31, 32.

10. Thavolia Glymph, *Out of the House of Bondage: The Transformation of the Plantation Household* (Cambridge: Cambridge University Press, 2008), 65.

11. Stephanie McCurry, *Masters of Small Worlds: Yeoman Households, Gender Relations, & the Political Culture of the Antebellum South Carolina Low Country* (New York: Oxford University Press, 1995), 6, 7. See also Elizabeth Fox-Genovese, *Within the Plantation Household: Black and White Women of the Old South* (Chapel Hill: University of North Carolina Press, 1988); Peter. W. Bardaglio, *Reconstructing the Household: Families, Sex, and the Law in the Nineteenth-Century South* (Chapel Hill: University of North Carolina Press, 1998); Cynthia A. Kierner, *Beyond the Household: Women's Place in the Early South, 1700–1835* (Ithaca: Cornell University Press, 1998); Elizabeth R. Varon, *We Mean to Be Counted: White Women and Politics in Antebellum Virginia* (Chapel Hill: University of North Carolina Press, 1998); Glymph, *Out of the House of Bondage.*

12. *Commonwealth vs. Mary,* John Floyd Executive Papers, 1830–1834. Accession 42665. Box 9, Folder 11. State Records Collection, The Library of Virginia, Richmond, Virginia.

13. *State vs. Violet,* Spartanburg District, Court of Magistrates and Freeholders, Case #160. South Carolina Department of Archives and History. Columbia, South Carolina.

14. *State vs. Dicey*, Laurens District Court of Magistrates and Freeholders, Case #39. South Carolina Department of Archives and History, Columbia, South Carolina.

15. George P. Rawick, ed., *The American Slave: A Composite Autobiography Texas Narratives* Supplement Series 2, Vol. 2, *Part. 1* (Westport: Greenwood Publishing Company, 1979), 67. Henceforth Rawick, ed., *Texas Narratives,* Sup. 2, Vol. 2, *Part 1*, 67.

16. *Commonwealth vs. Jane,* Henry A. Wise Executive Papers, 1856–1859. Accession 36710. Box 14, Folder 3. Misc. Reel 4209. State Records Collection, The Library of Virginia, Richmond, Virginia.

17. *Commonwealth vs. Jane,* Joseph Johnson Executive Papers, 1852–1855. Accession 44076. Box 2, Folder 6. State Records Collection, The Library of Virginia, Richmond, Virginia.

18. Glymph, *Out of the House of Bondage,* 67.

19. *Commonwealth vs. Catharine,* Henry A. Wise Executive Papers, 1856–1859. Accession 36710. Box 8, Folder 7. Misc. Reel 4203. State Records Collection, The Library of Virginia, Richmond, Virginia. Henceforth, *Commonwealth vs. Catharine* (LVA).

20. *Commonwealth vs. Catharine* (LVA).

21. *Commonwealth vs. Judy,* Henry A. Wise Executive Papers, 1856–1859. Accession 36710. Box 20, Folder 3. Misc. Reel 4216. State Records Collection, The Library of Virginia, Richmond, Virginia. Henceforth *Commonwealth vs. Judy* (LVA).

22. *Commonwealth vs. Judy* (LVA).

23. For an examination of the lifecycle of female slaves see Deborah Gray White, *Ar'n't I a Woman?: Female Slaves in the Plantation South* Revised Edition (1985; New York: W.W. Norton & Company, 1999), 91–118. For slaves at different ages see Marie J. Schwartz, *Born in Bondage: Growing Up Enslaved in the Antebellum South* (Cambridge: Harvard University Press, 2000); Wilma King, *Stolen Childhood: Slave Youth in the Nineteenth Century* (Bloomington: Indiana University Press, 1995); Stacey K. Close, *Elderly Slaves of the Plantation South* (New York: Garland Publishing, 1997).

24. Fox-Genovese, *Within the Plantation Household,* 153.

25. *Commonwealth vs. Judy* (LVA).

26. *Commonwealth vs. Judy* (LVA).

27. Glymph, *Out of the House of Bondage,* 91.

28. *Particulars of the Dreadful Tragedy in Richmond on the Morning of the 19th July 1852: Being a Full Account of the Awful Murder of the Winston Family: Embracing All the Particulars of the Discovery of the Bloody Victims, the Testimony Before the Coroner's Jury, and the Evidence of the Final Trials of the Murderess and Murderer, Jane and John Williams: Their Sentence, Confessions, and Execution Upon the Gallows: Together with the Funeral Sermon of the Rev. Mr. Moore on the death of Mrs. Winston and Daughter, And The Sermon of the Rev. Robert Ryland on the subject of the Murders* (Richmond: John D. Hammersley, Publisher, 1852), 5. Henceforth, *Dreadful Tragedy in Richmond,* 5, 6.

29. *Dreadful Tragedy in Richmond,* 5.

30. For an example of a typical ad see *Richmond Whig* (Richmond, VA), November 19, 1850.

31. *Richmond Whig* (Richmond, VA), January 14, 1848.

32. *Richmond Whig* (Richmond, VA), June 22, 1852.

33. *Richmond Dispatch* (Richmond, VA), July 20, 1852.

34. *Dreadful Tragedy in Richmond,* 4.

35. *Richmond Dispatch* (Richmond, VA), July 20, 1852.

36. For Jane's and John's testimony to the Coroner's Inquest see *Dreadful Tragedy in Richmond,* 7–9, 11–12, 14, 17–18.

37. *Richmond Dispatch* (Richmond, VA), July 20, 1852.

38. *Richmond Dispatch* (Richmond, VA), July 21, 1852.
39. *Richmond Dispatch* (Richmond, VA), July 22, 1852.
40. *Richmond Dispatch* (Richmond, VA), July 21, 1852. Emphasis in original.
41. *Richmond Dispatch* (Richmond, VA), July 22, 1852.
42. *Richmond Dispatch* (Richmond, VA), July 22, 1852.
43. *Richmond Dispatch* (Richmond, VA), July 20, 1852.
44. *Richmond Dispatch* (Richmond, VA), July 22, 1852.
45. *Richmond Dispatch* (Richmond, VA), July 20, 1852.
46. *Dreadful Tragedy in Richmond*, 19.
47. *Richmond Dispatch* (Richmond, VA), August 10, 1852.
48. *The Daily Picayune* (New Orleans, LA), August 17, 1852.
49. *Commonwealth vs. John Williams,* Joseph Johnson Executive Papers, 1852–1855. Accession 44076. Box 3, Folder 1. State Records Collection, The Library of Virginia, Richmond, Virginia.
50. *The Sun* (Baltimore, MD), September 16, 1852.
51. *Commonwealth vs. Amey,* James Barbour Executive Papers, 1812–1814. Accession 41557. Box 4, Folder 11. State Records Collection, The Library of Virginia, Richmond, Virginia. Henceforth *Commonwealth vs. Amey* (LVA).
52. *Commonwealth vs. Amey* (LVA).
53. *Richmond Enquirer* (Richmond, VA), September 7, 1838.
54. George Mayse, *1830 United States Federal Census*, Bath, Virginia; Series: M19; Roll: 189; Page: 195; Family History Library Film: 0029668. Accessed on Ancestry.com June 26, 2015; George Mayse, *1840 United States Federal Census*: Bath, Virginia; Roll: 551; Page: 122; Image: 252; Family History Library Film: 0029684. Accessed on Ancestry.com June 26, 2015.
55. *Richmond Enquirer* (Richmond, VA), September 7, 1838.
56. George P. Rawick, ed., *The American Slave: A Composite Autobiography Oklahoma Narratives,* Vol. 7 (Westport: Greenwood Press, 1972), 161–162. Henceforth, Rawick ed., *Oklahoma Narratives,* Vol. 7, 161–162.
57. Rawick, ed., *Unwritten History of Slavery, Fisk University,* Vol. 18, 287.
58. Glymph, *Out of the House of Bondage,* 46.
59. Rawick, ed., *Unwritten History of Slavery, Fisk University,* Vol. 18, 288.
60. *Commonwealth vs. Milly,* Henry County Court Records. Henry County (Va.) Commonwealth Causes, 1856–1859. Local Records Collection, The Library of Virginia, Richmond, Virginia. Henceforth *Commonwealth vs. Milly* (LVA).
61. *Commonwealth vs. Milly* (LVA).
62. *Commonwealth vs. Milly* (LVA).
63. *Richmond Dispatch* (Richmond, VA) in *Richmond Enquirer* (Richmond, VA), September 14, 1852.
64. *Richmond Dispatch* (Richmond, VA) in *Richmond Enquirer* (Richmond, VA), September 14, 1852.
65. *The Sun* (Baltimore, MD), September 13, 1852.
66. *Dreadful Tragedy in Richmond*, 23–24.
67. *The Daily Picayune* (New Orleans, LA), September 24, 1852.
68. *Richmond Dispatch* (Richmond, VA), October 23, 1852.

69. *Richmond Dispatch* (Richmond, VA), October 23, 1852.
70. *Dreadful Tragedy in Richmond,* 19.
71. *The Daily Picayune* (New Orleans, LA), July 31, 1852
72. *Richmond Enquirer* (Richmond, VA), July 23, 1852.
73. *Richmond Enquirer* (Richmond, VA), July 23, 1852.
74. *Richmond Dispatch* (Richmond, VA), October 25, 1852.
75. *Dreadful Tragedy in Richmond,* 19.
76. *Dreadful Tragedy in Richmond,* 32, 36.
77. *Richmond Dispatch* (Richmond, VA), July 5, 1880.
78. *Spectator* (Stanton, VA), reprinted in *Hampshire Gazette* (Northampton, MA) August 29, 1838.
79. *Richmond Enquirer* (Richmond, VA), September 7, 1838.
80. *Commonwealth vs. Jenny,* Henry A. Wise Executive Papers, 1856–1859. Accession 36710. Box 11, Folder 3. Misc. Reel 4206. State Records Collection, The Library of Virginia, Richmond, Virginia. Henceforth, *Commonwealth vs. Jenny* (LVA).
81. *Commonwealth vs. Jenny* (LVA).
82. Fox-Genovese, *Within the Plantation Household,* 308.
83. *Washington Star* reprinted in *The Liberator* (Boston, MA), January 29, 1858.
84. *Commonwealth vs. Judy* (LVA).
85. *Commonwealth vs. Judy* (LVA).
86. *Letter from John Moffat to the Honorable Governor Wise,* Henry A. Wise Executive Papers, 1856–1859. Accession 36710. Box 19, Folder 6. Misc. Reel 4216. State Records Collection, The Library of Virginia, Richmond, Virginia.
87. *Commonwealth vs. Judy* (LVA).
88. Glymph, *Out of the House of Bondage,* 6.

Chapter 5

Protecting White Supremacy

The last chapter demonstrated the ability of slave violence to destroy southern households. Enslaved women resisted their bondage by striking back against the institution of the household that demanded their obedience and submission. This chapter will look at the broader impact of physical confrontations. It will use three examples from Virginia's history to demonstrate how, under the right conditions, slave violence could reveal anxieties in the white community over protecting the institution of slavery. While these three cases occurred in three different decades and in three different counties, they share key features that justify examining them together. They all involve slave men accused of murder and sentenced to hang by local oyer and terminer courts. They all triggered petition campaigns from opposing factions within each county. When the governor commuted the sentences to transportation, white elites engaged in some form of extralegal action to ensure that the enslaved men kept their date with the hangman's noose.

This extralegal action was rare. In the vast majority of cases, white Virginians abided by the rulings of local oyer and terminer courts. They followed the laws of procedure governing the administration of slave trials. Accused slaves had attorneys who crossed-examined witnesses and organized appeals for pardons. After all, white Virginians followed the slave codes since they were written to protect slaveholders' property rights. As Philip Schwarz has written, "It was the legal status of slaves as property that influenced many judges to strive to identify accurately those responsible for actions defined as crimes. Indeed, this attempt helped to ensure, though it certainly did not guarantee, that slave courts would not necessarily be kangaroo courts."[1] Slave trials certainly were not fair by modern standards. But they did not exist merely to rubber stamp the convictions of slaves.

For their part, white legal scholars boasted of the fairness of slave trials. Thomas R.R. Cobb, the Georgia secessionist who wrote a lengthy history of slave law in the United States, hyperbolically claimed that "Capital offenses are, in most of the States, tried before the highest County Courts; and every guard, thrown around the citizen to protect his innocence, is allowed to the slave." While Cobb believed that slaves received the same fair trials as white defendants, his arguments were patently false. Enslaved defendants could not testify on their own behalf nor were they judged by a jury of their peers. Additionally, the racism of the time period infected every aspect of the legal system—even Cobb's supposed even-handed analysis. As Cobb himself demonstrated when he warned that slave confessions should be taken with a great deal of skepticism because "the habit of obedience in the slave compels him to answer all questions of idlest curiosity, while his mendacious disposition will always involve even the most innocent in the most contradictory inconsistencies."[2]

Yet slave laws did not solely exist in the law books that Cobb so admired. Rather southern slave codes represented an intersection of legal principles and practical concerns. As Ariela Gross has written, "rules of evidence and the language of legal argument shaped local disputes, but so did community norms." Gross noted that law "as it is actually experienced is created by a variety of lawmakers; not only by judges and legislators, but by the litigants, witnesses, and jurors in the courtroom."[3] Wishes of masters, prosecutors, justices of the peace, community members, and governors played an important role in shaping the legal outcome of slave confrontations. With so many competing interests involved in slave trials, conflicts arose. Diane Miller Sommerville has found that in antebellum rape cases, "towns and neighborhoods were frequently racked with discord as black rape trials played out. Typically, these splits fell along class lines."[4] Rarely, however, did these conflicts engender extralegal action on the part of white Virginians.

In the three cases to be discussed in this chapter, white Virginians all acted outside of the laws that they had previously obeyed. In Princess Anne County in 1819, a group of anonymous white citizens, which may have included several justices of the peace and the sheriff, orchestrated the murder of Mingo, a runaway slave convicted of arson. Mingo had led a band of runaways and terrorized the county for months. The white citizenry decided to protect themselves by killing Mingo even though he had been reprieved by the Governor. In 1828, in Louisa County, the commonwealth attorney, Lucian Minor, and five justices of the peace violated the laws governing slave trials to protect a number of prominent white men in the county. Sydnor, the enslaved man on trial, had kept a list of names the men who had paid for sex with Nancy Green, a young white girl. Minor and the justices hoped to ensure his execution and shield themselves from scandal. Finally, in 1852, in Richmond, a group of Richmond lawmakers and proslavery advocates used Governor Joseph Johnson's reprieve of a slave named Jordan Hatcher to protect their control over the commonwealth's political fortunes.

In other words, white Virginians, throughout the antebellum period, engaged in extralegal actions and violence to protect themselves, their political institutions, and ultimately, Virginia's slave society. They showed their devotion to white supremacy and the slave regime by violating the very laws they revered and swore to uphold.

FEAR OF CROSS-RACIAL ALLIANCES

On February 18, 1819, a group of white men from Princess Anne county ambushed Mingo, a slave convicted of arson, on the road to Norfolk. One of them shot at Mingo, placing a bullet through the center of his forehead, killing him instantly. The historical record does not indicate who fired the fatal shot that killed Mingo, but the two men escorting him to Richmond were caught in the crossfire. Both men eventually made it safely back to Richmond while nursing gunshot wounds of their own. While Virginia Governor James Preston wanted to bring Mingo's killer to justice, the potential suspect list was incredibly long and included the sheriff and several justices of the peace, all of whom wanted Mingo dead.

This specific type of extralegal execution was uncommon in antebellum Virginia. Whites killed African American slaves during confrontations or while attempting to capture runaways, but such violence was legal. White Virginians generally followed the dictates of the commonwealth's slave codes and abided by their outcomes. But the murder of Mingo, following his conviction and while on his way out of the county, was rare—lynching and other forms of extralegal violence only reached their zenith during the Jim Crow era.[5] Mingo's execution was the culmination of a years-long problem that had plagued the residents of Princess Anne County. As the leader of a band of runaways, Mingo had harassed, robbed, and attempted to kill numerous white men. In the fall of 1818, he even participated in the murder-for-hire plot.

The murder-for-hire was the breaking point for the white leaders of Princess Anne County. The justices of the peace investigating the crime discovered just how easily Mingo had crossed the boundaries between slavery and freedom. He frequently encountered whites and spoke of his desire to kill the county sheriff. Yet none of them tried to apprehend the fugitive slave. Mingo's fugitive status and the ease with which he moved between the white and enslaved communities represented an existential threat to the stability of the county. Poor whites and the enslaved had united once before in the colonial period and nearly upended Virginia's slave society. As far as the leaders of Princess Anne county were concerned, killing Mingo was the only way to make sure it did not happen again.

In November 1818, Mingo and Ned participated in the murder-for-hire of a white man named Alexander Taggert. Taggert, a wealthy native of South Carolina, had journeyed to the Pungo neighborhood of Princess Anne County to purchase slaves. One evening at the home of local resident William Gornto, Taggert met a young white farmer named Harper Ackiss. Ackiss insisted that Taggert stay at his home that evening, but Taggert refused. The following day Taggert met with Ackiss to discuss the purchase of some slaves. Taggert remained wary of the overly friendly Ackiss, but nonetheless agreed to spend the night at his house. As the evening dragged on and Ackiss suddenly announced his plan to go hunting in the middle of the night, Taggert became increasingly anxious. He worried that "the gang of negro desperadoes and runaways who infested the neighborhood and with whom Ackiss's negroes were known to be in league might seize the opportunity to murder him."[6] Taggert's concerns were well-founded. The next morning, after leaving Ackiss's house, Taggert disappeared.

Several days later, neighborhood residents found Taggert's horse wandering the road about three miles from Ackiss's house. The neighbors alerted the local authorities who convened a coroner's inquest. The members of the inquest began a search of the area and quickly found papers belonging to Taggert lying along the side of the road. A search of the nearby woods uncovered his saddle. The inquest soon discovered Taggert's body buried underneath a patch of newly dug earth. They also found a hoe that belonged to Harper Ackiss lying nearby. Taggert's money, an estimated fifteen or sixteen hundred dollars in cash, was missing. In his pockets, Taggert carried a copy of his commission as a captain in the South Carolina militia and his diploma certifying his status as a master mason.[7]

Taggert's concern about the band of runaways being a threat to his life proved correct. Ackiss himself had frequently conversed and collaborated with the runaways. He even hired Mingo and Ned to kill Taggert. At Mingo's trial, Joshua L. Hopkins, a neighborhood white man, revealed that after Ackiss announced his plan to go hunting, he had, in fact, gone to meet with Mingo and Ned. Hopkins testified that "Mingo told him that he and Ned Downs were in the swamp back of Harper Ackiss which was the night before that Taggart was killed and Harper Ackiss came in the swamp to them the night before."[8] Mingo also confirmed that he and Ned had met with Ackiss. Mingo testified that "Harper Ackiss offered him $100 and Ned $160 to do the deed—that he refused, but that Ned consented, and he saw Ned shoot Taggert while he was letting his horse drink at a run in the road."[9]

There was nothing unusual about Ackiss's familiarity with Ned and Mingo. Poor whites and slaves had frequent interactions across the boundaries between freedom and slavery. They gambled and drank together, sold each other food and other goods, and even engaged in petty crime together. They fought with one another and shared some mutual antagonisms toward elite whites who viewed African Americans as racially inferior and poor whites as socially undesirable. Yet the racial barrier that existed between the two groups prevented any sort of alliance against the elite white slaveowners who ruled antebellum Virginia. As a result, whites typically had little to worry except, as Jeff Forret has written, for "slave-poor white collusion in violent crime. Typically, this meant 'degraded' whites supplying news or material support to the slaves who actually committed violent acts."[10] Only when whites and slaves collaborated together to commit violent crimes did they represent a threat to white supremacy.

After Taggart's murder, white authorities in Princess Anne County sought to rid themselves of Ned and Mingo—and their frequent blurring of the color line—permanently. On December 7, 1818, two justices of the peace, Joseph McAlpine and William K. Land, drafted an order to Peter Land, the county sheriff and William's father. They wrote that they had "received satisfactory intelligence on oath that Negroes Mingo and Ned and other runaway negro slaves whose names and owners are unknown are lying out hid and lurking in swamps, woods and other obscure places." They further claimed that the slaves were "committing murder killing hogs and doing other injuries to the inhabitants of said County in the neighborhood of Pungo." The justices wanted Land to spare no man or expense in capturing the runaways. They wrote to the sheriff that he should "take with you such force and power of this County as you shall think fit and necessary for the effectual apprehending such out lying slaves and to go in search of them."[11] They further ordered Land to bring any captured slaves to the county jail for trial.

The geography of Princess Anne County was well suited for runaways. To the north and east lay the Atlantic Ocean and the entrance to Hampton Roads and the James River. The area along the Atlantic coast was dotted with swamps, inland lakes, and other bodies of water. To the west lay Norfolk County, best known for the Great Dismal Swamp, which extended across the coastal plains of Virginia and North Carolina. Throughout the colonial and antebellum periods, it was a well-known home to runaways and maroon communities.[12] In November 1823, one such runaway, Bob Ferebee, was convicted of murdering a white man named David Manning back in October 1818.[13] He had evaded capture for five years by hiding in the swamps and waterways. The *Norfolk Herald* reported his capture and trial with relief claiming that he was "chief of the party of outliers in the neighborhood of the Great Bridge, by whom so many atrocious outrages have been committed."[14]

Harriet Beecher Stowe even made the protagonist of her second anti-slavery novel, *Dred*, a maroon leader from the Great Dismal Swamp.[15]

To hunt down Mingo and Ned, sheriff Peter Land called out the militia of Princess Anne County. One hundred and forty infantry and cavalrymen met at the county seat of Kempsville and began their search. The militia men "set off, in squads, to scour the different swamps, and forests between that place and the southern edge of the county, in search of the gang of desperadoes who have so long kept that part of the county in a state of alarm." They searched the county from Kempsville to the Pungo Chapel, but came back empty-handed. The militia men resumed their efforts the next day, when a white man named Cox, joined one of the squads. He claimed that "he was intimate with one of the runaways named Mingo, and would engage to deliver him into their power, if they would secret themselves in his house."[16] The soldiers, likely tired after wading through swamps for two slave men in a county of over eight thousand residents and thirty-seven hundred slaves, agreed to Cox's plan.

Cox led the soldiers to the upper part of his cabin where they hid themselves. Cox left and shortly afterward returned with Mingo, "who appeared to be perfectly at home with Cox, and they drank together as old acquaintances." Cox planned to get Mingo drunk so that the militia men could swoop in and arrest him. While Cox and Mingo drank to their hearts' content, the soldiers quietly waited. Cox "took care to ply him with it until he thought he had produced the desired effect." To celebrate his escape from the soldiers, Mingo drunkenly shot his musket, his favorite weapon, into the air—avoiding the soldiers hiding above. Cox watched Mingo reload the weapon, but in the course of their drinking managed to get it out of the drunken bondsman's hands. Cox then signaled the soldiers to move in. The three men pounced on Mingo, but "he drew a dirk and wounded one of them severely; and even after they had tied him, he made a violent effort and maimed his friend Cox with his teeth and nails."[17] With Mingo now in custody, the authorities of Princess Anne began interrogating him and preparing for his trial.

Mingo had developed quite the reputation in the county as the result of his activities. After his capture, Mingo did not want to stand trial or go back into a life of slavery. Instead, he requested that "he might be turned loose and thirty of the soldiers be ordered to fire at him." A newspaper article describing Mingo's actions noted that "his ferocity and frequent depredations on the farms in the vicinity of his cruizing [sic] ground, have given rise to many strange stories among the inhabitants of that part of the county; which would furnish out a volume of no small dimensions and no little interest."[18] After escaping from his former master, Mingo had spent months hiding out in the swamps. Throughout the course of the interrogation, he confessed to a myriad of crimes, including burning down the haystacks and smokehouse of Henry

Capps and firing his musket at Capps when he tried to put the fire out. Mingo also admitted to shooting at justice of the peace William Land and his father, Peter. The militia, meanwhile, continued their search for Ned, while Mingo was taken to the county jail in Kempsville.

In early January 1819, the citizens of Princess Anne began the legal process of punishing Mingo for terrorizing the county for so many months. When Mingo stood trial for his crimes, the testimony of witnesses revealed the close relationship between the group of runaways and the white community, confirming the worst fears of the county's leaders. Numerous whites knew about Mingo's activities, had conversed with him, or aided him in some way. At his trial, eight different white men admitted to conversing with Mingo about his desire to kill Peter Land, the sheriff of Princess Anne County. Yet none of them had tried to apprehend him. William Gornto testified "that he went up to Mr. Thomas Ackiss's house and saw the said Mingo and Ned Downs there, he Mingo told me that he shot at Captain Land and missed him, but if ever he came across him he would kill him."[19] Mingo and Ned had moved within the white community of Princess Anne County with impunity. It was especially telling that a two-day search of county by one hundred and forty militiamen had yielded nothing, but Cox had found him in a matter of hours.

Elite white Virginians were not wholly irrational in their fears of collaboration between slaves and poor whites. Such a union had threatened the future of slavery in Virginia once before, in the late seventeenth century. In 1676, a group of settlers on the Virginia frontier rebelled against Governor William Berkeley. Berkeley had refused to retaliate against local Native American tribes for attacking frontier settlements. Nathaniel Bacon, a wealthy plantation owner, organized his own private militia and led raids against Native Americans. While Bacon himself was a member of the colonial elite, his rebellion attracted poor white indentured servants and slaves alike against the colony's government. The rebellion eventually petered out, but the union of the colony's poor, regardless of color, struck fear into the hearts of colonial elites. They worried, as Edmund Morgan has written, that "if freeman with disappointed hopes should make common cause with slaves of desperate hope, the results might be worse than anything Bacon had done."[20] In the ensuing decades, elite white Virginians molded the commonwealth's laws and cultural norms behind a racial ideology that prioritized white skin over black. Yet fears of a class rebellion lingered.

For some reason, a court of oyer and terminer acquitted Mingo of attempting to kill Peter Land, but convicted him of burning down the smokehouse of Henry Capps. The court sentenced Mingo to hang on February 19, 1819.[21] On January 16, 1819, however, Virginia Governor James Preston interceded in the case. A group of citizens had petitioned Preston to commute Mingo's sentence to transportation. As a result, Preston ordered that Mingo be brought to Richmond so he could be sold and transported out of the state. There was nothing unusual about this process. Ever since the 1801 law change allowing the governor to reprieve death sentences in favor of transportation, Virginia's chief executives had not been shy about using that power, especially when slaves were convicted of crimes against white property. As Philip J. Schwarz has explained, these cases revealed "the perception of oyer and terminer justices that slaves particularly dangerous to property alone could be removed safely by condemning them to death, with the full expectation that the governor and Council would commute the sentence to transportation."[22] Some citizens of Princess Anne County, however, had no intention of letting Mingo escape with his life.

William K. Land and other leading citizens of the county quickly crafted a petition asking Governor Preston to reconsider his decision. The petitioners expressed their "great regret" at Preston's actions. They believed that Preston "may not be fully apprised of his [Mingo's] character, they feel it their duty to trouble you with information upon the subject." They claimed that arson was "only one of the many crimes for which his life was forfeited to the law it is robbery at least that he has been now sold out of County and as often made his escape and returned to the said County." The petitioners claimed that Mingo and the other slaves in his gang waged "open war against the property and even being of our citizens." They listed Mingo's numerous crimes including shooting at William K. Land, threatening to kill Peter Land, and terrorizing the county. The petitioners believed that the "good of the County require that he should suffer the justice of the land."[23] The petition bore a staggering 663 signatures. This represented approximately 62 percent of the white male residents of Princess Anne County over the age of sixteen.[24]

Governor Preston refused to change his mind. He sent James W. Lord, who worked for the Commonwealth transporting prisoners from county jails to the State Penitentiary in Richmond, to retrieve Mingo from the Princess Anne County jail. On February 11, 1819, Lord arrived in Kempsville. The county jailor, however, refused to turn Mingo over without the permission of Sheriff Peter Land. Land had gone to Richmond to deliver the citizens' petition and would not return for another two days. Lord, not wanting to wait around in Kempsville, went back to Richmond empty-handed. Once Lord arrived back in the capital, Governor Preston ordered him back to Princess Anne County. Sensing trouble, Preston ordered him to solicit some help in guarding Mingo on the journey from Kempsville to Norfolk, where they would take a steamboat back to Richmond. On February 18, 1819, Lord, alongside John Wilson, the white man recruited to help him, arrived at Kempsville around 11:00 a.m. The men guarding Mingo refused to hand the bondsman over until the jailor, Mr. Williams, arrived and gave his permission. After a nearly four-hour wait,

Williams came to the jail and handed Mingo over. The three men then set out on the road to Norfolk.

The citizenry of Princess Anne County, however, refused to let Mingo be sold away and potentially return and terrorize them yet again. Several citizens threatened Mingo's life as John Wilson and James Lord took him from the jail. The two men tied Mingo to a horse drawn chair and rode on to Norfolk. When they were several miles outside of Kempsville, the men heard a gunshot from the nearby woods. Lord wheeled his head around to see where the shot had come from. Instead he "saw the head of Mingo fall forward, with his brains and blood running out, without a single struggle or a groan." Wilson rode off for assistance as Lord tried to free Mingo's body from the chair and unhitch the horse. Lord waited several hours for Wilson to return before finally riding off to Norfolk. The shot from the musket had struck Mingo in the head, killing him instantly. Other shots had wounded Lord and Wilson. Lord "received a ball just above the right hip bone and a buck shot below the wound."[25] He eventually made it home to Richmond but was unable to move his right thigh for some time afterwards.

The murder of Mingo and the attack on Lord and Wilson prompted a response from Governor Preston and the condemnation of local newspapers. The *Richmond Enquirer* recognized how Mingo had been "as great a curse as is represented to the citizens of the county of Princess Anne." But the paper wrote, "It is impossible for us not to regret in the strongest terms, this attack upon a prisoner." The paper stressed that "no citizen ought to have taken the law into his own hands, and sacrificed the life of the prisoner." The extralegal action taken by the residents of Princess Anne warranted a response from Governor Preston as well. He issued a proclamation promising a five-hundred-dollar reward for information leading to the arrest of whoever killed Mingo and wounded Wilson and Lord. Preston lamented the actions of the murderers "for wounding and endangering the lives of the innocent agents of the government, whilst in sacred performance of their duty; and for committing a cruel and atrocious murder on a defenseless slave, who had been reprieved under the law for transportation."[26] There is no indication in the county court records that anyone ever stood trial for Mingo's murder.

The residents of Princess Anne County decided that Mingo and Ned's violence had crossed the line of acceptable interaction across the color line. Their band of runaways had long plagued the county with the support of the poor white and slave communities. They burned down buildings, attempted to kill the county sheriff, and murdered a white man at the instigation of another white man. The whites of Princess Anne County, then, decided to rid themselves of these troublesome slaves. They arrested and convicted Mingo of arson and sentenced him to hang. When Governor Preston commuted Mingo's sentence and then refused to change his mind, a group of citizens decided to take the law into their own hands. Rather than risk Mingo potentially returning one day and again threatening the peace and quiet of Princess Anne County, they defied the Governor, ambushing Mingo while he was tied to a horse-drawn chair. Preserving the slave regime meant killing Mingo, even if James Lord and John Wilson got caught in the crossfire.

PROTECTING THE ELITES AND THE COLOR LINE

In the fall of 1825, Nancy Green, a thirteen or fourteen-year-old white girl from Louisa County, disappeared. Green's aunt and guardian, Susannah Kernal, last saw her heading out to retrieve wood with Clara, a hired slave woman belonging to a neighbor, Richard Sandidge. After Green failed to return home, Edmund Pendleton, a justice of the peace, began an investigation. He interrogated the Sandidge slaves and organized a search of the property, but came up empty. The case then went cold for three years until the discovery of a body that resembled Nancy Green's. Once again, the Sandidge slaves came under suspicion, only this time investigators had two suspects: Sydnor, Richard Sandidge's enslaved son and overseer, and Sydnor's sister, Eliza. Besides murdering Nancy Green, the county commonwealth attorney uncovered evidence of something much more shocking—that Nancy Green had secretly lived on the Sandidge property for some time after her disappearance. Even more shockingly, Green engaged in a sexual relationship with Sydnor and prostituted herself to local white men—including some prominent members of the Louisa county community—while splitting the profits with Sydnor and Eliza.

The implications of the investigation were scandalous. As discussed in Chapter 3, sex across the color line or even between a white man and a prostitute was permissible provided it remained discrete. The public airing of such behaviors would bring shame upon not only the men involved, but their families as well. In a famous example, after the family of South Carolina Governor James Henry Hammond found out he engaged in sexual liaisons with his nieces, Hammond saw his political prospects vanish overnight.[27] For his part, Sydnor had kept a list of the names of the men who had sex with Nancy but kept it to himself for fear of retribution. So what should Lucian Minor, the commonwealth attorney, and the county's justices of the peace do about these troublesome slaves?

Blaming Sydnor and Eliza for the murder of Nancy Green had its advantages. First, they were slaves and could be brought to trial quickly. Oyer and terminer courts were held on an as-needed basis; their trial could occur over the course of a single day. Secondly, Sydnor and Eliza could serve as convenient scapegoats. Their master, Richard Sandidge, had a reputation as an elderly eccentric who let his slaves do as they pleased, and was easily culpable for their behavior. Some details of the case would become public, like that Sydnor and Green had sex and that the slaves pimped her out but as long as Sydnor remained quiet about who precisely those men were, the county's prominent citizens would remain safely out of the spotlight. To accomplish this goal, however, the commonwealth attorney and the five justices of the peace who sat on Sydnor's case would have to violate the very laws that they had sworn to uphold.

Lucian Minor, the Louisa commonwealth attorney, put Eliza on trial first, before a court consisting of five justices of the peace: John Graves, James Michie, James Poindexter, Richard Wyatt, and Oliver Cross. From the beginning, there were issues with the case. The first being that John Poindexter, the Louisa County coroner, concluded that the two slaves had killed Green "with some cord or string hung by the neck."[28] By the time Eliza came to trial, however, white authorities had come up with a different cause of death. Lucian Minor charged that Sydnor and Eliza "violently make an assault with clubs, sticks, knives, and other weapons unknown" upon Nancy Green, killing her.[29] No one offered any explanation as to why the authorities changed the cause of death from strangulation to being assaulted with a wide range of weapons. Perhaps it was a way to cover up the fact that no one had any idea how Nancy Green had died.

Nor could anyone definitively state that the body they found actually belonged to Nancy Green. William Toler, one of the men who uncovered the body, testified that it was nothing but a pile of bones and rotting flesh. Green's aunt, Susannah Kernal, testified that she "verily believes (but will not swear positively)" that the body belonged to Nancy. She did state that "the features looked familiar." Several of Kernal's neighbors also claimed that they believed the body was Nancy's, but could not positively identify it. Mary Davis said, she "candidly believes it to be that of Nancy Green—tho she will not swear positively that it is." George Davis, who attended school with Nancy before she disappeared, said, "to the best of his belief, it was Nancy Green, but will not swear positively that it was."[30] A local doctor testified that a body buried in the ground would decompose within four or five weeks and after that it would be nearly impossible to identify visually. The lack of positive identification of the body, however, did not deter Minor from proceeding with the case.

In another bizarre move, the court heard evidence for three days in Eliza's trial before clearing her of all charges. Then Minor announced that he would put Sydnor on trial for Nancy Green's murder. Instead of summoning a new court of oyer and terminer and five new justices of the peace, Minor and the current court took it upon themselves to oversee Sydnor's trial. They later claimed this was done for the sake of expediency. The court decided to not resummon the witnesses and have them testify all over again. Instead, the five justices instructed the county clerk to copy the testimony from the record of Eliza's trial into Sydnor's. Furthermore, the court refused to allow Sydnor's attorneys to cross-examine the absent witnesses.

The only testimony that Minor offered linking Sydnor directly to Green's murder came from the newly acquitted Eliza. Eliza claimed that Sydnor had brought Nancy Green to Eliza's room in Sandidge's house, where he planned to hide her in the adjoining medicine closet. When Eliza objected and told her brother "he had no business to bring her there; he pulled out a pistol and pointed it at me saying God man your soul, if you don't hold your dam'd tongue or if you ever tell any one about her being here, I'll blow your damned brains out."[31] With a gun pointed at her face, Eliza agreed to Sydnor's demands and locked Green inside the medicine closet. The story then took an even more extraordinary and implausible turn.

One evening Sydnor left the key with Eliza, who took the opportunity to let Green out. As the two women sat by the fire, Eliza "saw the face of a white man looking through the glass." Fearing that it was her master, Eliza rushed to the door while Nancy extinguished the flames. After a knock at the door, Eliza inquired to the identity of the man. He answered, "a friend- let us come in, haven't you some girls here?" Nancy Green chatted with the two men and took one of them into the closet, leaving the other to wait by the fire. After a time, the two men left as inexplicably as they had come. The next morning Sydnor demanded to know what the white men had wanted. Surprised and confused by the entire situation, Eliza wondered how Sydnor knew about the nocturnal visitors. Eliza claimed that Sydnor concluded that "Nancy Green must stay no longer and that night he carried her again as he told me to the barn."[32] According to Eliza, Sydnor kept Nancy in the barn until sometime during the winter of 1825–1826.

When the barn became too cold, Sydnor moved Nancy back to the medicine closet, where she stayed through the summer, only coming out at night. Eliza made no mention of whether Green continued to receive any other nocturnal visitors. One evening, Sandidge came into Eliza's room seeking the key to the closet so he could retrieve some sulphur. Eliza told her master Sydnor had the key and a frustrated Sandidge left without his drugs. Eliza found Sydnor the next morning and told him what had happened. Sydnor conferred with Nancy and the two agreed to leave. Eliza recalled how Nancy "came and bade me farewell." When Sydnor returned the next morning, he told Eliza that he "had carried her over Brooks bridge and that she was on her way over the mountains." Eliza also claimed that Sydnor later admitted to killing Nancy. Sydnor had drunkenly boasted of a fortune teller who had predicted he would kill someone. When Eliza expressed fear for the safety of her mother, the inebriated Sydnor declared "'by God' it was too late for that now, for he had done it."[33]

The other key witness in the case was William Kimbrough, a local white man who had uncovered the body and had a lengthy relationship with the Sandidge family. In the fall of 1828, Kimbrough learned from Kitty, one of Sandidge's slaves, about the existence of a grave on Sandidge's property. Kimbrough testified that sometime in the late summer or early fall, "Kitty told me that Sydnor has shown her a burying ground, on enquiring of Sydnor, he told me Chainey had shown it to him and had said that she was shown it by Eliza, and he showed it to me."[34] Kimbrough spoke to Sydnor, who said that he believed the grave belonged to Nancy Green. Chainey, another slave belonging to Sandidge, claimed that Eliza had shown her the grave's location. Kimbrough believed that since so many of Sandidge's slaves knew the location of the grave, it would not remain a secret for much longer.

On October 7, 1828, Kimbrough sent a letter to Richard Sandidge, requesting a meeting. Kimbrough warned, "Mr. Sandidge, I think that it may be well for you to see me as quick as possible if you wish a part of your family well I wish them to have justice done them, if the laws of the land will do it." Sandidge ordered Sydnor to carry back a reply indicating his willingness to meet. By October 20, 1828, however, their meeting had not occurred, so Kimbrough penned a second letter. He wrote, "I repeat again, if you do not I must undertake I think something that may hang or take the years of some of your people."[35] Despite Kimbrough's repeated warnings, Sandidge never met with him.

The meeting never occurred because Kimbrough's letters had exacerbated the tensions in the household between the slaves. Richard Sandidge had a troubling reputation in the neighborhood. He was a seventy-year-old bachelor. As Sydnor's lawyer explained in a letter to Virginia Governor William Giles, Sandidge "in the folly of youth was so unfortunate as to become the father of this Sydnor." Sandidge had made Sydnor the overseer and also made him responsible for punishing the other slaves, including Eliza. She and Sydnor were also siblings, but he did not afford her any special treatment. As a result, the rest of the Sandidge slaves resented Sydnor for whipping them. Regarding the letters, Sandidge later recalled that "Eliza and the girls persuaded me not to go and Sydnor to go." Sydnor, however, "was very anxious for me to go and they had a great contention about it."[36] As a result of the tensions in the household, Sandidge never met with Kimbrough.

In November 1828, Kimbrough unsuccessfully searched for Green's grave by himself. On November 24, 1828, Kimbrough enlisted the aid of William Toler, a neighborhood white man. After another unproductive search, Toler suggested they ask Sydnor for help. Toler found Sydnor and brought him back to meet with Kimbrough who had been joined by another local white man, Anderson Trice. Sydnor spoke with Kimbrough who then led the other two men to a spot deeper in the woods. They began digging and quickly found the body of a white female buried a foot or so underneath the dirt. Toler later testified that she was "without coffin or shroud entirely naked." Toler described how "the legs were off at the knees, except a small ragged portion of the flesh and skin by which they hung." Toler also noted that "the end of the bone of one leg, instead of being round, looked square, as if cut off with some instrument."[37] The men believed they had found Nancy Green's body.

After the discovery of the body, William Kimbrough, William Toler, and Anderson Trice followed Sydnor back to Sandidge's house where Sandidge and Sydnor engaged in a verbal confrontation. Sandidge accused Sydnor of killing Nancy Green and unleashed a litany of complaints against his son. Sydnor proclaimed his innocence and tried to correct Sandidge's failing memory. Sandidge told Sydnor that "you know that you threatened my life." Sydnor reminded him that "your negroes told you I did, being angry with me for endeavoring to make them do what you had directed me, as their overlooker." Sandidge next claimed that Sydnor attacked him with a sword. Sydnor answered, "I never did. I found a cane with a sword in it and told you I thought it would suit you to walk with in your old age, and made you a present of it." Sandidge then resumed complaining about his son, claiming that Sydnor "threw brick bats at me and had liked to have knocked me in the head." Sydnor reminded Sandidge that he had put him in charge of his slaves to prevent them from hurling brickbats at one another. While on the stand, however, Sandidge admitted that he "never knew or heard any thing about Nancy Green" and was seventy years old with a failing memory.[38]

Two of Sandidge's other slaves offered conflicting testimonies. Ellison claimed that he "saw Nancy Green at Sydnor's house 3 or 4 times within 3 weeks last spring 12 months, in planting corn time, she seemed to hide herself from me." After asking Sydnor about her, Sydnor replied that "she had fits, and he did not know what to do with her." Ellison said that Sydnor then threatened to "blow my damned brains out" if he spoke out. Ellison also admitted that "I do not like him, but hate him; he has whipt me often!" Chainey testified that she had seen Nancy Green in Eliza's room and Eliza later admitted "that girl died in my room and I put her away in these woods as well as I could."[39] The slaves' testimony did little to clarify the exact circumstances that had led to Green's disappearance.

When the trial concluded, the court convicted Sydnor of murdering Nancy Green and sentenced him to hang on January 23, 1829. They had hoped that the conviction would bring this long and disturbing chapter in Louisa County history to a close. Instead, the verdict divided the white community, as supporters of Sydnor claimed that the justices railroaded him in an effort to bring the case to a quick and quiet conclusion. They pointed to the numerous legal improprieties conducted by the commonwealth attorney and the court. Lucian Minor and his supporters claimed that they had acted in the best interests of justice and the desires of the community. Both sides left it to Virginia Governor William Giles to sort out the mess.

As Sydnor's lawyers worked on a letter-writing campaign to spare bondsman's life, Lucian Minor and the five justices who comprised the oyer and terminer court launched their own efforts to ensure Sydnor's execution. Minor wrote to Governor Giles that in his discussions with the citizenry of Louisa County he had not "known any feeling so strong and so persistent among them (saving perhaps zeal for Genl Jackson during the late election) as is the feeling of discontent at the contemplated pardon of this convict." Minor warned the Governor that "the very consequence that I predicted when with you—an abated confidence in the efficacy of the penal laws- is even already beginning to show itself." If the governor spared Sydnor's life, the citizenry might abandon all faith in the legal system, Minor warned, "I have had one man say that we shall have no further use for courts: another that we may as well cut down our gallows."[40]

Minor defended the actions of the court and tried to convince Governor Giles to allow Sydnor's execution. Minor explained that the Governor might get the wrong impression about the evidence, because "there are in this case peculiar causes rendering the evidence as laid before the Executive, far more favorable to the accused than it was as presented in court upon the trial." Minor claimed that the court record failed to properly reflect the evidence in the trial because they had already heard much of the evidence against Sydnor during Eliza's trial. After Minor withdrew the charges against Eliza, he and the justices agreed that they did not need to hear the same witnesses again. They believed that with "the same court sitting on both trials, it was deemed unnecessary to have repeated in the second, all the <u>circumstantial</u> facts which had been detailed on the first trial because they were ineffaceably fixed on the minds of the court, and their repetition was thought superfluous for ensuring a conviction."[41] Minor admitted that much of the evidence that the court considered in rendering their verdict never made it into the trial record.

The commonwealth attorney, shockingly, did not believe that this action violated the law or denied Sydnor his right to a fair trial. Only after the case concluded, did Minor and the five justices realize how badly they had mangled the entire case. Minor explained that "it was then perceived that many facts trivial and inconclusive in themselves yet when connected with the principal mass, supplying its chasms, and greatly increasing its strength, were in admissible upon the record, altho' they had naturally and legally conduced to influence the operation of the court." Minor noted that these omissions in the court record meant that significant pieces of evidence were "then precluded from the consideration of the Executive on the record."[42] Despite admitting to violating Virginia's legal codes regarding the presentation of evidence, Minor defended the fairness of the trial and asked Governor Giles to allow the execution to go forward.

Minor assured Governor Giles that the presentation of the case had been much more convincing than the record indicated. He claimed he had offered more evidence about "the decrepit frame and confessed intellect of Mr. Sandidge the master—his solitary and singular bachelor life—the peculiar and scandalous relation in which he stands to the accused." Minor attacked Sydnor's character by pointing out "the species of discipline or rather the total absence of discipline as of other, property and good morals, that prevailed on his domain—and the high hand with which the accused governed there." He noted that Eliza gave a particularly remarkable performance as a witness. Minor praised her "impressive tones her strongly emphatic gestures, and the solemn earnestness of her whole manner betokened her consciousness of the portentous truth, which she had never till that occasion dared to divulge." He assured the Governor of the "incalculable difference between oral and written testimony—especially whether testimony abridged" and how the written record failed to convey the power of the witnesses' testimony. Minor and the justices reiterated their belief in the strength of the case. They argued that "few stronger cases of guilt proved by mere circumstantial testimony have ever been presented to a court of justice."[43] Contrary to legal principles, Minor stressed that any prosecutorial errors should favor the Commonwealth and not the accused.

Any sympathy that Governor Giles may have felt for Sydnor because of the prosecution's legal blunders, Minor and the five justices warned, would undermine faith in Virginia's criminal justice system. They lamented "the mercy (almost to a fault) in which criminal justice is administered by our county courts." They further claimed that executive clemency led to criminals escaping "the just consequences of their crimes." Such mercy also gave encouragement to "future offenders by the impunity of their precursors." Commuting Sydnor's sentence threatened to undermine the white community's faith in the judicial process. Minor and the justices explained that a pardon or reprieve would impair the "confidence of the community in the administration of public justice." They rejected transportation as a viable alternative for Sydnor, noting "its inefficacy in either reforming the offender, striking a salutary terror into others, or ridding society at large of annoyance and danger from his subsequent outrages (the criminal cuts off all punishment)."[44] Lucian Minor and the five justices of the peace expressed their expectation that Governor Giles would uphold the verdict.

With Sydnor now sentenced to hang for murder, his lawyers, John McPherson and Garrett Quarles, tried to convince Governor Giles to pardon the bondsman or, at least, commute his sentence to transportation. On December

17, 1828, shortly after the trial, McPherson penned a letter hoping to draw Giles's attention to the peculiar circumstances of the case. Since the justices had sentenced Sydnor to hang without recommending mercy to the Governor, McPherson wrote, "I beg leave to draw you serious attention to it, as in my humble opinion the evidence was not satisfactory to condemn the prisoner to death." He hoped to convince Giles that the numerous flaws in the commonwealth's case, including the conflicting witness testimonies and the failure to articulate exactly when and how Nancy Green died, warranted sparing Sydnor the hangman's noose. In another letter, Quarles wrote that "Eliza was the person who brought Nancy Green to the house of Richard Sandidge and kept her in her room for the purpose of sharing with her the profits ensuing from an illicit intercourse with the young men in the neighborhood."[45] Both lawyers steadfastly argued for Sydnor's innocence.

McPherson warned Giles that while the evidence against Sydnor was weak, a powerful group of white citizens had arrayed themselves against him. McPherson informed Governor Giles that he had wanted to ask the court to recommend Sydnor for mercy. But one member of the court informed him "that a majority seemed to think example necessary. The people were excited in turn against every one who was taken up (which was 3 besides Sydnor) in the offense they said required that some one should be hanged." McPherson himself did not believe that his client had killed Nancy Green. He, however, explained that many county residents wanted Sydnor hanged. He was unsure "whether or not they are the most numerous, one thing I do know, they cry the loudest and many join who have but a hearsay knowledge of the matter and will sign the paper urging you to hang him." He also informed the Governor that the court had excluded favorable evidence to Sydnor from the trial. McPherson wrote that Edmund Pendleton, the justice of the peace who investigated the initial disappearance of Nancy Green in 1825, stated that "he would not have voted for his condemnation."[46] McPherson also presented a statement from the deputy sheriff of Louisa County, Nicholas Poindexter, contradicting much of Eliza's testimony.

Quarles and McPherson also attached a statement from Sydnor where the bondsman offered his own sensationalistic account of Nancy Green's life after her disappearance. He explained that Nancy had run away with Eliza to Sandidge's because her aunt had mistreated her and she did not want to return home. Shortly after Green vanished, white authorities questioned Eliza about the young girl's disappearance. While Eliza avoided arrest, Sydnor claimed she panicked, fearing the consequences of being caught with the missing white girl. Sydnor believed "she was afraid of losing her ears for secreting her." He explained how Eliza had a small hiding place attached to Sandidge's house where she kept Nancy out of sight. Eliza kept the girl there "for the purpose of making money out the white men that came there to visit her." Sydnor offered a different explanation for orphan girl's death. He wrote "Nancy Green took sick and died there, and Eliza had her put away." Eliza, however, grew increasingly alarmed about anyone discovering the body. She was afraid that "the offense of concealing her would be nearly as bad as if she had murdered her."[47] So she buried the body in the woods to cover up her crime.

In his statement, Sydnor claimed that he knew the identities of most of the men who had come to Sandidge's house to sexually exploit Green, but "was afraid to name them." One such white man had told Sydnor that if he "mentioned his coming there he would kill him." Sydnor provided a list of the names to his attorney, John McPherson. In a letter acknowledging the existence of the list to Governor Giles, McPherson refused to share it with the governor because it included "among the most respectable in the County" and McPherson deemed it "improper to name them." Jugurtha Johnson, a neighborhood white man, testified at Sydnor's trial that Sydnor admitted that "he had a girl concealed not only for his own use but for others."[48] Remarkably no one disputed that Sandidge's slaves had pimped Nancy Green out to the white residents of the neighborhood or that Sydnor kept a list of their names.

McPherson and Quarles, Sydnor's attorneys, attacked the actions of the court and the ferocity with which Minor and the five justices of the peace were pursuing Sydnor's execution. The attorneys described how Minor and members of the court's actions were "unusual and to our minds has more the appearance of warm partisans pursuing with unrelenting vengeance the life of their most deadly enemy, than that of a dignified attorney and impartial and unprejudiced justices, seeking for truth in a legal manner and administering the criminal laws of the Country impartially and in mercy." Quarles and McPherson noted that "on some occasions when the defending counsel objected to the illegality of the evidence about to be elicited by the Court, the Attorney was appealed to say whether it was legal, or not, he would decide that it was illegal, yet the Court persisted contrary to the opinion of their Attorney and would make the witness give the evidence." They noted that "so great was the zeal of some members of the Court, that the counsel deciding more than once reminded them of that humane maxim of the law 'that the Court should be of Counsel for the accused' and to say to them, that so far from pursuing that maxim they were taking on themselves the office of prosecutors."[49]

Quarles and McPherson then turned to one of the most pertinent legal matters at hand, the influence of Eliza's trial on Sydnor's. Sydnor's lawyers complained that "what the evidence was, which the Court heard in the tryal [sic] of Eliza, that had so much influence on their minds, on the tryal [sic] of Sydnor, and which was not repeated on his Sydnor's tryal [sic], Mr. Attorney, nor the Justices, have not thought proper to tell us, we wish they had as we cannot divine." McPherson and Quarles had reasonably believed that Eliza's trial was separate from Sydnor's. They had "supposed the court would not transfer the evidence heard in her tryal [sic] to the account of another prisoner, and permitted it to have weight on their minds. It never entered into the minds of the defending counsel to conceive or image that the evidence heard against Eliza was to operate against Sydnor unless it was heard in his case." McPherson and Quarles, at first, refused to believe that the justices of the peace allowed the evidence from one case to influence the outcome of another "but for having said so themselves."[50]

This admission represented a major breach of legal practice. As McPherson and Quarles wrote, "Would it not, violate every rule of law and justice?" They continued their attack on Minor's arguments, "What! Condemn a human being to death, on evidence not heard in his tryal? The Spanish Inquisition is far preferable." Quarles and McPherson turned to another key issue: Sydnor's legal status. While Sydnor lacked the legal rights of a white man, Virginia's slave code allowed him to confront his accusers and hear all of the evidence against him. Quarles and McPherson quipped that "if the evidence on which his is to be condemned or acquitted is not to be heard by the counsel: of what possible service could counsel be."[51] No fact, they argued, could be taken on face value unless proven by a witness or other suitable evidence before the court. Quarles and McPherson asked Giles to spare Sydnor's life by granting him a pardon or commuting his sentence to transportation.

Governor Giles also received a pair of petitions on February 9, 1829; one in favor of the execution, the other opposed. On February 14, 1829, six days before his scheduled execution, Giles reprieved Sydnor's sentence to transportation. The Commonwealth paid out $350 in compensation to Garrett Quarles for the value of Sydnor, closing one of the most bizarre legal cases that the Commonwealth had ever seen.[52]

So why did whites in Louisa County, who knew that Nancy Green was alive and having sex across the color line, do nothing about it? And why did the discovery of her body in 1828 suddenly spur them to flagrantly violate the laws of the commonwealth in order to railroad Sydnor? The answer stems from two interconnected factors. The first is how white southerners handled sexual liaisons between black men and white women. The second addresses how white elites, like those in Louisa County, viewed poor women. Prior to emancipation, patriarchy and class issues dictated just how much toleration elites afforded interracial sex. If liaisons produced children, as Martha Hodes, has written, "two important social categories were eroded: racial categories were eroded because the children would be of mixed European and African ancestry, and categories of slavery and freedom were eroded because free people of African ancestry endangered the equation of blackness and slavery."[53] Since Sydnor's liaison with Nancy did not produce children, white elites were less likely to interfere since it did not challenge the southern racial and social order. Additionally, revealing the nature of Sydnor and Nancy's relationship would expose their own knowledge and participation in Green's disappearance.

Additionally, class distinctions played a key role in white responses to relationships between white women and black men. Elite white men and women had long looked down upon their lower-class counterparts. Southern views on femininity stressed how white women should not work outside of the household and certainly not for wages. This was not a new phenomenon in antebellum Virginia. Class consciousness among whites descended from European traditions. In the new world, however, these classist notions took on a racial component. As Victoria Bynum has pointed out, southern ideas on race associated menial labor with African Americans. As a result, Bynum writes, "To be poor was even more shameful for white women because it violated norms of white femininity."[54] The liaison between Nancy Green and Sydnor did not meet either of the conditions that would lead to the white community to intervene. Green and Sydnor did not have any children together that could blur the lines between race-based slavery and freedom. Additionally, as a poor orphan girl, Green had no reputation or honor in need of protection. Instead she bore responsibility for her own predicament. As Hodes noted, "In the dominant visions of the antebellum South, then, black women seduced white men, and poorer white women were capable of seducing black men."[55]

The public revelation of the complicity of Louisa County's unnamed "respectable" men likely drove the desire to prosecute Sydnor and Eliza. A liaison between a male slave, himself the son of a disreputable white man, and an orphan girl did not warrant the attention of local authorities. Yet when that liaison implicated the local elites, who paid money to two slaves to sexually exploit Nancy Green, the threat of scandal proved too much to bear. Publicly, white men, as Bertram Wyatt-Brown has explained, "were supposed to fall in love, honor and cherish their mates, and live upright, Christian lives in conventional fashion."[56] As a result, elite white men sought younger and compliant wives. When such women proved difficult to find, since white southern women had their own ideas about marriage, elite men naturally looked elsewhere for sexual gratification. They often sexually exploited their slave women and as long as such affairs were kept out of the public view, they did not ruin a man's reputation.

White southerners believed that having sex was an important part of becoming a man. But if a man decided to have sex outside of marriage or his social class, he should be discrete about it. As a result, white men often targeted slave women who had little ability to reject their sexual advances as Richard Sandidge had done. But Sandidge had acknowledged his relationship to his enslaved children. As a result, other whites described how Sandidge "in the folly of youth was so unfortunate" to father Sydnor.[57] Words like "folly" and "unfortunate" indicate that Sandidge had crossed the boundaries of acceptable behavior. Nancy Green, a poor orphan white girl, could also serve as a suitable substitute for a slave girl. Her sexual availability provided elite white men with a sexual outlet. As Wyatt-Brown argued, "Prostitutes performed that convenient service in free societies; fallen women, it was thought, kept the rest of the world in good moral order."[58] Such sexual liaisons were permissible as long as they remained out of the public eye.

The disappearance and death of Nancy Green revealed a shocking case of sexual exploitation by whites and African Americans alike. Rather than acknowledge their own responsibility in Green's case, Lucian Minor, the five justices of the peace, and other elite whites of Louisa county chose to scapegoat Sydnor and Eliza. They tried and condemned an unpopular slave to death to cover up the sexual exploitation of Nancy Green. They channeled the white community's anger against Sydnor, Eliza, and Richard Sandidge in order to pretend that color line remained firmly intact. This desire led Minor and the five justices to engage in grossly illegal behavior, denying Sydnor the right to a fair trial and the right to confront his accusers. Sydnor's attorneys, James McPherson and Garrett Quarles managed to spare Sydnor's life, but Lucian Minor and the other whites succeeded in removing Sydnor from Louisa County permanently. Their desire to protect themselves and the ideology of white supremacy that meant sacrificing the life of one unpopular slave. As their letters to Governor Giles indicated, it was a sacrifice that they had no trouble making.

PROTECTING SLAVE POWER

On February 25, 1852, Jordan Hatcher, a slave, engaged in a physical confrontation with Nathaniel Jackson, the overseer at the Walker and Harris tobacco factory in Richmond. Their altercation, like many between bondsmen and overseers, began after Jackson disciplined Hatcher for his poor work habits. Two days later, Jackson died of his wounds and Hatcher was put on trial for murder. After a Richmond Hustings Court sentenced Hatcher to hang, Governor Joseph Johnson, reprieved Hatcher's sentence to transportation. Johnson, the commonwealth's first democratically elected governor, came from the sparsely populated western portion of the state. Additionally, Hatcher was part of the increasing number of hired-out slaves working in Richmond's factories who competed with the newly enfranchised poor whites for jobs. A new governor, new voters with no allegiance to the slave regime, and an increasing population of hired-out slaves, led Virginia's planter class to worry about maintaining their grip on power. So they unleashed a political firestorm in Richmond, organizing a protest meeting outside of the Executive Mansion that erupted into mob violence.

The confrontation began on the morning of February 25, 1852, when Nathaniel Jackson challenged Jordan Hatcher about his poor work habits. Hatcher's job at the Walker and Harris factory involved removing stems from tobacco leaves. Jackson had previously chastised Hatcher for leaving dirty stems on his work bench and threatened to punish him if he did it again. After being yelled at by the overseer, Hatcher begged Jackson to not whip him. The bondsman promised that "he would try to do better if he would not whip him." Jackson refused to show mercy and struck Hatcher several times with his whip. Hatcher resisted, grabbing the whip as the two men battled one another. As the fight continued, Hatcher "picked up an iron poker . . . and struck Mr. Jackson a blow with it on the forepart of the head, which caused Mr. Jackson to fall."[59] Hatcher fled into the streets before being arrested a short time later.

Jackson received a visit from a doctor before resuming his work at the factory. Dr. John Cunningham examined him and found no signs of a serious head injury. Jackson himself did not complain of any pain or illness. At the end of the work day, Jackson returned home where he lived with his parents, ate dinner and went to bed. As he prepared to go to work the next morning, his mother convinced him to stay home. She summoned Dr. Cunningham again. Only now, the prognosis was dire. Cunningham "saw that Mr. Jackson was suffering from a very severe injury to the brain." Cunningham consulted with another physician who agreed that they would have to operate on Jackson's skull. Cunningham recommended that they call for a third doctor, James Bolton, to perform the surgery. Bolton, who a few months later would be called upon to examine the comatose Joseph Winston, examined Jackson and found "that the skull had been broken, and portions of it forced in upon the brain."[60] Bolton operated and removed the broken parts of Jackson's skull. The doctors, however, had acted too late. By the next morning, the nineteen-year-old Jackson had died, two days after his confrontation with Hatcher.

On March 12, 1852, Hatcher stood trial in a Hustings Court in Richmond. In major cities, Hustings Courts handled cases of violent slave crime and served the same function as oyer and terminer courts. After hearing testimony from several witnesses, four Richmond aldermen found Hatcher guilty of Jackson's murder and sentenced him to hang on April 23, 1852. The court valued Hatcher at $600 and ordered the state to pay out compensation to a Mrs. P.O. Godsey of Chesterfield County, Hatcher's owner.[61]

Shortly after Hatcher's conviction, a number of leading citizens of Richmond petitioned Governor Joseph Johnson to spare the bondsman's life. The signers of the petition included lawyers, ministers, and leading businessmen.

S.S. Baxter, a former attorney general, William McFarland, the president of the Farmer's Bank of Virginia, W.M. Elliot, editor of the *Richmond Whig*, and G. A. Myers, the president of the Richmond City Council all lent their names to the petition. The petitioners did not dispute that Hatcher's blow had killed Jackson. They, however, claimed that the "consequence was neither expected nor desired by him." They furthered argued that "All of the facts of the case tend to establish that the blow was struck under circumstances tending greatly to aggravate the boy, without premeditation and with no design to kill. There is no malignant, willful or deliberate purpose developed by the proofs to commit murder." The petitioners did not believe that Hatcher should die for his crime. Rather they saw the case as "precisely one of those cases upon which a sound discretion would induce the exercise of some degree of executive clemency."[62] They also cited Hatcher's youth as a reason to mitigate his death sentence.

While a number of leading citizens worked to spare Hatcher's life, a counter petition began to circulate asking Governor Johnson to let the death sentence stand. The petitioners expressed their displeasure at any effort to commute Hatcher's execution. They also claimed that "nothing in his favor has been elicited since his trial" and there were no mitigating circumstances warranting clemency. They wrote, "We believe, for the protection of our lives and property, that examples should be made of all such offenders, and the change of punishment asked for in the present instance will, we are satisfied, fail to produce any satisfactory effect whatsoever." The petitioners offered an ominous warning to Governor Johnson if he decided to pardon Hatcher. They warned that "a growing spirit of insubordination amongst of the negroes of this city has been manifested for several years and particularly amongst those employed in the tobacco factories, who number some two or three thousand." The petitioners also claimed that the situation had grown so bad that "the managers of those establishments can now rarely correct the negroes for the gravest offenses, without hazarding their lives."[63] The commonwealth of Virginia, they argued, stood at a precipice of slave rebelliousness and only decisive action by Governor Johnson could stem the tide.

The complaints of the counter-petitioners about the need to execute Jordan Hatcher reflected a growing concern from Richmond citizens about the rapidly transforming city. The city's tobacco factories had grown as part of a burgeoning industrial sector. By 1852, Richmond housed numerous tobacco factories, flour mills, and the Tredegar Iron Works. Recently built railroads connected the commonwealth's agricultural regions to newly emerging industrial centers like Richmond, Norfolk, and Petersburg. As a result, thousands of hired-out slaves worked in the city's factories under the supervision of largely poor white overseers. Here poor whites participated in the labor force alongside African Americans creating tensions between the two groups.

This growing population of hired-out slaves increased the number of African Americans in the capital and heightened white fears regarding slave violence and insurrection. So many slaves moving freely about the city and mixing with poor whites and free African Americans could only lead to trouble.[64] Throughout the history of slavery in Virginia, whites feared that any change to the political or social order would result in the dissolution of slavery. In light of this changing reality, the counter-petitioners argued that Governor Johnson needed to act decisively to protect the slave regime.

At first glance, there was nothing unusual about Governor Johnson considering reprieving Hatcher's sentence to transportation. Since the 1801 law change, Virginia governors had the right to reprieve death sentences if they believed the circumstances of the case warranted it. Often governors spared the lives of slaves who did not intend to kill whites. They believed that transportation was sufficient to remove the threat to the white population. In similar, albeit non-fatal, confrontations that occurred before and after 1852, Virginia governors granted reprieves to slaves convicted of attacking their overseers in tobacco factories. In 1847, Governor William Smith reprieved the death sentence of a slave who slashed the face of his overseer with a knife at a Lynchburg tobacco factory.[65] In 1859, Governor Henry Wise spared the lives of two different slaves convicted of trying to kill their overseers at Richmond tobacco factories. One bondsman, Robert, had resisted punishment and attacked his overseer.[66] Another named David had stabbed his overseer, Robert Allen, in the temple with a knife he had concealed in his pocket.[67] In Hatcher's case, the only difference was in the outcome, not the form of the confrontation.

Shortly before Hatcher's execution, Governor Johnson issued a temporary reprieve until May 7. Then on May 5, 1852, Johnson commuted Hatcher's punishment to transportation. Johnson's political opponents quickly mobilized against the governor. Richmond newspapers, led by the *Richmond Republican*, published notices of an "indignation meeting" to be held at City Hall on the evening of Friday May 7th at 8 o'clock. The organizers called on "all good citizens who are willing at all times ready to stand by the institutions of the South and especially Virginia laws" to gather to express their outrage. The notice included further incendiary language: "Come one, come all, and protect your firesides by putting down all those who uphold murder." The *Republican* claimed that "the news had spread like electricity throughout the various ramifications of the city, and all sections, classes and vocations of the people, had poured out their hundreds to express their great indignation at the course pursued by Governor Johnson."[68]

On May 7, outraged citizens gathered outside the Governor's mansion. They listened to a few speakers before getting to the business of the meeting. They passed a resolution claiming that Governor Johnson "abused the trust confided to him by the Constitution, has outraged the feelings of the community, and has given an encouragement to insubordination and crime, which calls for the indignant reprobation of the people of Virginia."[69] Having expressed their disapproval of the Governor's actions, the meeting then broke up.

Many in the crowd, however, refused to disperse and instead, as the *Richmond Enquirer* reported, began "to invade the private grounds of the Governor's Mansion, and to degrade themselves and the city of their residence by the most gross breach of hospitality, the most shameful abuse of personal sanctity, and the rudest intrusion upon domestic quiet that ever degraded this commonwealth." Many of the participants were white men between the ages of fifteen and twenty, the same age range as deceased Nathaniel Jackson.[70] These poor white men were angered by the death of one of their own and the refusal of the Governor to execute Jackson's killer. The *Enquirer* claimed that "we only speak the truth when we say that it was a MOB and not a deliberative assembly." The crowd who attacked the Governor's mansion wanted "to make a row and uproar, closing their ears to truth and facts." The paper explained that "our laws confer the power of remitting the death-penalty upon the Executive, impose upon one man that gravest of all responsibilities, the responsibility of deciding between the life and death of a fellow creature in the last resort."[71] The *Enquirer* defended Governor Johnson and condemned the mob for attempting to impose their will on the rest of the state.

Petition campaigns and public meetings had a long history in Virginia. Violent attacks on the governor's mansion? Not so much. In the antebellum era, mob violence became an increasingly prominent part of public life. Beginning in the 1830s, the mobilization of abolitionists in the North prompted an uptick in mob violence. White mobs consisting of a mix between poor whites and "gentlemen of property and standing" attacked African Americans, abolitionists, and their meeting houses in Philadelphia, Utica, Boston, and elsewhere. Angry South Carolinians burned abolitionist literature on the docks in Charleston. Pro-slavery and anti-slavery forces engaged in increasingly violent confrontations along the border between free and slave states.[72] Richmond, however, was not flooded with abolitionists threatening the very fabric of Virginia's slave regime. Rather, as the rioters feared, the threat to slavery was coming from inside the Governor's mansion.

Many white Virginians, especially from the Eastern part of the commonwealth, were already suspicious of Governor Johnson and whether he would fight to preserve slavery. The commonwealth's new constitution, approved in 1851, granted the vote to all white men, not just those who owned property. The constitution also made the governorship open to the popular vote for the first time in the commonwealth's history. As a result of these changes, the Western part of the state, with its large numbers of poor whites gained more political power at the expense of the landed Eastern elites. Governor Johnson had been born in New York and moved to Bridgeport, Virginia (now West Virginia) at the age of 16. Johnson's home county, Harrison, had only 488 slaves out of a population of 11,728 according to the 1850 census.[73] Because of his background, Johnson's claims of wanting to protect and preserve slavery did little to assuage the fears of his political adversaries, who were largely from the east. They saw his actions as failing to quell the rebellious attitude among the commonwealth's slaves and even encouraging further violence.

After the riot, Johnson decided to write a message to the Virginia Legislature explaining his actions. His justification, however, failed to alleviate the tensions caused by the reprieve. Johnson explained that he believed that Hatcher "had no intention of committing murder or taking the life of his overseer, Mr. Jackson in some way." He further argued that Hatcher's single blow with the iron poker was "given at a moment of great excitement and suffering." Since Hatcher had not planned or intend to kill Jackson, Johnson had spared the enslaved man's life. Johnson believed that the death sentence was "against the spirit of our laws and of the age, as it is contrary to mercy and humanity." Then the governor pushed his argument too far for his political opponents. He claimed that "if Hatcher had been a white man, the utmost he could have been charged with would have been justifiable homicide, or involuntary manslaughter; and in this case it was but manslaughter, without intent to kill."[74] With this logic, Johnson, as William A. Link has written, argued "that the standards of justice existed above race."[75] Johnson made it seem that he cared more about the equal application of the law than maintaining white supremacy. Rather than extinguishing the debate, Johnson's comments only fanned the flames.

By arguing that equality under the law should prevail over white supremacy, Johnson confirmed the worst fears of his political enemies. On May 19, Johnson issued a second message to the Legislature clarifying his position. He wrote to the legislators complaining that "the terms in which those reasons were expressed have been misconstrued and my views upon the delicate relations existing between master and slave, misapprehended." Johnson denied that he suggested that "the slave would under any circumstances be excused for justified in resisting the legal authority of his master." He described the right of masters or their representatives to punish slaves as "necessary for wholesome discipline and restraint." He rejected the idea that slaves had the right to resist their masters' punishment in any way. He further clarified his position on the balance between slavery and justice. Johnson wrote that "I did not intend to convey the idea that the relative positions of the white citizen and the slave, to the laws of the country, were the same." Johnson further stated that "I did not intend to express the conviction of my mind that a slave should not suffer death for offenses below the grade of murder."[76] Johnson sought to reassure the Legislature of his devotion to the protection of slavery.

Johnson's clarification failed to settle the debate over his actions. In the legislature, the two parties divided along geographic lines. Whigs, from the eastern part of the commonwealth, accused Johnson of being a secret abolitionist and demanded that he crack down on slave violence. As William A. Link explained, "To many easterners, the Hatcher case revealed western hostility for or indifference towards slavery." Johnson's Democratic supporters from the western parts of the commonwealth rejected the attacks on the Governor's character. As Link argued, men from the western part of the state, like Governor Johnson, "had long borne a grudge against the eastern slaveocracy."[77] Exacerbated by the entire situation, Charles Lewis, a Johnson supporter, even proposed the formation of a committee to investigate moving the capital away from the coast to a more centralized location within the state. The political crisis eventually passed, but not before revealing the fears over the future of slavery that threatened to tear the commonwealth apart.

In the cases of Mingo, Sydnor, and Jordan Hatcher, white Virginians professed their love and respect for the laws of the commonwealth. They demanded that the commonwealth's executive branch refuse to show mercy to the condemned slaves. But when their pleas fell on deaf ears, they took matters into their own hands.

Mingo's repeated crimes and the ease with which he crossed the color line prompted a group of angry Princess Anne county citizens to shoot him through the head while tied to a chair. Their desire to kill Mingo ran so strong that they shot indiscriminately, wounding the white men whose only crime was following the orders of the governor to escort Mingo to Richmond. In 1828, the county elites of Louisa county banded together and illegally tried Sydnor for the murder of Nancy Green. Relying on shoddy evidence and a desire to cover up their own complicity in Green's sexual exploitation, the commonwealth attorney and the justices of the peace that comprised the oyer and terminer court convicted Sydnor of murder. They hoped that a quick execution would rid the county of a troublesome slave and any further questions about this case of sex across the color line. In 1852, a mob of angry Richmond citizens, concerned about the city's growing slave population and burgeoning factories, rioted outside of the Governor's mansion rather than allow Jordan Hatcher to be transported. This potential for blurring the color line proved too much for Richmond's citizens to bear.

When confronted with the choice between abiding by the laws that governed the commonwealth and slave crime, white Virginians throughout the 19th century generally followed the law. They adjudicated thousands of cases ranging from petty crime to murder. When physical confrontations, however, intersected with concerns about maintaining and perpetuating white supremacy, white Virginians sacrificed their legal principles in order to preserve and protect their slave society.

NOTES

1. Philip J. Schwarz, *Twice Condemned: Slaves and the Criminal Laws of Virginia, 1705–1865* (Baton Rouge: Louisiana State University Press, 1988), 47.
2. Thomas R.R. Cobb, *An Inquiry Into the Law of Negro Slavery in the United States of America: To Which is Prefixed An Historical Sketch of Slavery* (Philadelphia: T. & J.W. Johnson & Co., 1858), 268, 271.
3. Ariela J. Gross, *Double Character: Slavery and Mastery in the Antebellum Southern Courtroom* (Princeton: Princeton University Press, 2000), 5.
4. Diane Miller Sommerville, *Rape and Race in the Nineteenth Century South* (Chapel Hill: University of North Carolina Press, 2004), 4.
5. The literature on lynching is extensive, but prominent works include: Allen W. Trelease, *White Terror: The Ku Klux Klan Conspiracy and Southern Reconstruction* (Baton Rouge: Louisiana State University Press, 1971); George C. Wright, *Racial Violence in Kentucky: Lynchings, Mob Rule, and 'Legal Lynchings'* (Baton Rouge: Louisiana State University Press, 1990); W. Fitzhugh Brundage, *Lynching in the New South* (Urbana: University of Illinois Press, 1994); W. Fitzhugh Brundage ed., *Under Sentence of Death: Lynching in the South* (Chapel Hill: University of North Carolina Press, 1997); Philip Dray, *At the Hands of Persons Unknown: The Lynching of Black America* (New York: Modern Library, 2003).
6. *Alexandria Herald* (Alexandria, VA), Dec. 9, 1818.
7. *Alexandria Herald* (Alexandria, VA), Dec. 9, 1818.
8. *Commonwealth vs. Mingo*, James P. Preston Executive Papers, 1816–1819. Accession 41737. Box 11, Folder 10. State Records Collection, The Library of Virginia, Richmond, Virginia. Henceforth *Commonwealth vs. Mingo*, (LVA).
9. *Baltimore Patriot and Mercantile Advertiser* (Baltimore, MD), Dec. 21, 1818.
10. Jeff Forret, *Race Relations at the Margins: Slaves and Poor Whites in the Antebellum Countryside* (Baton Rouge: Louisiana State University Press, 2008), 180.
11. *Commonwealth vs. Mingo*, (LVA).
12. See Daniel O. Sayers, *A Desolate Place for a Defiant People: The Archaeology of Maroons, Indigenous Americans, and Enslaved Laborers in the Great Dismal Swamp* (Gainesville: University Press of Florida, 2014).
13. *Commonwealth vs. Bob*, James Pleasants Executive Papers, 1822–1825. Accession 42046. Box 2, Folder 4. State Government Records Collection, The Library of Virginia, Richmond, Virginia.
14. *Norfolk Herald* (Norfolk, VA), June 25, 1823, reprinted in *Spectator* (New York, NY) July 1, 1823.
15. Harriet Beecher Stowe, *Dred: A Tale of the Great Dismal Swamp* (Boston: Phillips, Sampson and Co., 1856).

16. *Baltimore Patriot and Mercantile Advertiser* (Baltimore, MD), Dec. 21, 1818.
17. *Baltimore Patriot and Mercantile Advertiser* (Baltimore, MD), Dec. 21, 1818.
18. *Baltimore Patriot and Mercantile Advertiser* (Baltimore, MD), Dec. 21, 1818.
19. *Commonwealth vs. Mingo,* (LVA).
20. Edmund Morgan, *American Slavery, American Freedom: The Ordeal of Colonial Virginia* (New York: W.W. Norton & Company, 1975), 328
21. *Commonwealth vs. Mingo,* James P. Preston Executive Papers, 1816–1819. Accession 41737. Box 6, Folder 12. State Records Collection, The Library of Virginia, Richmond, Virginia. This file may now be located in Box 11, Folder 10. I found it while searching for another case and requested that the archive place it with the other papers related to Mingo's case.
22. Philip J. Schwarz, *Slave Laws in Virginia* (Athens: University of Georgia Press, 1996), 108.
23. *Commonwealth vs. Mingo,* (LVA).
24. Calculations taken from the 1820 Census, *Abstract of the Returns of the Fifth Census* (Washington: Duff Green, 1820).
25. *American Beacon and Norfolk and Portsmouth* (Norfolk, VA), March 1, 1819.
26. *American Beacon and Norfolk and Portsmouth Daily Advertiser* (Norfolk, VA), March 1, 1819.
27. Drew Gilpin Faust, *James Henry Hammond and the Old South: A Design for Mastery* (Baton Rouge: Louisiana State University Press, 1982), 241–254.
28. *Inquest of Nancy Green,* Princess Anne County (Va.) Coroners' Inquisitions, 1810–1927. Local Records Collection, Virginia Beach (City)/Princess Anne County Court Records. The Library of Virginia, Richmond, Virginia.
29. *Commonwealth vs. Sydnor,* William B. Giles Executive Papers, 1827–1830. Accession 42310. Box 6, Folder 5. State Records Collection, The Library of Virginia, Richmond, Virginia. Henceforth *Commonwealth vs. Sydnor,* (LVA).
30. *Commonwealth vs. Sydnor,* (LVA).
31. *Commonwealth vs. Sydnor,* (LVA).
32. *Commonwealth vs. Sydnor,* (LVA).
33. *Commonwealth vs. Sydnor,* (LVA).
34. *Commonwealth vs. Sydnor,* (LVA).
35. *Commonwealth vs. Sydnor,* (LVA).
36. *Commonwealth vs. Sydnor,* (LVA). The court record does not indicate whether they shared both sets of parents or were half siblings. Eliza and Sydnor were at least twenty years apart in age, suggesting that they were half siblings and Sandidge was their father.
37. *Commonwealth vs. Sydnor* (LVA).
38. *Commonwealth vs. Sydnor* (LVA).
39. *Commonwealth vs. Sydnor* (LVA).
40. *Commonwealth vs. Sydnor* (LVA).
41. *Commonwealth vs. Sydnor* (LVA).
42. *Commonwealth vs. Sydnor* (LVA).
43. *Commonwealth vs. Sydnor* (LVA).

44. *Commonwealth vs. Sydnor* (LVA).
45. *Commonwealth vs. Sydnor* (LVA).
46. *Commonwealth vs. Sydnor* (LVA).
47. *Commonwealth vs. Sydnor* (LVA).
48. *Commonwealth vs. Sydnor* (LVA).
49. *Commonwealth vs. Sydnor* (LVA).
50. *Commonwealth vs. Sydnor* (LVA).
51. *Commonwealth vs. Sydnor* (LVA).
52. *Commonwealth vs. Sydnor* (LVA).
53. Martha Hodes, *White Women, Black Men: Illicit Sex in the 19th Century South* (New Haven: Yale University Press, 1997), 4.
54. Victoria E. Bynum, *Unruly Women: The Politics of Social and Sexual Control in the Old South* (Chapel Hill: University of North Carolina Press, 1992), 6.
55. Hodes, *White Women, Black Men*, 5.
56. Bertram Wyatt-Brown, *Southern Honor: Ethics and Behavior in the Old South* (New York: Oxford University Press, 1982), 200.
57. *Commonwealth vs. Sydnor* (LVA).
58. Wyatt-Brown, *Southern Honor*, 297.
59. *Richmond Enquirer* (Richmond, VA), May 11, 1852.
60. *Richmond Enquirer* (Richmond, VA), May 11, 1852.
61. *Richmond Enquirer* (Richmond, VA), May 11, 1852.
62. *Richmond Enquirer* (Richmond, VA), May 11, 1852.
63. *Richmond Enquirer* (Richmond, VA), May 11, 1852.
64. For the history of Richmond's industry and the particular type of slavery it helped foster see Midori Takagi, *Rearing Wolves to Our Own Destruction: Slavery in Richmond Virginia, 1782–1865* (Charlottesville: The University Press of Virginia, 1999), especially 71–95.
65. *Commonwealth vs. Augustus*, William Smith Executive Papers, 1846–1848. Accession 43708. Box 6, Folder 1. State Records Collection, The Library of Virginia, Richmond, Virginia.
66. *Commonwealth vs. Robert*, Henry A. Wise Executive Papers, 1856–1859. Accession 36710. Box 20, Folder 6. Misc. Reel 4217. State Records Collection, Library of Virginia, Richmond, Virginia.
67. *Commonwealth vs. David*, Henry A. Wise Executive Papers, 1856–1859. Accession 36710. Box 17, Folder 6. Misc. Reel 4217. State Records Collection, Library of Virginia, Richmond, Virginia.
68. *Richmond Enquirer* (Richmond, VA), May 11, 1852.
69. *Richmond Enquirer* (Richmond, VA), May 11, 1852.
70. William A. Link, *Roots of Secession: Slavery and Politics in Antebellum Virginia* (Chapel Hill: University of North Carolina Press, 2003), 84.
71. *Richmond Enquirer* (Richmond, VA), May 11, 1852.
72. See Leonard L. Richards, *"Gentlemen of Property and Standing": Anti-Abolition Mobs in Jacksonian America* (New York: Oxford University Press, 1970); Paul A. Gilje, *The Road to Mobocracy: Popular Disorder in New York City, 1763–1834* (Chapel Hill: Omohundro Institute of Early American History and Culture and the

University of North Carolina Press, 1987); David Grimsted, *American Mobbing, 1828–1861: Towards Civil War* (New York: Oxford University Press, 1998).

73. "Table of Counties; Districts, and Parishes in the United States 1850" in *The Seventh Census of the United States* (Washington: Robert Armstrong, Public Printer, 1853), xcviii. Accessed online: https://www2.census.gov/library/publications/decennial/1850/1850a/1850a-14.pdf#

74. *Richmond Enquirer* (Richmond, VA), May 14, 1852.

75. William A. Link, "The Jordan Hatcher Case: Politics and 'A Spirit of Insubordination in Antebellum Virginia," *The Journal of Southern History* 64, No. 4 (November 1998): 632. See also Harrison M. Etheridge, "The Jordan Hatcher Affair of 1852: Cold Justice and Warm Compassion," *The Virginia Magazine of History and Biography* 84, No. 4 (October 1976): 446–463.

76. *Richmond Enquirer* (Richmond, VA), May 21, 1852.

77. Link, "The Jordan Hatcher Case," 635.

Epilogue

What Violence Meant to the Enslaved

Notions of patriarchy, honor, slavery, and a political tradition that emphasized the violent defense of individual rights had granted nineteenth-century white male Virginians—especially rich ones—near exclusive claim over the legitimate use of violence. In their day-to-day affairs, white men could beat their wives, children, other white men—especially poorer ones—and enslaved African Americans. In their political struggles, white Virginians invoked America's history of violence against oppression to decry the actions of their political opponents—whether they be rabble-rousing Northern abolitionists, insufficiently pro-slavery officials, or whomever else the moment demanded. These claims of violence in defense of themselves were wholly self-serving, justifying all manner of abuses and rejecting any challenges to the racial, gender, political, and economic status quo. White Virginians did not have to solely rely on rhetoric or their own individual behavior to protect their interests. Rather Virginia's political, social, and economic institutions—the House of Burgesses, the courts, Virginia's churches—all legitimized white men's exclusive claims to violence and power.

Since legally the enslaved had no independent will separate from their owners, they had no legitimate claims to engaging in violence. As the southern legal scholar Thomas R.R. Cobb explained, "The slave, in a state of pure or absolute slavery, is totally deprived, being, as to life, liberty and property, under the absolute and uncontrolled dominion of his master." Cobb's claim, which has existed in some form dating back to Aristotle, was always untenable. In reality, enslaved people exerted their will contrary to that of their owners. Eventually slave laws recognized this reality—begrudgingly. Cobb noted there was an exception to the use violence, if bondspeople were in danger for their lives. As Cobb wrote, "If, however, the life or limb of the slave is endangered, he may use sufficient force to protect and defend himself, even if in doing so he kills the aggressor."[1] In the end, even the laws of slavery could not deny the humanity of enslaved people and their right to use violence in defense of themselves.

The day-to-day interactions between whites and enslaved people in antebellum Virginia reveal the myriad ways in which white Virginians recognized enslaved persons' claims to violence. In one instance, a group of slaves belonging to William Boulware attacked John Dodd, their overseer, after he whipped Betty, a sick slave. For his part, Boulware believed his slaves acted appropriately in Betty's defense. Instead, Boulware blamed Dodd for instigating the slaves to action in the first place rather than acknowledging Betty's history of health problems.[2] Daniel Warwick had similarly become enraged at his overseer, Albert Jenkins, when Jenkins engaged in a physical confrontation with Edward, one of his slaves. Edward was deaf and his violence in response to the overseer storming into his cabin and attacking him seemed appropriate.[3] These few instances, however, were too infrequent to challenge white Virginians views that they alone had the right to employ violence against whoever they wished.

While white southerners had plenty of opinions on slave violence and its illegitimacy, ex-slaves had their own, different views on the subject. The formerly enslaved who wrote autobiographies represented a narrow subset of slaves—they were largely young, male, and from the Upper South—but their autobiographies show how bondspeople framed their violence in the broader debate over slavery in antebellum America. On the most basic level, ex-slaves viewed their physical confrontations as essential to gaining or maintaining their desire for freedom. Through their writings, ex-slaves placed themselves in the American tradition of men being willing to fight for their liberty. Some ex-slaves took the argument even further, arguing that physical confrontations showed the importance of the collective struggle against slavery.

Runaways like James Watkins, John Brown, and Leonard Black emphasized the transformative power of violence in their journeys to freedom. Watkins, an ex-slave from Maryland, fought two men and a woman during his escape. They had attempted to capture him and claim a two-hundred-and-fifty dollar bounty. Watkins described, "One of the men, however, took me by the collar, and we had a struggle together. I struck him a heavy blow and he fell to the ground, when the second man engaged me, who, at the same time, gave me an awful blow on my head." Rather than surrender, the confrontation furthered Watkins' desire to be free. He wrote, "I had now determined to be freed from them all, and I felled him to the ground. I was then tackled by the woman, who hung on to me by the leg."[4] Watkins broke away from the woman and continued his successful flight to freedom.

Rather than submit to the whites chasing him, Watkins resisted and gained his freedom.

John Brown similarly highlighted how a violent confrontation gave him the courage to escape. After failing in a previous escape attempt, Brown attempted to fool his master, De Cator Stevens, into believing that he had given up hope of freedom. Brown had planned to "delude my master into the belief that I was cured of running off, and by appearing very humble and submissive, first gain his confidence." Initially the plan worked. As Brown explained, "Every thing he bade me do, I did, until at length he got to think the last flogging he had given me, had done me good, and made me submissive. Then he would chuckle and crow over me, thinking it a great victory to have succeeded, as he thought, in breaking down my spirit." Stevens, believing that he had broken Brown, enlisted his help in punishing two other recalcitrant slaves. When the two bondsmen escaped, Stevens turned his anger toward Brown. After Stevens accused the bondsman of aiding in their escape and called for his gun, Brown attacked. He struck his master and "tipped him down off my shoulders, and he fell to the ground, severely hurting his neck."[5] After striking his master, Brown fled to the woods for three days.

After being recaptured, Stevens savagely beat Brown for his resistance. Stevens hung him from a beam and whipped him repeatedly with the aid of two other slaveholders. For the next three months, Stevens affixed bells and horns around Brown's head, preventing any further escape attempts. The confrontation and its aftermath, however, failed to dissuade Brown from making another flight for freedom. Brown wrote, "I still held to my resolution to make another venture as soon as I could see my way of doing it." During that time, Brown collected clothes, flint and steel, and a tinder-horn. Despite threats from his master and the three-month long humiliation, Brown's desire for freedom never deserted him. He explained, "I clung to hope, with a tenacity which now surprises me. It was a blessed consolation, and only for it I must have died."[6] Rather than submit, Brown revealed how his confrontation helped further his desires for freedom.

Leonard Black, an ex-slave from Maryland, ran away from his master in 1837. During his escape, he engaged in a physical confrontation with a tavern owner. The man attempted to lure Black into the tavern, but the bondsman sensed a trap. When he refused to enter, the tavern owner "took hold of my collar, but I threw him down, for I was resolved to whip the devil out of the way, if possible." Black described, "The white man fought me, and I fought him with any thing that came handy, with fists and with stones. I told him he might kill me or I would kill him. Finally, I whipped him." Joy overwhelmed Black following his confrontation and escape from the tavern owner. He wrote, "My words are inadequate to express my joyful feelings at my deliverance. God alone could know my feelings."[7] Leonard Black's willingness to use violence permitted his escape and helped him win his freedom.

Other runaways like Andrew Jackson compared their violence to American revolutionaries. During Jackson's escape attempt, a man on a horse approached him and commanded him to stop. Jackson halted, knowing that the man had identified him as a runaway. Jackson had obeyed the man's order and drew "back my trusty hickory, and by a well directed blow sent him reeling from his unsaddled horse. He soon recovered, however, as the blow only stunned him for a moment, and renewed the pursuit." Jackson picked up a stone and threw it at the man, again temporarily stunning him. Jackson eventually escaped from his pursuer. He defended his violence, writing, "I was after a prize, for which I was willing to risk my life. And I doubt not, any one who reads this, would have done the same." Jackson invoked America's revolutionary history of violently overthrowing oppression and tyranny to justify this escape. He argued, "And if it was right for the revolutionary patriots to fight for liberty, it was right for me, and it is right for any other slave to do the same." He further claimed that slaves should fight for their freedom. He explained that "were I now a slave, I would risk my life for freedom. 'Give me liberty or give me death,' would be my deliberate conclusion."[8] Andrew Jackson claimed his desire for freedom justified violent confrontation.

By linking violence and their desires for freedom, the enslaved tapped into a deeper vein of American thought regarding violence and freedom. Southern writers and orators frequently justified the American Revolution by noting their willingness to use violence to defend themselves and their rights. Southern orators, as Dickson Bruce Jr. has argued, believed that "the American Revolution had been a period in which the noble passions had stood up to the violent force which would have crushed lesser feelings." They could easily defend the actions of their ancestors in the founding of the United States and draw comparisons with the present. The founding generation provided a clear example of noble and masculine behavior in defense of the rights of men. As Bruce noted, "In the violence of the Revolution, all that had been noble in men had met the challenge put to them."[9] Ex-slaves, adopted the same tone and arguments as their white southern counterparts. In doing so, they laid claim to an American tradition that held that violence was necessary to win and safeguard individual freedom.

Ex-slave turned minister Henry Highland Garnet unequivocally embraced slave violence as a means to end bondage. In a famous address, Garnet listed the crimes that whites had committed against African Americans, from stealing them from their homes in Africa and transporting them across the ocean, to enslaving Africans and their descendants for generations. Garnet told slaves, "You should therefore now use the same manner of resistance, as would have been just in our ancestors, when the bloody foot prints of the first remorseless soul thief was placed upon the shores of our fatherland." Garnet also believed that it would better to die while resisting than live as slaves. He wrote, "Inform them that all you desire, is FREEDOM, and that nothing else will suffice. Do this, and for ever after cease to toil for the heartless tyrants, who give you no other reward but stripes and abuse. If they then commence the work of death, they, and not you, will be responsible for the consequences. You had far better all die—*die immediately,* than live slaves, and entail your wretchedness upon your posterity."[10]

For his part, Frederick Douglass emphasized how his physical confrontation was a turning point in his life as a slave. During the altercation, Douglass wrote that he had not planned to resist his hired-out owner Edward Covey, "but at this moment—from whence came the spirit I don't know—I resolved to fight." Douglass gained the upper hand in his fight with Covey and managed to avoid punishment. He also won better treatment for himself. After fighting back, Covey never tried to whip him again. Douglass described the altercation as not only improving the day-to-day experiences of his life but also reviving his spirit and desire to be free. He wrote, "My long-crushed spirit rose, cowardice departed, bold defiance took its place; and I now resolved that, however long I might remain a slave in form, the day had passed forever when I could be a slave in fact. I did not hesitate to let it be known of me, that the white man who expected to succeed in whipping, must also succeed in killing me."[11]

With the publication of his second autobiography, *My Bondage, My Freedom*, Douglass expanded the meaning and importance of his violence to include his fellow slaves as well. He emphasized how his individual confrontation had broader consequences for himself and the other slaves under Covey's control. In this revised autobiography, Douglass especially stressed the role of the other slaves in refusing to help Covey. During their confrontation, Covey called on Bill, another slave, to help subdue Douglass, "Bill replied, with spirit, 'My master hired me here, to work, and not to help you whip Frederick.' It was now my turn to speak. 'Bill,' said I, 'don't put your hands on me.' To which he replied, 'MY GOD! Frederick, I aint goin' to tech ye,' and Bill walked off, leaving Covey and myself to settle our matters as best we might."[12] Douglass stressed that Bill risked punishment from Covey by refusing to help punish Douglass.

Douglass also added another participant to the confrontation in *My Bondage, My Freedom*. Caroline, the only slave owned by Edward Covey, also refused to aid in Covey's efforts to punish Douglass. In his first autobiography, Douglass had only mentioned Caroline in passing and she did not play role in the confrontation. This time around Douglass wrote that "Caroline answered the command of her master to 'take hold of me,' precisely as Bill had answered, but in her, it was at greater peril so to answer; she was the slave of Covey, and he could do what he pleased with her." According to Douglass, Covey later whipped Caroline for her intransigence. By describing how his fellow slaves refused to aid Covey, Douglass shifted the focus from his individual act of resistance to a more communal one. He wrote, "We were all in open rebellion, that morning."[13] Including the actions of his fellow slaves allowed Douglass to shift the importance of the confrontation from his own transformation to a broader demonstration of the evils of slavery.

Douglass also defended his actions in confronting Covey to his readers. He wrote, "He only can understand the effect of this combat on my spirit, who has himself incurred something, hazarded something, in repelling the unjust and cruel aggressions of a tyrant. Covey was a tyrant, and a cowardly one, withal. After resisting him, I felt as I had never felt before." Douglass referred to his confrontation with Covey as "undignified" yet necessary. In claiming that readers needed to experience the tyranny of slavery firsthand, Douglass attempted to deflect criticisms of his violent actions. He admitted a distaste for violence, but it had proven necessary to secure his freedom. He reminded his readers, "A man, without force, is without the essential dignity of humanity. Human nature is so constituted, that it cannot honor a helpless man, although it can pity him; and even this it cannot do long, if the signs of power do not arise."[14] Finally, Douglass stressed to his readers the necessity of violence in ending his own enslavement and potentially to end the institution itself.

In terms of the institution of slavery, physical confrontations like Douglass's did little to deter its growth and expansion. Resident masters, smaller holdings, and a substantial armed white population prevented slave rebelliousness from reaching the level of a Saint Domingue. Yet bondspeople found other ways to resist like engaging in physical confrontations. These physical confrontations, as the words of Douglass, Jackson, and others suggest, provided enslaved people with hope against a system of oppression designed to destroy their humanity. They also pushed back against the worst excesses of bondage, resisting white intrusion into the most intimate of relations—between husbands and wives and parents and children—and in controlling the day-to-day rhythms of work. By resisting such interference, enslaved Virginians gave themselves much needed breathing room—to create families, communities, and the institutions necessary for survival under brutal oppression. Their violence carried implications not only for themselves—often times individuals were whipped, transported, or executed—but for other slaves as well. While those who engaged in confrontations often suffered, they passed the benefits on to others. Their violence, while occurring largely on the individual level, resonated for far longer and with a larger number of people than whites or the enslaved could have possibly imagined.

NOTES

1. Thomas R.R. Cobb, *An Inquiry Into the Law of Negro Slavery in the United States of America: To Which is Prefixed An Historical Sketch of Slavery* (Philadelphia: T. & J.W. Johnson & Co., 1858), 83, 94.

2. *Commonwealth vs. Ben, Tom, George, Robert, Moore, & Edmund,* Henry A. Wise Executive Papers, 1856–1859. Accession 36710. Box 9, Folder 2, Misc. Reel 4203. State Records Collection, The Library of Virginia, Richmond, Virginia.

3. *Commonwealth vs. Edward,* James McDowell Executive Papers, 1843–1845. Accession 43559. Box 6, Folder 4. State Records Collection, The Library of Virginia, Richmond, Virginia. Henceforth *Commonwealth vs. Edward,* (LVA).

4. James Watkins, *Narrative of the Life of James Watkins, formerly a "Chattel" in Maryland, U. S. Containing an Account of His Escape from Slavery, Together with an Appeal on Behalf of Three Millions of Such "Pieces of Property," Still Held Under the Standard of the Eagle* (Bolton, Eng.: Kenyon and Abbatt, 1852), 22.

5. John Brown, *Slave Life in Georgia: A Narrative of the Life, Sufferings, and Escape of John Brown, a Fugitive Slave, Now in England.* Ed. Louis Alexis Chamerovzow (London: W. M. Watts, 1855), 82–85.

6. Brown, *Slave Life in Georgia,* 89.

7. Leonard Black, *The Life and Sufferings of Leonard Black, a Fugitive from Slavery. Written by Himself* (New Bedford: Benjamin Lindsey, 1847), 25–27.

8. Andrew Jackson, *Narrative and Writings of Andrew Jackson, of Kentucky; Containing an Account of His Birth, and Twenty-six Years of His Life While a Slave; His Escape; Five Years of Freedom, Together with Anecdotes Relating to Slavery; Journal of One Year's Travels, Sketches, Etc. Narrated by Himself; Written by a Friend* (Syracuse: Daily and Weekly Star, 1847), 13–14.

9. Dickson D. Bruce Jr., *Violence and Culture in the Antebellum South* (Austin: University of Texas Press, 1979), 185.

10. Henry Highland Garnet, "An Address to the Slaves of the United States of America. Rejected by the National Convention 1848," in Stanley Harrold, *The Rise of Aggressive Abolitionism: Addresses to the Slaves* (Lexington: University Press of Kentucky, 2004), 184–185.

11. Frederick Douglass, *Narrative of the Life of Fredrick Douglass: An American Slave* (1845: New York: Oxford University Press, 1999), 67–68.

12. Frederick Douglass, *My Bondage and My Freedom: Part I. Life as a Slave. Part II. Life as a Freeman* (New York: Miller, Orton & Mulligan, 1855), 245.

13. Douglass, *My Bondage, My Freedom,* 245.

14. Douglass, *My Bondage, My Freedom,* 246–7.

Bibliography

PRIMARY SOURCES

Library of Virginia, Richmond, Virginia
James Monroe Executive Papers, 1799–1802.
John Tyler, Sr. Executive Papers, 1808–1811.
James Barbour Executive Papers, 1812–1814.
James P. Preston Executive Papers, 1816–1819.
Thomas Randolph Executive Papers, 1819–1822.
James Pleasants Executive Papers, 1822–1825.
John Tyler Executive Papers, 1825–1827.
William B. Giles Executive Papers, 1827–1830.
John Floyd Executive Papers, 1830–1834.
Littleton Tazewell Executive Papers, 1834–1836.
Wyndham Robertson Executive Papers, 1836–1837.
David Campbell Executive Papers, 1837–1840.
John M. Gregory Executive Papers, 1842–1843.
James McDowell Executive Papers 1843–1846.
William Smith Executive Papers 1846–1849.
John B. Floyd Executive Papers, 1849–1852.
Joseph Johnson Executive Papers, 1852–1856.
Henry A. Wise Executive Papers, 1856–1859.
John Letcher Executive Papers, 1859–1864.
Virginia Auditor of Public Accounts, Records of Condemned Blacks Executed or Transported, 1781–1865.
Henry County (Va.) Commonwealth Causes, 1856–1859.
Princess Anne County (Va.) Coroners' Inquisitions, 1810–1927.

South Carolina Department of Archives and History, Columbia, South Carolina
Spartanburg District, Court of Magistrates and Freeholders.
Laurens District Court of Magistrates and Freeholders.

Historic Natchez Foundation, Natchez, Mississippi
    Adams County Court Records.

Newspapers
    Louisiana
    The Daily Picayune (New Orleans)
    Massachusetts
    Boston Recorder (Boston)
    Hampshire Gazette (Northampton)
    Salem Gazette (Salem)
    The Liberator (Boston)
    Maryland
    Baltimore Patriot and Mercantile Advertiser (Baltimore)
    The Sun (Baltimore)
    New York
    Ballston Spa Gazette (Ballston)
    The Spectator (New York City)
    Pennsylvania
    National Gazette and Literary Register (Philadelphia)
    Virginia
    Alexandria Herald (Alexandria)
    American Beacon and Norfolk and Portsmouth Daily Advertiser (Norfolk)
    Norfolk Herald (Norfolk)
    Richmond Dispatch (Richmond)
    Richmond Enquirer (Richmond)

Richmond Whig (Richmond)
    Spectator (Stanton)
    Washington D.C.
    Washington Star

Internet Databases
    Ancestry. http://www.ancestry.com/.
    Celia, A Slave. University of Missouri-Kansas City Famous Trials Series. http://law2.umkc.edu/faculty/projects/ftrials/celia/celiahome.html.
    America's Historical Newspapers. http://www.readex.com/content/americas-historical-newspapers.
    Library of Virginia: Virginia Newspapers. http://www.virginiamemory.com/collections/virginia_newspapers.

Published Primary Sources
Abstract of the Returns of the Fifth Census. Washington: Duff Green, 1820.
Anderson, William. *Life and Narrative of William J. Anderson, Twenty-four Years a Slave; Sold Eight Times! In Jail Sixty Times!! Whipped Three Hundred Times!!! or The Dark Deeds of American Slavery Revealed. Containing Scriptural Views of the Origin of the Black and of the White Man. Also, a Simple and Easy Plan to Abolish*

Slavery in the United States. Together with an Account of the Services of Colored Men in the Revolutionary War-Day and Date, and Interesting Facts. Chicago: Daily Tribune Book and Printing Office, 1857.

Black, Leonard. *The Life and Sufferings of Leonard Black, a Fugitive from Slavery. Written by Himself.* New Bedford: Benjamin Lindsey, 1847.

Bibb, Henry. *Narrative of the Life and Adventures of Henry Bibb, an American Slave, Written by Himself.* New York: The Author, 1849.

Brown, John. *Slave Life in Georgia: A Narrative of the Life, Sufferings, and Escape of John Brown, a Fugitive Slave, Now in England.* Ed. Louis Alexis Chamerovzow. London: W. M. Watts, 1855.

Brown, William Wells. *Narrative of William W. Brown, a Fugitive Slave, Written by Himself.* Boston: American Anti-Slavery Society, 1847.

Bruce, Henry Clay. *The New Man: Twenty-Nine Years a Slave. Twenty-Nine Years a Free Man.* York: P. Anstdat & Sons, 1895.

Cartwright, Samuel. "Natural History of the Prognathous Species of Mankind." In *Cotton is King, and Pro-slavery Arguments: Comprising the Writings of Hammond, Harper, Christy, Stringfellow, Hodge, Bledsoe, and Cartwright,* edited by E.N. Elliot, 704–716. Augusta: Pritchard, Abbott & Loomis, 1860.

Cary, Virginia. *Letters on Female Character: Addressed to a Young Lady on the Death of Her Mother.* Richmond: A. Works, 1828.

Catterall, Helen Tunnicliff ed. *Judicial Cases Concerning American Slavery and the Negro,* Vol. 1–5. Washington, D.C.: Carnegie Institution of Washington, 1926.

Clarke, Lewis. "'Leaves from a Slave's Journal of Life,' Published in two parts in National Anti-Slavery Standard, October 20, 27 (1842)." In *Slave Testimony: Two Centuries of Letters, Speeches, Interviews, and Autobiographies,* edited by John Blassingame, 151–164. Baton Rouge: Louisiana State University Press, 1977.

———. *Narrative of the Sufferings of Lewis Clarke: During a Captivity of More Than Twenty-Five Years, Among the Algerines of Kentucky, One of the So Called Christian States of America. Dictated by Himself.* Boston: David H. Ela, 1845.

Cobb, Thomas R.R. *An Inquiry into the Law of Negro Slavery in the United States of America.* Philadelphia: T. & J.W. Johnson & Company, 1858.

Collins, Robert. *Essay on the Treatment and Management of Slaves: Written for the Seventh Annual Fair of the Southern Central Agricultural Society.* Boston: Eastburn's Press, 1853.

Douglass, Frederick. *My Bondage and My Freedom: Part I. Life as a Slave. Part II. Life as a Freeman.* New York: Miller, Orton & Mulligan, 1855.

———. *Narrative of the Life of Fredrick Douglass: An American Slave.* 1845 reprint. New York: Oxford University Press, 2009.

Duties of an Overseer, De Bow's Review, Vol. 18, Issue 3 (March 1855): 339–345.

Equiano, Olaudah. *The Interesting Narrative and Other Writings.* New York: Penguin Books, 2003.

Fitzhugh, George. *Cannibals All! Or, Slaves Without Masters.* Richmond: A. Morris, 1857.

Garnet, Henry Highland. "An Address to the Slaves of the United States of America. Rejected by the National Convention 1848." In *The Rise of Aggressive*

Abolitionism: Addresses to the Slaves, edited by Stanley Harrold, 179–188. Lexington: University Press of Kentucky, 2004.

Harper, William. *Memoir on Slavery: Read Before the Society for Advancement of Learning of South Carolina at its Annual Meeting at Columbia.* Charleston: James S. Burges, 1838.

Henson, Josiah. *The Life of Josiah Henson, Formerly a Slave, Now an Inhabitant of Canada, As Narrated by Himself.* Boston: A. D. Phelps, 1849.

Hinks, Peter ed. *David Walker's Appeal: To the Coloured Citizens of the World.* University Park: The Pennsylvania State University Press, 2000.

Jackson, Andrew. *Narrative and Writings of Andrew Jackson, of Kentucky; Containing an Account of His Birth, and Twenty-six Years of His Life While a Slave; His Escape; Five Years of Freedom, Together with Anecdotes Relating to Slavery; Journal of One Year's Travels. Sketches, Etc. Narrated by Himself; Written by a Friend.* Syracuse: Daily and Weekly Star, 1847.

Jacobs, Harriet. *Incidents in the Life of a Slave Girl.* Eds. Nellie Y. McKay and Frances Smith Foster. 1861 reprint. New York: W.W. Norton & Company, 2001.

Keckley, Elizabeth. *Behind the Scenes or Thirty Years a Slave, and Four Years in the White House.* 1868 reprint. New York: Oxford University Press, 1988.

Loguen, Rev. J. W. *The Rev. J. W. Loguen, as a Slave and as a Freeman. A Narrative of Real Life.* Syracuse: J.G.K. Truair & Company, 1859.

Mandeville, Sir John. *The Voyages and Travels of Sir John Mandeville.* London: Cassell & Company, Limited, 1886.

Northup, Solomon. *Twelve Years a Slave. Narrative of Solomon Northup, a Citizen of New-York, Kidnapped in Washington City in 1841, and Rescued in 1853, from a Cotton Plantation near the Red River, in Louisiana.* Ed. David Wilson. Auburn: Derby and Miller, 1853.

Olmsted, Frederick Law. *A Journey in the Seaboard Slave States with Remarks on the Economy.* New York: Mason Brothers, 1861.

Page, Thomas Nelson. *Social Life in Old Virginia Before the War.* New York: Charles Scribner's Sons, 1897.

Particulars of the Dreadful Tragedy in Richmond on the Morning of the 19th July 1852: Being a Full Account of the Awful Murder of the Winston Family: Embracing All the Particulars of the Discovery of the Bloody Victims, the Testimony Before the Coroner's Jury, and the Evidence of the Final Trials of the Murderess and Murderer, Jane and John Williams: Their Sentence, Confessions, and Execution Upon the Gallows: Together with the Funeral Sermon of the Rev. Mr. Moore on the death of Mrs. Winston and Daughter, And The Sermon of the Rev. Robert Ryland on the subject of the Murders. Richmond: John D. Hammersley, Publisher, 1852.

Perdue Jr. Charles L., Thomas E. Barden, & Robert K. Phillips eds. *Weevils in the Wheat: Interviews with Virginia Slaves.* Charlottesville: University Press of Virginia, 1976.

Picquet, Louisa and Hiram Mattison. *Louisa Picquet, the Octoroon, or, Inside Views of Southern Domestic Life.* New York: The Author, 1861.

Rawick, George P. ed. *The American Slave: A Composite Autobiography Vol. 1–19.* Westport: Greenwood Press, 1972.

---. *The American Slave: A Composite Autobiography Supplement Series 1, Vol. 1–12*. Westport: Greenwood Press, 1977.
---. *The American Slave: A Composite Autobiography Supplement Series 2, Vol. 1–10*. Westport: Greenwood Press, 1979.
Seventh Census of the United States. Washington: Robert Armstrong, Public Printer, 1853.
Smith, Harry. *Fifty Years of Slavery in the United States of America*. Grand Rapids: West Michigan, 1891.
Steward, Austin. *Twenty-two Years a Slave and Forty Years a Freeman; Embracing a Correspondence of Several Years, While President of Wilberforce Colony, London, Canada West*. Rochester: W. Alling, 1857.
Stowe, Harriet Beecher. *Dred: A Tale of the Great Dismal Swamp*. Boston: Phillips, Sampson and Co., 1856.
Thompson, John. *The Life of John Thompson, a Fugitive Slave; Containing His History of 25 Years in Bondage, and His Providential Escape. Written by Himself*. Worcester: J. Thompson, 1856.
Watkins, James. *Narrative of the Life of James Watkins, Formerly a "Chattel" in Maryland, U. S.; Containing an Account of His Escape from Slavery, Together with an Appeal on Behalf of Three Millions of Such 'Pieces of Property,' Still Held Under the Standard of the Eagle*. Bolton: Kenyon and Abbatt, 1852.
Weld, Theodore Dwight. *American Slavery As It Is: Testimony of a Thousand Witnesses*. New York: American Anti-Slavery Society, 1839.

SECONDARY SOURCES

Andrews, William L. *To Tell A Free Story: The First Century of Afro-American Autobiography, 1760–1865*. Urbana: University of Illinois Press, 1986.
Aptheker, Herbert. *American Negro Slave Revolts: 50th Anniversary Edition*. New York: International Publishers, 1993.
Ayers, Edward L. *Vengeance and Justice: Crime and Punishment in the 19th Century American South*. New York: Oxford University Press, 1984.
Bailey, David Thomas. "A Divided Prism: Two Sources of Black Testimony on Slavery." *Journal of Southern History* 46, No. 3 (August 1980): 381–404.
Baptist, Edward E. "'Cuffy,' 'Fancy Maids,' and 'One-Eyed Men': Rape, Commodification, and the Domestic Slave Trade in the United States." *American Historical Review* CVI (December 2001): 1619–1650.
---. "The Absent Subject: African American Masculinity and Forced Migration to the Antebellum Plantation Frontier." In *Southern Manhood: Perspectives on Masculinity in the Old South*, edited by Craig Thompson Friend and Lorri Glover, 136–176. Athens: University of Georgia Press, 2004.
Bardaglio, Peter. W. *Reconstructing the Household: Families, Sex, and the Law in the Nineteenth-Century South*. Chapel Hill: University of North Carolina Press, 1998.
Bauer, Raymond A. and Alice H. Bauer. "Day-to-day Resistance to Slavery." *Journal of Negro History* 27, No. 4 (1942): 388–419.

Berlin, Ira, Steven F. Miller, and Leslie S. Rowland. "Afro-American Families in the Transition from Slavery to Freedom." *Radical History Review* 42 (1988): 89–121.

Bernhard, Virginia, Betty Brandon, Elizabeth Fox-Genovese, and Theda Purdue eds. *Southern Women: Histories and Identities*. Columbia: University of Missouri Press, 1992.

Blassingame, John W. *The Slave Community: Plantation Life in the Antebellum South Revised & Enlarged Edition*. New York: Oxford University Press, 1979.

———. "Using the Testimony of Ex-Slaves: Approaches and Problems." *The Journal of Southern History* 41, No. 4 (November 1975): 473–492.

Bleser, Carol K. "Southern Planter Wives and Slavery." In *The Meaning of South Carolina History: Essays in Honor of George C. Rodgers Jr.*, edited by David R. Chestnut and Clyde N. Wilson, 104–120. Columbia: University of South Carolina Press, 1991.

Boles, John B. ed. *Masters & Slaves in the House of the Lord: Race and Religion in the American South, 1740–1870*. Lexington: University Press of Kentucky, 1988.

Breen, T.H. and Stephen Innes. *Mine Own Ground: Race and Freedom on Virginia's Eastern Shore*. New York: Oxford University Press, 1980.

Brown, Kathleen. *Good Wives, Nasty Wenches, & Anxious Patriarchs: Gender, Race, and Power in Colonial Virginia*. Chapel Hill: Published for the Institute of Early American History and Culture, Williamsburg, Virginia by the University of North Carolina Press, 1996.

Bruce Jr., Dickson D. *Violence and Culture in the Antebellum South*. Austin: University of Texas Press, 1979.

Brundage, W. Fitzhugh. *Lynching in the New South*. Urbana: University of Illinois Press, 1994.

——— ed., *Under Sentence of Death: Lynching in the South*. Chapel Hill: University of North Carolina Press, 1997.

Bynum, Victoria E. *Unruly Women: The Politics of Social and Sexual Control in the Old South*. Chapel Hill: University of North Carolina Press, 1992.

Callahan, Allen Dwight. *The Talking Book: African Americans and the Bible*. New Haven: Yale University Press, 2006.

Camp, Stephanie M.H. *Closer to Freedom: Enslaved Women and Everyday Resistance in the Plantation South*. Chapel Hill: University of North Carolina Press, 2004.

Campbell, Stanley W. *The Slave Catchers: Enforcement of the Fugitive Slave Law, 1850–1860*. Chapel Hill: University of North Carolina Press, 1970.

Chabris, Christopher and Daniel Simons. *The Invisible Gorilla: How Our Intuitions Deceive Us*. New York: Broadway Books, 2009.

Clinton, Catherine. *The Plantation Mistress: Woman's World in the Old South*. New York: Pantheon Books, 1982.

Close, Stacey K. *Elderly Slaves of the Plantation South*. New York: Garland Publishing, 1997.

Cornelius, Janet Duitsman. *Slave Missions and the Black Church in the Antebellum South*. Columbia: University of South Carolina Press, 1999.

Davis, Thomas J. *A Rumor of Revolt: The "Great Negro Plot" in Colonial New York*. New York: Free Press, 1985.

Dray, Philip. *At the Hands of Persons Unknown: The Lynching of Black America.* New York: Modern Library, 2003.

Dubois, Laurent. *Avengers of the New World: The Story of the Haitian Revolution.* Cambridge: Belknap Press of Harvard University Press, 2004.

Egerton, Douglas R. *Gabriel's Rebellion: The Virginia Slave Conspiracies of 1800 and 1802.* Chapel Hill: University of North Carolina Press, 1993.

———. *He Shall Go Out Free: The Lives of Denmark Vesey.* Madison: Madison House, 1999.

Elkins, Stanley M. *Slavery: A Problem in American Institutional and Intellectual Life Second Edition.* Chicago: University of Chicago Press, 1968.

Ellison, Mary. "Resistance to Oppression: Black Women's Response to Slavery in the United States." *Slavery and Abolition* 4, (May 1983): 56–63.

Escott, Paul D. *Slavery Remembered: A Record of Twentieth Century Slave Narratives.* Chapel Hill: University of North Carolina Press, 1979.

"Estimates: Broad Embarkation Regions, North America." *Voyages: The Transatlantic Slave Trade Database,* http://www.slavevoyages.org/assessment/estimates (accessed: December 13, 2018).

Etheridge, Harrison M. "The Jordan Hatcher Affair of 1852: Cold Justice and Warm Compassion." *The Virginia Magazine of History and Biography* 84, No. 4 (October 1976): 446–463.

Faust, Drew Gilpin. *James Henry Hammond and the Old South: A Design for Mastery.* Baton Rouge: Louisiana State University Press, 1982.

Fehrenbacher, Don E. *The Slaveholding Republic: An Account of the United States Government's Relations to Slavery.* New York: Oxford University Press, 2001.

Finkleman, Paul ed. *Slavery & the Law.* Madison: Madison House Publishers, 1997.

Flanigan, Daniel J. "Criminal Proceedings in Slave Trials in the Antebellum South." *Journal of Southern History* 40, No. 4 (November 1974): 537–564.

Fogel, Robert William and Stanley L. Engerman. *Time on the Cross: The Economics of American Negro Slavery.* Lanham: University Press of America, 1984.

Forret, Jeff. "Conflict and the 'Slave Community': Violence among Slaves in Upcountry South Carolina." *The Journal of Southern History* 74, No. 3 (August 2008): 551–588.

———. *Race Relations at the Margins: Slaves and Poor Whites in the Antebellum Southern Countryside.* Baton Rouge: Louisiana State University Press, 2006.

———. *Slave Against Slave: Plantation Violence in the Old South.* Baton Rouge: Louisiana State University Press, 2015.

Fox-Genovese, Elizabeth. *Within the Plantation Household: Black And White Women of the Old South.* Chapel Hill: University of North Carolina Press, 1988.

Franklin, John Hope and Loren Schweninger. *Runaway Slaves: Rebels on the Plantation.* New York: Oxford University Press, 1999.

Fraser, Rebecca. "Negotiating Manhood: Masculinity Amongst the Enslaved in the Upper South, 1830–1861." In *Black and White Masculinity in the American South,* edited by Sergio Lussana and Lydia Plath, 76–94. Newcastle upon Tyne: Cambridge Scholars Publishing, 2009.

French, Scot A. *The Rebellious Slave: Nat Turner in American Memory.* Boston: Houghton Mifflin, 2004.

Frey, Sylvia R. *Water from the Rock: Black Resistance in a Revolutionary Age.* Princeton: Princeton University Press, 1991.

Frey, Sylvia R. and Betty Wood. *Come Shouting to Zion: African American Protestantism in the American South and British Caribbean to 1830.* Chapel Hill: University of North Carolina Press, 1998.

Gaspar, David Barry and Darlene Clark Hine eds. *More than Chattel: Black Women and Slavery in the Americas.* Bloomington: University of Indiana Press, 1996.

Genovese, Eugene D. *From Rebellion to Revolution: Afro-American Slave Revolts in the Making of the Modern World.* Baton Rouge: Louisiana State University Press, 1979.

———. *Roll, Jordan, Roll: The World the Slaves Made.* New York: Vintage Books, 1974.

Gilje, Paul A. *The Road to Mobocracy: Popular Disorder in New York City, 1763–1834.* Chapel Hill: Omohundro Institute of Early American History and Culture and the University of North Carolina Press, 1987.

Glover, Lorri. *Southern Sons: Becoming Men in the New Nation.* Baltimore: Johns Hopkins University Press, 2007.

Glymph, Thavolia. *Out of the House of Bondage: The Transformation of the Plantation Household.* Cambridge: Cambridge University Press, 2008.

Gorn, Elliott J. "'Gouge and Bite, Pull Hair and Scratch': The Social Significance of Fighting in the Southern Backcountry." *American Historical Review* 90 (February 1985): 18–43.

Greenberg, Amy S. *Manifest Manhood and the Antebellum American Empire.* Cambridge: Cambridge University Press, 2005.

Greenberg, Kenneth S. *Honor & Slavery: Lies, Duels, Noses, Masks, Dressing as a Woman, Gifts, Strangers, Humanitarianism, Death, Slave Rebellions, The Proslavery Argument, Baseball, Hunting, and Gambling in the Old South.* Princeton: Princeton University Press, 1996.

———. *Nat Turner: A Slave Rebellion in History and Memory.* New York: Oxford University Press, 2003.

Grimsted, David. *American Mobbing, 1828–1861: Towards Civil War.* New York: Oxford University Press, 1998.

Gross, Ariela J. *Double Character: Slavery and Mastery in the Antebellum Southern Courtroom.* Princeton: Princeton University Press, 2000.

Gutman, Herbert. *The Black Family in Slavery and Freedom 1750–1925.* New York: Vintage Books, 1976.

Hadden, Sally E. *Slave Patrols: Law and Violence in Virginia and the Carolinas.* Cambridge: Harvard University Press, 2001.

Harding, Vincent. *There Is a River: The Black Struggle for Freedom in America.* New York: Harcourt Brace Jovanovich, 1981.

Harrold, Stanley. *The Rise of Aggressive Abolitionism: Addresses to the Slaves.* Lexington: University Press of Kentucky, 2004.

Hartman, Saidiya V. *Scenes of Subjection: Terror, Slavery, and Self-Making in Nineteenth-Century America.* New York: Oxford University Press, 1997.

Hine, Darlene Clark. "Rape and Inner Lives of Black Women: Thoughts on the Culture of Dissemblance." In *Hine Sight: Black Women and the Re-Construction of American History*, edited by Darlene Clark Hine, 37–48. Brooklyn: Carson Publishing Company, 1994.

Hine, Darlene Clark and Earnestine L. Jenkins. "Black Men's History: Towards a Gendered Perspective." In *A Question of Manhood: A Reader in U.S. Black Men's History and Masculinity Vol. 1*, edited by Darlene Clark Hine and Earnestine L. Jenkins, 1–58. Bloomington: Indiana University Press, 1999.

Hindus, Michael Stephen. *Prison and Planation: Crime, Justice, and Authority in Massachusetts and South Carolina, 1767–1878*. Chapel Hill: University of North Carolina Press, 1980.

Hodes, Martha. *White Women, Black Men: Illicit Sex in the 19th Century South*. New Haven: Yale University Press, 1997.

Hoffer, Peter Charles. *Cry Liberty: The Great Stono River Slave Rebellion of 1739*. New York: Oxford University Press, 2010.

Hoffer, Peter Charles and William B. Scott eds. *Criminal Proceedings in Colonial Virginia: Richmond County, 1710/11–1754. American Legal Records Series, Vol 10*. Athens: University of Georgia Press, 1984.

Horton, James Oliver and Lois E. Horton, "Violence, Protest, and Identity: Black Manhood in Antebellum America." In *A Question of Manhood: A Reader in U.S. Black Men's History and Masculinity Vol. 1*, edited by Darlene Clark Hine and Earnestine L. Jenkins, 382–389. Bloomington: Indiana University Press, 1999.

Isaac, Rhys. *The Transformation of Virginia, 1740–1790*. Chapel Hill: Published for the Institute of Early American History and Culture, Williamsburg, Virginia by the University of North Carolina Press, 1982.

Johnson, Michael P. "Denmark Vesey and his Conspirators." *William and Mary Quarterly* 58 (October 2001): 913–976.

———. "Forum: The Making of a Slave Conspiracy." *William and Mary Quarterly* 59 (January 2002): 135–202.

Johnson, Paul E., ed. *African-American Christianity: Essays in History*. Berkeley: University of California Press, 1994.

Johnson, Walter. *Soul by Soul: Life Inside the Antebellum Slave Market*. Cambridge: Harvard University Press, 2001.

Jones, Jacqueline. *Labor of Love, Labor of Sorrow: Black Women, Work, and the Family from Slavery to the Present*. New York: Basic Books, 1985.

Jordan, Winthrop D. *Tumult and Silence at Second Creek: An Inquiry into a Civil War Slave Conspiracy*. Baton Rouge: Louisiana State University Press, 1993.

———. *White Over Black: American Attitudes Towards the Negro, 1550–1812*. New York: W.W. Norton & Company, 1968.

Kaye, Anthony E. "Neighborhoods and Nat Turner: The Making of a Slave Rebel and the Unmaking of a Slave Rebellion." *Journal of the Early Republic* 27, No.4 (2007): 705–720.

Kierner, Cynthia A. *Beyond the Household: Women's Place in the Early South, 1700–1835*. Ithaca: Cornell University Press, 1998.

King, Wilma. *Stolen Childhood: Slave Youth in the Nineteenth Century.* Bloomington: Indiana University Press, 1995.

Kolchin, Peter. *American Slavery 1617–1877.* New York: Hill and Wang, 2003.

———. "Reevaluating the Antebellum Slave Community: A Comparative Perspective." *Journal of American History* 70 (December 1983): 579–601.

———. *Unfree Labor: American Slavery and Russian Serfdom.* Cambridge: Belknap Press of Harvard University Press, 1987.

Kulikoff, Allan. *Tobacco and Slaves: The Development of Southern Cultures in the Chesapeake, 1680–1800.* Chapel Hill: Published for the Institute of Early American History and Culture, Williamsburg, Virginia by the University of North Carolina Press, 1986.

Lepore, Jill. *New York Burning: Liberty, Slavery, and Conspiracy in an Eighteenth-Century Manhattan.* New York: Alfred A. Knopf, 2005.

Link, William A. *Roots of Secession: Slavery and Politics in Antebellum Virginia.* Chapel Hill: University of North Carolina Press, 2003.

———. "The Jordan Hatcher Case: Politics and 'A Spirit of Insubordination in Antebellum Virginia." *The Journal of Southern History* 64, No. 4 (November 1998): 615–648.

Lussana, Sergio. *My Brother Slaves: Friendship, Masculinity, and Resistance in the Antebellum South.* Lexington: University Press of Kentucky, 2016.

McElya, Micki. *Clinging to Mammy: The Faithful Slave in Twentieth Century America.* Cambridge: Harvard University Press, 2007.

McLaurin, Melton A. *Celia, A Slave.* Athens: University of Georgia Press, 1991.

Martin, Jonathan D. *Divided Mastery: Slave Hiring in the American South.* Cambridge: Harvard University Press, 2004.

McCurry, Stephanie. *Masters of Small Worlds: Yeoman Households, Gender Relations, and the Political Culture of the Antebellum South Carolina Low Country.* New York: Oxford University Press, 1995.

Morgan, Edmund S. *American Slavery, American Freedom: The Ordeal of Colonial Virginia.* New York: W.W. Norton & Company, 1975.

Morgan, Jennifer L. *Laboring Women: Reproduction and Gender in New World Slavery.* Philadelphia: University of Pennsylvania Press, 2004.

Morris, Thomas D. *Southern Slavery and the Law.* Chapel Hill: University of North Carolina Press, 1996.

Morton, Patricia ed. *Discovering Women in Slavery: Emancipating Perspectives on the American Past.* Athens: University of Georgia Press, 1996.

Moynihan, Daniel Patrick. *The Negro Family: The Case for National Action.* Washington D.C.: Office of Policy Planning and Research, U.S. Department of Labor, 1965.

Mullin, Gerald W. *Flight and Rebellion: Slave Resistance in Eighteenth-Century Virginia.* New York: Oxford University Press, 1972.

Oakes, James. "The Political Significance of Slave Resistance." *History Workshop* 22 (1986): 89–107.

Oates, Stephen B. *The Fires of Jubilee: Nat Turner's Fierce Rebellion.* New York: Harper & Row, 1975.

Painter, Nell Irving. *Soul Murder and Slavery*. Waco: Baylor University Press, 1995.
Parent, Anthony S. *Foul Means: The Formation of a Slave Society in Virginia, 1660–1740*. Chapel Hill: Published for the Omohundro Institute of Early American History and Culture, Williamsburg, Virginia, by the University of North Carolina Press, 2003.
Patterson, Orlando. *Slavery and Social Death: A Comparative Study*. Cambridge: Harvard University Press, 1982.
Phillips, Ulrich B. *American Negro Slavery: A Survey of the Supply, Employment and Control of Negro Labor as Determined by the Plantation Regime*. New York: D. Appleton and Company, 1918.
Raboteau, Albert J. *Canaan Land: A Religious History of African Americans*. New York: Oxford University Press, 2001.
———. *Slave Religion: The 'Invisible Institution' in the Antebellum South*. New York: Oxford University Press, 1978.
Rasmussen, Daniel. *American Uprising: The Untold Story of America's Largest Slave Revolt*. New York: Harper, 2011.
Remini, Robert V. *Andrew Jackson: The Course of American Empire, 1767–1821*. Baltimore: Johns Hopkins University Press, 1998.
Richards, Leonard L. *"Gentlemen of Property and Standing": Anti-Abolition Mobs in Jacksonian America*. New York: Oxford University Press, 1970.
Rose, Willie Lee. "The Domestication of Domestic Slavery." In *Slavery and Freedom*, edited by William W. Freehling, 18–36. New York: Oxford University Press, 1982.
Rothman, Joshua D. *Notorious in the Neighborhood: Sex and Families Across the Color Line in Virginia, 1787–1861*. Chapel Hill: University of North Carolina Press, 2003.
Rucker, Walter C. *The River Flows On: Black Resistance, Culture, and Identity Formation in Early America*. Baton Rouge: Louisiana State University Press, 2006.
Sayers, Daniel O. *A Desolate Place for a Defiant People: The Archaeology of Maroons, Indigenous Americans, and Enslaved Laborers in the Great Dismal Swamp*. Gainesville: University Press of Florida, 2014.
Scarborough, William K. *The Overseer: Plantation Management in the Old South*. Baton Rouge: Louisiana State University Press, 1966.
Schafer, Judith Kelleher. *Slavery, the Civil Law, and the Supreme Court of Louisiana*. Baton Rouge: Louisiana State University Press, 1997.
Schwalm, Leslie A. *A Hard Fight for We: Women's Transition from Slavery to Freedom in South Carolina*. Urbana: University of Illinois Press, 1997.
Schwartz, Marie J. *Born in Bondage: Growing Up Enslaved in the Antebellum South*. Cambridge: Harvard University Press, 2000.
Schwarz, Philip J. *Slave Laws in Virginia*. Athens: University of Georgia Press, 1996.
———. *Twice Condemned: Slaves and the Criminal Laws of Virginia, 1705–1865*. Baton Rouge: Louisiana State University Press, 1988.
Scott, Ann Firor. *The Southern Lady: From Pedestal to Politics, 1830–1930 25th Anniversary Edition*. Charlottesville: University of Virginia Press, 1995.

Scott, James C. *Domination and the Arts of Resistance.* New Haven: Yale University Press, 1990.
———. *Weapons of the Weak: Everyday Forms of Peasant Resistance.* New Haven: Yale University Press, 1985.
Sidbury, James. *Ploughshares into Swords: Race, Rebellion, and Identity in Gabriel's Virginia, 1730–1810.* New York: Cambridge University Press, 1997.
Smith, Mark M. *Stono: Documenting and Interpreting a Southern Slave Revolt.* Columbia: University of South Carolina Press, 2005.
Sobel, Mechal. *Trabelin' on: The Slave Journey to an Afro-Baptist Faith.* Westport: Greenwood Press, 1979.
Sommerville, Diane Miller. *Rape and Race in the Nineteenth-Century South.* Chapel Hill: University of North Carolina Press, 2004.
Stampp, Kenneth M. *The Peculiar Institution: Slavery in the Ante-Bellum South.* New York: Alfred A. Knopf, 1956.
Stevenson, Brenda. *Life in Black and White: Family and Community in the Slave South.* New York: Oxford University Press, 1996.
Takagi, Midori. *Rearing Wolves to Our Own Destruction: Slavery in Richmond Virginia, 1782–1865.* Charlottesville: The University Press of Virginia, 1999.
Thornton, John K. "African Dimensions of the Stono Rebellion." *American Historical Review* 96 (October 1991): 1101–13.
Trelease, Allen W. *White Terror: The Ku Klux Klan Conspiracy and Southern Reconstruction.* Baton Rouge: Louisiana State University Press, 1971.
Trussell, James and Richard Steckel, "The Age of Slaves at Menarche and Their First Birth." *The Journal of Interdisciplinary History* 8, No. 3 (1978): 477–505.
Tushnet, Mark V. *The American Law of Slavery, 1810–1860: Considerations of Humanity and Interest.* Princeton: Princeton University Press, 1981.
Varon, Elizabeth R. *We Mean to Be Counted: White Women and Politics in Antebellum Virginia.* Chapel Hill: University of North Carolina Press, 1998.
Webber, Thomas L. *Deep Like the Rivers: Education in the Slave Quarter Community, 1831–1865.* New York: W.W. Norton & Company, 1978.
Weiner, Marli F. *Mistresses and Slaves: Plantation Women in South Carolina, 1830–1880.* Urbana: University of Illinois Press, 1998.
West, Emily. *Chains of Love: Antebellum Slave Couples in South Carolina.* Urbana: University of Illinois Press, 2004.
White, Deborah Gray. *Ar'n't I a Woman? Female Slaves in the Plantation South.* New York: W.W. Norton & Company, 1985.
Wood, Kirsten E. *Masterful Women: Slaveholding Widows from the American Revolution through the Civil War.* Chapel Hill: University of North Carolina Press, 2004.
Wood, Peter H. *Black Majority. Negroes in Colonial South Carolina from 1670 through the Stono Rebellion.* New York: Alfred A. Knopf, 1974.
Woodward, C. Vann. "Review: History from Slave Sources." *The American Historical Review* 79, No. 2 (April 1974): 470–481.
Wright, George C. *Racial Violence in Kentucky: Lynchings, Mob Rule, and 'Legal Lynchings.'* Baton Rouge: Louisiana State University Press, 1990.

Wyatt-Brown, Bertram. "Mask of Obedience: Male Slave Psychology in the Old South." *The American Historical Review* 93, No. 5 (December 1988): 1228–1252.

———. *Southern Honor: Ethics and Behavior in the Old South.* New York: Oxford University Press, 1982.

Yetman, Norman R. "Ex-Slave Interviews and the Historiography of Slavery." *American Quarterly* 36, No. 2 (Summer 1984): 181–210.

Young, Jason R. *Rituals of Resistance: African Atlantic Religion in Kongo and the Lowcountry South in the Era of Slavery.* Baton Rouge: Louisiana State University Press, 2007.

Index

Ackiss, Harper, 122–23
Africa: white views of, 69–70
African slave trade, 65
American Revolution: enslaved men linking violence to, 34–35, 154–55; and necessity of violence, 35
American slavery: compared to elsewhere, xv, 1
Anderson, William, 21
Aristotle, 151
Auditor of Public Accounts (Virginia), xii, 74
autobiographies (slave), xiii–xiv, 15–16, 32–33, 39, 152

Bacon's Rebellion, 125
Bibb, Henry, 75–76
Black, Leonard, 152, 153–54
Blassingame, John, xiii, 43
Brown, Henry "Box", xv
Brown, John (ex-slave), 152, 153
Brown, William Wells, 35, 52, 64, 68
Bruce, Henry Clay, 39
Bruce Jr., Dickson, 35, 154
Bynum, Victoria, 138

Cartwright, Samuel, 70
Cary, Virginia, 90–91, 113–14
Celia, 72–74, 75

Chabris, Christopher, xiv
childhood. *See* slave children
Christianity (enslaved). *See* slave religion
Christianity (white). *See* religion (white)
Clarke, Lewis, 35, 67
Cobb, Thomas R.R., xi, 1, 70–71, 120, 151–52
Collins, Robert, 30
color-line: economic interactions across, 123; and fear of alliance between enslaved and poor whites, 125; sex across, 128, 137–39
Cudgo and Randall, 36–37

De Bow's Review, 11, 66
Douglass, Frederick, xiv, xv, 4, 5, 6, 15–16, 52, 53; assertion of masculinity, 33–34, 155; changes in autobiographies, 155–56; fight with Edward Covey, xvii, 4, 32–33, 155–56

Edwards, Isaac, ix–x, xii, xx
Edwards, Thomas, ix–x, xiv–xv, xx–xxi
Eliza (in *Twelve Years a Slave*), 42–43, 64, 67
Eliza (Louisa County), 128–32, 134–37
Elkins, Stanley, xii–xiii, xvi

Engerman, Stanley, 5
Epps, Edwin, 71–72, 77–78
Equiano, Olaudah, 29–30
Executive Council (Virginia), xi–xii, 73–74, 79
Executive Papers (Virginia), xiv
extralegal violence, 119

Fancy Trade, 66–67
Federal Writer's Project. *See* Works Progress Administration narratives
Fitzhugh, George, 16
Floyd, John, 14–15, 72, 73–75
Fogel, Robert, 5
Forret, Jeff, 40, 123
Fox-Genovese, Elizabeth, 63, 96, 111
Francis, John, 63–69, 71–72, 74–75, 79, 80
Fraser, Rebecca, 34, 45

Gabriel's Plot, xv
Garnet, Henry Highland, 34–35, 154–55
gender. *See* masculinity
Genovese, Eugene, 2, 3–4, 19, 47
George, Newsom, 72–73
Giles, William, 18, 19, 131, 133–37, 139
Glover, Lorri, 29, 38
Glymph, Thavolia, 92, 94, 96–97, 104
Gone with the Wind, xii, xiv
governors (Virginia). *See* entries by individual name
Great Dismal Swamp, 123
Green, Nancy, 120–21, 128–33, 135–39, 145; difficulty identifying body of, 129; disappearance of, 128; discovery of body, 131–32
Greenberg, Kenneth, 41
Gross, Ariela, 75, 120

Hamlin, John, 16–18, 19, 21–22
Hammond, James Henry, 128
Harper, William, 70
Hatcher, Jordan, xx, 121, 139–45
Henson, Josiah, 43–44

heroic slave archetype, 34–35
Hine, Darlene Clark, 30
hired-out owners: dislike of by slaves, 15–16, 39; and paternalism, 10; slaves resisting authority of, 10–11
hiring out, 10–11; prospects for enslaved, 11
Hodes, Martha, 137, 138
honor culture: enslaved men's claims to, 32–53; external validation, 37; and familial protection, 43, 45; importance of bodily protection, 52–53; importance of familial protection, 42–49; lack of protection for poor women, 138; and poor households, 105; and protection from public humiliation, 49–52; and protection of white women's sexuality, 76; and white manhood, 37; and willingness to defend manhood, 32; and verbal communication, 40
household: animosity between slaves in, 100; conflict between enslaved women and mistresses, 89–114; and confrontations over punishment, 93–94; failures of, 108–10; idealized views of, 89–90; importance of enslaved women's labor in, 91; and inability to explain enslaved women's violence, 94–96; limited power of mistresses in, 97, 103–5; as organizing unit of southern society, 92–93, 113–14; rationalizing away enslaved women's violence in, 106–13; tensions within, 97–106; tenuous status of poor, 106; violence as disorder, 94, 113–14; white women's use of violence to control, 90–91
Humphrey and Thornton, 20–21

Jackson, Nathaniel, 139–40
Jacobs, Harriet, xv, 33, 34, 53, 73, 75, 79, 80, 90, 91
Jamaica, 1
Jenkins, Earnestine L., 30

Jezebel archetype, 69–71, 79–80, 82
Johnson, Joseph, 121, 139, 140–45
Johnson and Jim, ix–xii, xiv, xx–xxi
Jordan, Winthrop, 69–70
Judy, 95–96, 111–12

Keckley, Elizabeth, 80–81, 91
Kimbrough, William, 131–32
Kolchin, Peter, xiii, xv, 3, 15, 66

Land, Peter, 123–26
Land, William K., 123, 125–26
legal system. *See* Oyer and Terminer, Courts of
Link, William A., 144
Longuen, Jermain W., 81
Lord, James, 127–28
Lost Cause, xix
Louverture, Touissant, 34

mammy, 89–90
manhood. *See* masculinity
marriage. *See* slave marriage
Martin, Jonathan D., 10
masculinity: affirmation of (from other slaves), 35–36; assertions of by enslaved men, 31, 32–42; and avenging punishment of children, 45–47; and avenging punishment of siblings, 47–48; and avenging sexual assault of wives, 43–44; and bodily protection, 52–53; of elite white men, 29; enslaved men reasserting, 42–53; enslaved women recognizing, 37–38; and familial protection, 42–49; and heroic slave archetype, 34–35; and honor culture, 32–53; and insults, 40–41; limits of enslaved men's, 30–31, 38–39, 42; and protecting selves from public humiliation, 49–52; and refusal to submit to unworthy whites, 39–41; and slavery, 29–30; types of enslaved men, 30; violence used to assert, 31–42; white denial of, 29–30, 53

masters: angry at enslaved women's resistance to sexual exploitation, 71–72; denial of enslaved men's masculinity, 29–30, 53; failing to live up to paternalistic obligations, 16–22; fear of slave violence and rebellion, 19–20; hiding sexual exploitation of enslaved women, 75; hiring attorneys to defend slaves, 14–15; interaction with oyer and terminer courts, 20; interest in enslaved women's sexual reproduction, 66; limits of power, 16; not punishing enslaved enough, 4–5; reluctance to sexually exploit enslaved women, 75; skeptical of overseers, 15; troubled by slave violence, 19–20; views of enslaved women's sexuality, 69–71
McCurry, Stephanie, 92
McPherson, John, 134–37
men (enslaved): affirmation of masculinity, 35–36; asserting masculinity, 31–42; avenging punishment of children, 45–47; avenging punishment of siblings, 47–48; avenging sexual assault of wives, 43–44; claims to honor culture, 32–53; claims to violence, 151–52; economic and social interactions with poor whites, 123; and familial protection, 42–49; limits of masculinity, 30–31, 38–39, 42; not sympathizing with sexually exploited women, 75–76; protecting selves from public humiliation, 49–52; reasserting masculinity, 42–53; refusal to submit to unworthy whites, 39–41; view of violence, 151–56; violence regarding violation of rights, 3–9
men (white): American revolution important to asserting manhood, 35; angry at enslaved women rejecting them, 71–72; denial of enslaved

men's masculinity, 29–30, 53; fear of alliance between enslaved and poor whites, 125; fear of slave violence and rebellion, 19–20; hiding sexual exploitation of enslaved women, 75; and importance of sex, 138–39; publicly punishing enslaved as warning, 20; sex with poor white women, 138; views of enslaved women's sexuality, 69–71

Mingo, xx, 120, 121–28

Minor, Lucian, 120, 128–29, 133–34, 139

mistresses: bitterness of enslaved women towards, 79, 91; and confrontations over punishment, 93–94; confrontations with enslaved women, 89–114; descriptions of enslaved women's violence, 94; idealized depictions of, 89–90; inability to explain enslaved women's violence, 94–96; and lack of alliance with enslaved women, 60, 76–77; lashing out at enslaved women and children, 77–78; limited power of in households, 97, 103–5; limits of power, 16; punishing enslaved women, 93–94; reliance on enslaved women's labor, 91; tensions with enslaved women, 97–106; use of violence to control households, 90–91; viewing enslaved women's violence as disorder, 113–14

mobs, 143

Monroe, James, 14

Nat (Turner), xv, 34

Ned, 122–24

New Orleans, 63–64, 66, 67, 71, 75; threat of sale to, 64, 68

Northup, Solomon, 6–7, 10–11, 39, 42, 64, 66, 68, 71–72, 77–78

Olmsted, Frederick Law, 66

overseers: authority undercut by masters, 15; complicating master-slave relationship, 10–12; confrontations with slaves, 5–6, 8, 12–16, 20–22, 33, 36, 38, 39–41, 44, 45–46, 47–48, 60, 62–63, 105–6, 139–40, 142; disagreements with owners, 13, 14–15; dislike of by slaves, 15–16, 32, 39; injuries of, 13–14; sexually assaulting enslaved women, 76–77, 81

Oyer and Terminer, Courts of, xi, xiv–xv, xx, xxin5, 119–20, 126, 128–29; as sources for physical confrontations, xiv–xv

Page, Thomas Nelson, 89–90

Painter, Nell Irving, 78, 80

paternalism, xvii–xviii, 1–3; defined, 1, 23n3; enslaved view of, 2, 3–4; and hired-out owners, 10; masters failing to live up to obligations, 16–22; and overseers, 10; and reciprocity, 2, 16; violating basic rights of slaves, 3–9; as white generosity, 3–4; white view of, 2, 3–4

Patsey, 71–72, 77–78

Peggy, 63–66, 67–69, 72, 74–75, 79

petitions, xi–xii, 5, 14, 73–75, 112, 125–26, 137, 140–42

physical confrontations: and American Revolution, 35; appealing to North for support, 34–35; avenging punishment of children, 45–47; avenging punishment of siblings, 47–48; avenging sexual assault of wives, 43–44; causing class tensions between whites, 105–6; cost of, 35–36, 49; between enslaved and overseers, 5–6, 8, 12–16, 20–22, 33, 36, 38, 39–41, 44, 45–46, 47–48, 60, 62–63, 105–6, 139–40, 142; enslaved not trying to kill whites, 5; enslaved women's similar to men's, 60–63; and food, 5–7; with hired out owners, 10–11; historical analysis of, xii–xiii; impact of, xvi–xvii, xx–xxi, 20–21, 156; inability to overthrow slavery, xvi; and insults, 40–41; between mistresses and enslaved women, 89–114; with overseers, 12–16; as proof of racial inferiority, 92; protecting families, 42–49; protection from public humiliation, 49–52; refusal to accept punishment, xii, 4–5; refusal to submit to unworthy whites, 39–41; setting limits on slavery, xvi–xvii, xviii, 3, 9, 10; sources for, xii–xv; in tobacco factories, 142; transformative power of, 152–54; as a type of resistance, xv

Picquet, Louisa, 81–82

Pleasants, James, xi–xii, 5

poor whites: confrontations with enslaved men, 12–16; economic and social interactions with enslaved, 123; enslaved men's hatred towards, 15–16, 39; tensions with owners and elite whites, 13–15, 105–6; tensions with the enslaved, 141–42; tenuous status of, 105–6; violence similar to slaves, 31

Preston, James, 121, 125–26, 127–28

punishment: avoiding, 12, 33, 39, 81, 97, 104, 106; and the body, 52; enslaved expectations regarding, xvi; enslaved women's bodies exposed during, xviii–xix, 67, 82; enslaved women's confrontations over, 60–63, 93–94, 96–97, 104; inability to avoid, 33–34, 35–36; negotiating out of, 12; no longer accepting, 38–39; protecting family members from, 43–49; resistance to, xviii, 4–6, 10–11, 142, 155–56; running away as response to, xvi; of wives, 44–45

Quarles, Garrett, 134–37

rape. *See* sexual exploitation
rebellion. *See* slave resistance
religion (slave). *See* slave religion
religion (white), 90–91, 112

runaways. *See* running away

running away, xiv, xv–xvi, 5, 17, 120, 121–24, 125, 152–54; as intermediate form of resistance, xv–xvi

Saint Domingue, 1, 156

Sandidge, Richard, 128–29, 130, 131–32, 134, 138–39

Schwarz, Philip, 119

sexual exploitation, xviii; enslaved women's responses to, xviii–xix; masters' initial reluctance to, 75

Simons, Daniel, xiv

slave children, 48–49

slave code (Virginia), xi, xvii, 119, 121, 134, 137; grants executive review 1801, xi–xii, 126, 142

slave codes, xi, 120

slave community, xii; weakness of, xvi–xvii, xviii

slave diet, 5–7; complaints about lack of food, 6–7

slave families, 2, 7–9, 22, 42–43; confrontations over visiting, 7–9; protection and honor culture, 45

slave holdings, xv, xvii, 1, 22, 49, 156

slave marriage, 44

slave religion, 2–3, 23n8

slave resistance, xv–xvi, xxiiin27; day-to-day resistance, xv, xxivn31; and paternalism, 1–22; physical confrontations as a type of, xv–xvi; running away as a type of, xv–xvi; slave rebellion as a type of, xv, xxiiin28

slavery in Virginia, xvii; development of, xvivn36; diversity of slave experience in, 141–42; divisions within over slavery, 139–45

slave sources, xiii–xiv

slave trials, xi–xii, 119–21

Smith, Harry, 36

Smith, William, 142

Sommerville, Diane Miller, 75, 120

Steward, Austin, 36

Sydnor, 128–37; appeals to Governor Giles, 133–34; trial of, 129–33

Taggert, Alexander, 122
Thompson, John, 33–34, 35–36
Tibeats, John, 10–11, 39
Tredegar Iron Works, 141

Vesey, Denmark, 34
violence. *See* physical confrontations

Walker, David, 34–35
Watkins, James, 52, 152–53
West, Emily, 9, 44
White, Deborah Gray, 59, 71, 82
white supremacy, xx, 119–21, 145–46; fears of cross-racial alliance, 121–28; use of violence to uphold, 119–46
Williams, Jane, 97–101, 107–10
Williams, John, 99–101, 108–9
Wilson, John, 126–28
Winston, Joseph, 97–98, 99, 101, 106, 107, 108–10, 111, 113
Winston, Virginia, 97–98, 99, 101, 107, 109
Wise, Henry, 15, 19, 112, 142
women (enslaved): apologizing to Northerners for trying to control sexuality, 79–81; birth rate of, 65; conflicts with mistresses, 89–114; confrontations similar to enslaved men's, 60–63; control over sexuality, 65–66; engage in relationships to ward off sexual exploitation, 81; exposure of bodies, 67; and Jezebel archetype, 69–71, 79–80, 82; lack of sympathy from enslaved men, 75–76; lack of sympathy from white women, 76–78; masters' interest in sexual reproduction of, 66; precarious position of, 59; resentful of mistresses, 91; resentful of white women, 79; similarities to enslaved men's confrontations, 60–63; successfully resisting sexual exploitation, 81–82; threat of sale to New Orleans, 64, 68; threat of sexual exploitation, 59–60; violence in households, 91–92, 113–14; violence towards white children, 102–3; white men's anger towards, 71–72; and whites rationalizing away their violence, 106
women (white): afraid of husbands, 78–79; aiding in sexual exploitation, 77; bitterness of enslaved women towards, 79, 91; and lack of alliance with enslaved women, 60, 76–77; lashing out at enslaved women and children, 77–78; limits of power, 103–5; poor women and sex, 138; punishing enslaved women, 93–94; role as mistresses, 92–93; sexuality, 76; status in southern society, 78; tenuous status of poor, 106
Woodward, C. Vann, xiv
Works Progress Administration (WPA) narratives, xiv
Wyatt-Brown, Bertram, 37, 52, 75, 138–39

About the Author

Christopher H. Bouton is a historian and researcher. He graduated with a bachelor's degree in history from Hamilton College and earned his PhD in history from the University of Delaware. He grew up in Beverly, Massachusetts, and now lives in Natchitoches, Louisiana. He is married and has a dog, Mayday, and a rabbit, Hillary. In his spare time, he reads, cooks, and writes about baseball.

www.ingramcontent.com/pod-product-compliance
Lightning Source LLC
Chambersburg PA
CBHW050906300426
44111CB00010B/1398